Books by W. Timothy Gallwey

The Inner Game of Tennis
Inner Tennis: Playing the Game
Inner Skiing (with Robert Kriegel)
The Inner Game of Golf

THE
INNER GAME
OF GOLF

THE INNER GAME OF GOLF

W. Timothy Gallwey

Random House New York

Grateful acknowledgment is made to the
following for permission to reprint previously
published material:

A. S. Barnes & Company, Inc.: Excerpts from
Power Golf by Ben Hogan, published by A. S.
Barnes & Company, Inc. Copyright 1948, 1976
by Ben Hogan. Reprinted by permission of the
publisher. All rights reserved.

A portion of this work was previously published in *Golf Magazine*.

Library of Congress Cataloging in Publication Data
Gallwey, W Timothy.
The inner game of golf.
1. Golf—Psychological aspects. I. Title.
GV979.P75G34   796.352′01   80-6019
ISBN 0-394-50534-4

Manufactured in the United States of America
02468B97531

To Guru Maharaj Ji,
in gratitude for teaching me the one thing
I most needed to learn

*If I always want an experience in life,
first I must find a constant source of experience.*

GURU MAHARAJ JI

Preface

If human beings did not have a tendency to interfere with their own ability to perform and learn, there would be no Inner Game. Similarly, if golfers hit every shot as well as they did their best ones, there would be no Inner Game of golf. But the fact is that because of self-interference, few of us perform up to the level of our potential for more than brief moments at a time. Learning to get out of one's way is the purpose of the Inner Game.

Because self-interference is a purely human phenomenon, and one not limited to any particular culture, the Inner Game is as ancient as man itself. It has been played well by all those who have achieved excellence in any field, and poorly by those who fail to achieve their potential. But the most important fact to recognize is that the game has always been there, and that it can be played consciously.

This is not a book about the mechanics of the swing, nor is it one on strategy. These are the province of the Outer Game and have received sufficient attention in golf literature. The subject of this book is the mental side of golf—namely, the learning of the "inner skills" that enable the player to decrease the mental obstacles that prevent him from playing his best. Yet the fact that concentration and confidence are discussed more than posture and swing mechanics does not mean that I don't believe that the fundamentals of golf are important. But my experience in teaching the Inner Game over the past ten years has proven to me that there is a superior approach to learning the fundamentals of any game than the practices commonly used.

I believe that we have reached a point of diminishing returns in the study of golf technique. Although this technique, taught by professionals, will remain important, the breakthroughs, if there are to be any, will come from study of the mental aspects of the game—specifically, *how* to learn and how to overcome the self-interference of tension, self-doubt, fear of failure, anxiety and a limiting self-image.

As golfers and their teachers undertake to play the Inner Game consciously and to develop skills of relaxed concentration, significant breakthroughs in how golf is performed, learned and enjoyed will inevitably follow. Furthermore, as a player learns to reduce the mental interference with his golf, he stands to reduce not only his golf handicap significantly, but also the ways in which he handicaps himself in the performance of every activity in his life. As he gains a measure of self-control he wins a measure of freedom.

Acknowledgments

This book was completed with the help of more people than I can name. I acknowledge and thank the few below who generously contributed time and energy.

Jane Blalock
Marilyn Bowden
Tom Capelety
Tony Coleman
Ed Gallwey
Sally Gallwey
Al Geiberger
Molly Groger

Arch McGill
Michael Murphy
Tom Nordland
Gary Peterson
D.P.S. Rawat
Linda Rhodes
Prentiss Uchida

Contents

Preface   xi

1   Golf: The Danger and the Challenge   1

2   Breaking 90: Finding the Bounce-Hit of Golf   13

3   Overtightness: The Most Common Cause of Error   29

4   Self-Doubt and the Trying Mode   39

5   Learning Golf in the Awareness Mode   55

6   The Art of Relaxed Concentration and the Performance Triangle   75

7   Inner Putting and Inner Chipping   101

8   Inner Swinging   121

9   Of Slumps and Streaks: The Self-Image Barrier   145

10   "Breaking 80" and Other Stories   161

11   Breaking the Golf Illusion   191

1
GOLF:
THE DANGER AND
THE CHALLENGE

As I laid down my tennis racket and cleaned off golf clubs scarcely used in twenty-five years I felt two emotions. On the one hand, I had a keen sense of expectancy about exploring the application of Inner Game methods and principles developed on the tennis courts and ski slopes to the "royal and ancient" game of golf. On the other, I felt distinct uneasiness about grappling with the notorious mental obstacles evoked by the game. Somehow I sensed that, for me, golf could prove to be a dangerous game.

My uneasiness did not stem from a lack of confidence in the Inner Game. I knew that it had a real contribution to make; that its principles were grounded in basic truth; and that the methods and techniques had produced dramatic results not only in tennis and skiing, but also in such varied worlds as music, business, education, health and family life. Furthermore, I had received letters from many golfers who had read *The Inner Game of Tennis* and reported that they had not only significantly lowered their handicaps but considerably increased their enjoyment. I sincerely felt that the Inner Game would help golf and golfers in general, and from time to time even indulged in wishful daydreams about instant mastery of the game.

But golf is different from tennis, a sport that I had excelled in, having played it all my life. My intention was to take up the game and in a short period of time see how much I could improve my present hacker level. I knew that helping others overcome the doubts, fears and frustrations that prevent excellence in performance always seemed easy to me, but that teaching was a challenge very different from performing. In learning golf *I* would be the student. Sometimes my mind felt the pressure of possible failure, but I comforted myself with the knowledge that if I really played the Inner Game I could not help learning a great deal more than simply about golf, and thus I could not really lose. Results would inevitably follow learning.

"The Only Game I Play That I Can't Lick"

One of the first rounds of golf I played on my return to the game was at the Hillcrest Club in Los Angeles in a foursome that included Dr. F., one of the best-known surgeons in California. Somehow Dr. F, whom I had met at a celebrity tennis tournament, found time to play three times a week. On the first tee I felt nervous in this unfamiliar atmosphere, and admired Dr. F's seeming self-assurance. On the second tee, however, after a par on the first hole, he pushed two successive drives out of bounds. Exasperated with himself, he slammed his driver to the ground and exclaimed disgustedly, "This is the most frustrating damned game ever concocted by the mind of man!"

Sensing that his outburst did not come out of short acquaintance with the game, I naïvely asked, "Then why do you play so often?"

Dr. F. paused, then finally answered, "Because I can't lick it." He seemed surprised by his remark, and thought about it for a moment before repeating firmly, "Yes, it's the only game I play that I can't beat!"

It soon became apparent that Dr. F. was frustrated not only by drives. Seeing him stand tensely over four-foot putts, I reflected that if he held his scalpel with as much apprehension and self-doubt as his putter, I'd never want to be on his operating table. Obviously, performing delicate surgery demands far more dexterity than is required to sink a four-foot putt, quite apart from the added dimension that the patient's life is at stake. Yet, clearly, golf unnerved Dr. F. more. Somehow I just couldn't imagine him angrily throwing his scalpel on the operating-room floor and calling himself a clumsy oaf, but this is exactly what happened on more than one three-putt green. Watching all this, my respect for the challenge of the game was not diminished.

Dr. F. was not alone in frustration. Though I'd learned better in tennis, after almost every mis-hit golf shot I found myself subjecting my swing to critical analysis. I knew very little about the mechanics of the swing, but I tried to figure out what had gone wrong. Had I been off balance? Swung too hard? Maybe I'd been either too early or too late with my wrists. On the next shot I would try to correct whatever I thought had caused the mistake. But it seemed that every time I managed to fix one flaw two more would emerge. The harder I tried to control my swing, the more mechanical and less rhythmic it became. The resulting shots were erratic, and provoked my desire to try even harder for self-correction. Before long this cycle proved to be more like self-destruction than self-correction.

Away from the golf course, I took a fresh look at the game and asked myself what it was all about. The single word that came to mind was *control*. Basically, it seemed to be a matter of getting your body to do what you want it to do so that you can make the golf ball do what you want *it* to do. I saw the game as a stark challenge to a person's ability to control his own body. Since I had learned something from my experience in tennis about the problem of control, I decided to find a way of translating this understanding to golf.

What I Learned on the Tennis Court

In short, what I learned on the tennis court was that the way most of us are taught to control our bodies simply doesn't work. Telling our bodies how to do something is not the most effective way to improve performance. Our muscles don't understand English, and our thinking minds don't really understand hand-eye coordination. Trying to make their bodies conform to the instructions of their last lesson, most tennis players inhibit free movement of their bodies and interfere with coordination rather than assist it. Get your racket back early . . . Meet the ball in front of you . . . Don't roll the racket over on the follow-through . . . they say furiously to themselves during a match. Even when these drill-instructor commands are obeyed, they are usually performed with the stiffness and self-consciousness of a rebellious recruit, and in a way that prohibits true excellence.

The quality of my teaching and of my students' performance took a major step forward the day I realized the extent of the disrupting effects of overinstruction. When my pupils' minds were free from both external and internal instructions, they could follow the ball better and had significantly better feel of their rackets. As a natural consequence, better results followed. In those early days of exploration of the Inner Game I was surprised at the improvement that would result after giving students the sole instruction "Forget everything you think you know about how to hit a tennis ball." Unable to forget anything they *really* knew, they could only forget what they *thought* they knew, and a natural ease would enter their game. But the Inner Game is not won with a single instruction, the inner opponent being far too crafty and well entrenched in our psyche to be dethroned so easily.

After several years the premise of the Inner Game of tennis emerged clearly. The prime causes of error in tennis are within the mind of the player—in doubt, tension and lapses of concentration more than in ignorance of mechanics. For this reason, as coach I found it far more effective to work from the inside out, trying to resolve the mental causes of error rather than to correct all the external symptoms. Over and over I observed that the removal of a single self-doubt could result immediately in numerous technical improvements in a tennis player's swing and overall game. The changes were spontaneous and unforced; they required neither technical instruction nor the constant demand for self-analysis that had characterized my early teaching.

On the tennis courts, methods for combating most mental problems facing tennis players had been found and proven effective. Now the challenge was to find practical ways to do the same under the physical requirements and mental pressures of the game of golf.

Golf Is an Inner Game

As I began to play golf more regularly I realized that it would be a unique challenge of Inner Game effectiveness. What other game invites such tension and mental anguish? Like one's own children, golf has an uncanny way of endearing itself to us while at the same time evoking every weakness of mind and character, no matter how well hidden. The common purpose served is that we either learn to overcome the weaknesses or be overwhelmed by them. Few games provide such an ideal arena for confronting the very obstacles that impair one's ability to learn, perform and enjoy life, whether on or off the golf course. But to take advantage of this opportunity, the golfer must accept the challenge to play the Inner Game as well as the Outer Game. He must recognize not only sand traps and OB markers but the reality of mental hazards as well.

Perhaps the first task for the player of the Inner Game is to become aware of the mental factors evoked by golf. I found them to be many and multifaceted, but essentially they seemed to fall into five categories: the lure of the game to the ego; the precision it requires; the competitive pressures on the golfer; the unique pace of the game; and the currently prevailing obsession with the mechanics of the swing.

The Lure of Golf

There is, I soon discovered, a seductive quality to golf found in few other sports. In moments of frustration many players vow to quit, but few are able to. For some reason, the two or three "triumphs" during a round are remembered long after the exasperating failures and dull mediocrity are forgotten.

I could see that some of the attraction of the game lay in the results that could sometimes be achieved by sheer luck. Golf is one of the few sports in which a novice can, on occasion, perform like a champion. A non-athlete playing golf for the first time can sink a fifty-foot putt on the first green and conclude that it is an easy game. Overconfidence can run rampant. Likewise, a reasonably well coordinated twenty-year-old may hit his first drive two hundred fifty yards straight down the middle of the fairway, and by the time he's walked up to his ball his ego is telling him that it will probably be only a short time before he's ready for the PGA tour. On a given day my seventy-five-year-old father can break 80, scoring better than Jack Nicklaus does on his worst. The trick, of course, is consistency.

After only a few hours on the driving range I realized that the compelling attraction of the game for me was also its major frustration. Even though I had played relatively little golf since I was thirteen, on occasion I would drive two hundred thirty yards, right on target. The sight of the ball soaring high and true was exhilarating; it filled me with a sense of mastery and power. The frustration lay in the fact that I couldn't repeat the experience at will. Fed by seemingly undying hope, I repressed my annoyance at failure and would reach for ball after ball. I wanted that feeling back, and to prove to myself that I could repeat what my body had shown me it was capable of doing. I was getting hooked by the game.

As I looked around the practice range I could see that others were caught in the same snare; there we were, spending hours and dollars trying for that elusive, but tantalizing perfect swing that would give predictable results. Yet time and time again we were all faced with the dismal truth that we simply didn't have the self-control we wanted and which we somehow felt we should have. It wouldn't have hurt so much if we hadn't hit some excellent shots, giving us that cruel knowledge that the ability was there within us somewhere.

I began to understand and share Dr. F's fascination with the game. Golf seemed to raise my hopes only to dash them, to puff up my ego only to squash it. What kind of fun was this supposed to be? Could the game be beaten? What would that mean? Could I at least learn to enjoy the game and to play without frustration? I felt that to do only this would not be an insignificant victory.

The Demands of Precision

The most agonizing aspect of my own game was clearly its inconsistency. I was perfectly capable of hooking a ball forty yards left of center on one shot, and then, with what seemed to be the same swing, slicing an equal distance on the next. Even more disconcerting was hitting a long drive down the middle on one hole, followed by a topped ball that barely dribbled off the tee on the next. I was used to inconsistency in tennis, but nothing on that order of magnitude! Although I might serve an ace and follow it with a serve four feet out, I wouldn't hit the bottom of the net with one shot and the fence on the fly with the next. Yet that's what golf felt like on some days.

It seemed to me that the precision required to play good golf demanded much greater mental discipline than was necessary for good tennis. The reason for the low margin of error was not hard to discover: the speed of the club head that is necessary to hit the ball a long distance. The speed of the golfer's arms on the downswing is not much greater than the speed of the tennis player's arm on the serve, because of the greater length and flexibility of the golf club, but the club-head speed is much greater. If a club head traveling over 100 mph contacts the ball with a face open a mere degree or two, the ball can be sent off-target many tens of yards. With those odds, it's amazing that the ball ever does go exactly where we want it to.

In tennis, the serve is the only shot in which the player *initiates* the action, whereas in golf he does so on every shot. It is interesting to note that if you miss your first serve in tennis, you get another try. Golf is not so forgiving! Further, in tennis a much larger surface hits a much larger ball a much shorter distance. Moving from tennis to golf was definitely going to require some fine-tuning of my concentration.

The greater precision required in golf is also reflected in the manner in which the player addresses the ball. A tennis player can be pretty casual, or even a little flamboyant, as he sets up the service line, bounces the ball a few times and serves. Most professional golfers display much more self-discipline. They seem to approach the ball in the same controlled, almost ritualistic way every time. Even their dress seems more meticulous. (I've often felt I could pick out the golfers from the tennis players at a cocktail party.)

Meticulousness has never been my strong suit. There isn't a family picture of me as a boy in which at least one shoe wasn't untied. I could usually solve all the problems given me on a math test, but would seldom make a perfect score because of careless mistakes in computation. I wondered if I'd ever be able to achieve the degree of discipline that the game of golf seemed to call for. At the outset my only hope was to look at the game as a challenge to my ability to enhance this particular quality of mind. I can't say that I looked forward to the task.

The precision required in golf doesn't allow for release of the pent-up anger and frustration that one can find in more aggressive sports. Golf produces frustration, but requires that you learn to deal with it in some way other than in your next shot. This presents a fascinating Inner Game challenge.

Pressure of Competition

If I have a mediocre day on the tennis court and lose a match 6–3, 6–3, I can always lessen the humiliation to my ego by telling myself that my opponent was playing particularly well that day. But the golfer stands alone. Blame or credit for his score rests on him, and usually there are three other people around to pass judgment. The ego thrives and dies in such a setup.

Every shot I take in golf counts. In tennis I can lose three straight points and still win the game; many lost points will never show up in the final score. Tennis forgives a few mistakes; golf forgives none. Thus, pressure is constant.

Because the game of golf is inherently a game of the golfer against himself, the Inner Game is intensified. The ego is both more challenged and more threatened. The player's spirits tend to rise or sink in direct proportion to his score, the sole product of his own efforts. Although I have seen many golfers avoid this pressure by blaming various weather and course conditions, golf clubs, balls, other players, family or business affairs, I feel that few can fool themselves for long before facing the fact that golf is a game played only against the course and oneself, and that one's score is a pretty true indication of skill.

Although I have seen many "fry" under this kind of pressure, I have also noticed that often it is this very same pressure that attracts golfers to the game. As a rule, most golfers prefer the tougher courses to easy ones, and like to add to the existing pressure by betting money on the result "just to make the game more interesting."

Learning to perform at one's best under pressure is a clear goal of the Inner Game. The challenge of sinking a five-foot putt on the eighteenth hole to save par and the match is clearly a lot more mental than it is physical. And the player who can learn to perform with precision and power under such pressure will learn an inner skill that can help him to cope with other situations in his life.

Pace

The pace of golf is unique, and in obvious contrast to that of most sports. In tennis, for example, if my mind begins to entertain a flow of self-critical or negative thoughts, it is cut short abruptly by the need to respond to the oncoming ball.

But in golf we have too much time to think. Between shots a negative train of thought can become entrenched: What went wrong on that last shot? How do I correct my slice? What will happen to my score if I hit the next shot out of bounds? There is endless time to overanalyze and become confused, discouraged or angry.

The tennis player is constantly caught up in the action—moving toward or hitting the ball. In four hours on the court I may play about sixty-four games or about four hundred points in perhaps twelve hundred to fifteen hundred separate shots. During the same length of time in golf I will hit—I hope—less than one hundred shots. If each golf shot takes me two seconds, then I am engaged in swinging the golf club for a total of only three minutes out of four hours of play.

Therefore concentration in golf requires a unique kind of effort. In the first place, the ball just sits there, and the pace of the game demands that the golfer be at an intense peak of concentration at the exact moment of the swing, supremely challenging his ability to keep from being distracted during the long intervals between shots. In tennis my concentration tends to build as the point progresses, reaching its peak as I become "lost in the action." But in the long stretches between golf shots it is easier to become lost in the thoughts on the surface of our minds.

I concluded that the walk between shots is one of the most critical parts of the game. Though this period of time is recognized by some pros as a potential mental hazard as well as a benefit, I feel its importance in most golfers' minds is generally undervalued. It is most often in the interval between shots that both the inner and the outer game are won or lost. It is during this time that the golfer's mental equilibrium can be destroyed by the momentum of his negative thoughts, or employed to shake off the tension of the last shot and to prepare for the next. The inner golfer learns to use the time between shots to relax his mind and to prepare it for the total concentration he'll need during the two seconds of his next swing. (This subject will be dealt with further in Chapter 8.)

Obsession with Tips and Technique

I had long thought that the mechanics of the tennis swing had been exhaustively analyzed until I took a look at existing golf manuals. I wouldn't be surprised if more has been written about the mechanics of the golf swing than just about any other human movement. It has been dissected into amazingly minute segments and the information passed along to the already overloaded minds of students of the game. Hearing that I was taking up the game, a friend presented me with three volumes: *295 Golf Lessons by Bill Casper, 395 Golf Lessons by Gary Player, 495 Golf Lessons by Arnold Palmer.*

It is not difficult to see how superstition thrives on the modern golf course. So many players are in constant search of "the secret," and endless magic formulas are propagated by true believers. Ready to try anything to relieve frustration, the golfer finds his hopes rising as he hits a few good shots after trying a given tip. It works! he thinks to himself. "I've got the game licked," he exclaims, as my father has so many times confessed to feeling. But how long does any single magic formula help a given player? "The secret" is dropped after a few poor shots occur and hope wanes. Soon the golfer is open for the next tip. Of course, some modest tips can be truly helpful, but the all-encompassing ones only raise one's hopes for conquering a game that can *never* be mastered by a single tip. I am convinced that the happiest and best golfers are those who have realized that there is no single gimmick that works, and that good golf is attained only by patience and humility, and by continually practicing both outer and inner game skills.

So here is the mental situation, as I see it, facing the brave soul who plunges innocently into the awesome game of golf. His ego will be attracted to the rich psychic rewards offered by success in the sport, and it will fear the imagined devastation that failure to perform up to a reasonable norm may bring. After he has played a few rounds, he will have hit enough good shots to provoke unquieting thoughts of heroism—if only he can learn to repeat consistently what he has shown that he can do on occasion. But unknown to the novice player, the mechanics of the game dictates that the probabilities of hitting those shots consistently are almost nil. Furthermore, he will be surrounded by prophets with both mental and technical golfing keys promising to deliver him from his evils, and to unlock the gates leading into the heaven of good golf. Confused by the long lists of dos and don'ts, ranging from sound fundamentals to superstitious mental magic, he will tend to analyze each shot and to try to compensate for each mistake. Then he will compensate for the compensation. Between failures he will have all the time in the world to think, and while doing so to increase his tension and doubt, while after success he won't be able to resist the temptation to analyze how to repeat it. Put this all together in the head of one man or woman who is already suffering the tensions of twentieth-century life, and what you have is an intriguing but dangerous game.

It is the thesis of this book that the secret to increasing control over our bodies lies in gaining some measure of control over our minds. A basic understanding of mechanics can help, and, of course, a certain amount of physical coordination is required to play good golf. But differences in talent do not account for the fact that most of us hit much better on the practice range than we do in the thick of battle on the course, nor for the wide variations in our individual scores. The aim of the Inner Game is to close the unnecessarily wide gap between our potential and our actual performance and to open the way to higher and more constant levels of enjoyment of the game.

The Inner Game of Golf

Thus, the challenge of golf lies as much in the relatively unexplained aspects of the Inner Game as it does in the Outer Game. There is a growing interest in the mental side of golf that is reflected in current books and magazine articles on the subject. Asking me to speak at a PGA meeting, a regional PGA educational director said that there was a general consensus that teaching pros were reaching a point of diminishing returns on analysis of the mechanics of golf, and were turning their attention to the mental side of the sport. "We know a lot about the swing," one college golf coach said to me, "but not much about how to help golfers learn it."

This is not merely a matter of words. The issues of how to overcome self-doubt, lapses in concentration, self-anger and low self-esteem are very real. Facing these handicaps for some is like noticing an unwelcome bedfellow; we'd rather roll over and forget that he or she is there.

But to play the Inner Game is not really a matter of choice. It is always going on, and we are playing it constantly in our various outer games. The only question is whether we are playing it consciously or not, and whether we are winning it or losing it. Anyone who feels his performance is always equal to its actual potential, and fully enjoys and learns from his golf experience, has my hearty congratulations for winning the Inner Game. As for all others, including myself, though we may play very different outer games in different circumstances, there is still an enemy within, and thus an Inner Game to be played.

The fundamental challenge to the golfer is to recognize the existence of interference, and that winning the Inner Game may be more to the point than simply defeating the golf course.

This book describes practical ways to bring Inner Game principles and techniques to your golf game. These exercises are neither gimmicks nor tips; rather, they are ways to increase three primary Inner Game skills: concentration, confidence and willpower. Because many of these exercises were developed as I attempted to improve my own golf game, some of this book comprises a narrative of my own story as a golfer—a saga that I can assure you contains at least my fair share of mental obstacles.

The next chapter begins that narrative, and includes the Inner Game concentration technique with which I was first able to find enough consistency to begin breaking 90. There are four chapters that deal with the fundamentals of the Inner Game approach to learning and performance, which, though discussed in terms of golf, are easily relatable to any Outer Game. Chapters 7 and 8 concentrate on developing an Inner Game technology for improvement of putting, chipping and swinging. Chapter 9 deals with slumps, streaks and the problem of self-image in golf. The last part of Chapter 10 was written only after I succeeded in breaking 80, and it tells about my difficulties in doing so. The final chapter deals with the Inner Game perspective of golf, and some of my ideas on the future of the game.

2
BREAKING 90: FINDING THE BOUNCE-HIT OF GOLF

Over the last twenty-five years my involvement in golf had been slight. From four to six times a year, whenever I visited my parents, I would play at least one round with my father at the Rancho Canada Golf Club, a pleasant and interesting course in the Carmel Valley with a degree of difficulty off the regular tees of 70.3. If I completed the eighteen holes with a 95, I felt I had done well enough. Dad generally shot in the high 80's.

My game was not hard to characterize. I hit a fairly long drive, but consistency proved elusive. Out of ten drives three would be straight, four would have a moderate to severe slice, and three would be dubbed or hooked. Such variety was not encouraging.

My midirons and short irons were a little more reliable—but only a little. Sometimes I sank a long putt, but more often I would three-putt. I usually expected the best of myself, and was amazed and disappointed when I didn't achieve it. Though I didn't know what a "yip" was, that inexplicable little mid-swing jerk that ruined about one-third of my wedge shots was exasperating.

My game was not a cautious one. If I had a chance to cut off distance on a dogleg or hit through a flock of trees for the green, I would almost always go for it. I hated to play it safe—or sometimes even rationally.

My swing was relatively natural, perhaps because I had played some golf between the ages of nine and thirteen. But I had never taken a lesson or played often enough to feel in a groove of any kind. The word that best characterized my swing also described my results: inconsistent. The power was there, even though I am relatively slender (about 145 pounds at five eleven), but it came mostly from my tennis arm, the wrist and biceps of which are nearly twice the size and strength of my left. (One of the drawbacks of tennis is that it is so one-sided.) For this reason it seemed natural to try to generate power in my golf swing in somewhat the same way as I did on my right-handed serve. If I connected just right, the ball would go a mile, but more often than not I would overtighten my right arm in an attempt to produce power, and would end up hitting the turf before the ball. Or I would restrict the movement of my wrists and hips and produce my all-too-common slice.

Still, hope was kept alive by the two or three spectacular shots I would hit every eighteen holes. Deep down I saw no reason why I couldn't do the same thing every time, and my experience with Inner Game successes in other fields gave me hope that it was possible.

Each time I would return home from Rancho Canada with my average 95, I'd be greeted by Mom's standard question, "How did you do?" While I hemmed and hawed, Dad would interject, "We had a lot of fun. Tim hit some great shots and did pretty well for someone who never plays!"

So my basic problem with my Outer Game was clear-cut: my swing *felt* inconsistent and my game *was* inconsistent. I began to understand why professional golfers seemed so disciplined. Unfortunately, I never thought of myself as the disciplined type. Creative, perhaps, even hard-working, but never self-disciplined.

As I began thinking about this, I realized that I *had* been conscientious and determined at certain points in my life. As a junior tennis player, I had achieved enough consistency to be ranked number seven nationally. But I also recognized the price I had paid to achieve that consistency. Over the course of a single summer I must have hit close to half a million tennis balls.

By fifteen I had enough consistency and self-confidence to hold up pretty well under the pressures of tournament play. No wonder! As an adult, when someone asked me if I was a good tennis player, I did not consider it bragging to reply, "You bet I am. You would be, too, if you'd spent the time and effort that I did as a kid."

During those same years I'd hit no more than a couple of thousand golf shots, and since then only about five or six hundred shots a year. If consistency were solely a result of practice, it was pretty obvious why my golf game was so erratic. I realized that the pros on the tour had attained their consistency with the same kind of dedication that I had put into tennis. Their 70's that looked so easy, and of which I stood in awe, were achieved only at the expense of thousands of hours of practice and instruction. From this perspective their achievement seemed less awesome.

I also realized that at this point in my life I had neither the determination nor the time to pursue excellence in golf with dedication equal to the pros'. The challenge I put to myself was to attain as much consistency as I could while practicing no more than the average golfer has time for. The goal would not be to break par, but to see how much I could improve within the limitations of only a few hours a week.

At the outset I decided on the following regimen: eighteen holes of golf per week, with forty minutes' practice with woods and irons on the driving range and twenty minutes on the putting green. One lesson per month. Miscellaneous chipping on the front lawn during writing breaks.

In spite of the pressure I was feeling, I started this golfing experiment with high expectations. Somewhere in the more naïve part of my mind I entertained thoughts that perhaps I could discover such an effective concentration exercise for golf that I would be shooting par in a couple of weeks.

Needless to say, my dreams of instant mastery were quickly shattered. Out on the course, away from the familiar environs of the tennis court, everything seemed different. Finishing my first round at Rancho Park in Los Angeles with a 98, I realized that despite my confidence as a tennis professional and Inner Game adherent, my ability did not automatically transfer to golf. I would have to work to develop ways to concentrate that could overcome the unique pressures of the game.

I noticed that I frequently experienced mental lapses right in the middle of my swing. I would start with a nice slow backswing and have a pretty good sense of feel, and then the lights would go out. I'd lose the feel of what my club was doing, develop a jerking motion on the downswing, and finish the shot trying to recover my balance. On short pitches and chips my practice swing would be as smooth as silk, but over the ball my arms would tighten, more often than not, just before hitting and the club would jerk stiffly. Sometimes I'd hit the ground a couple of inches behind the ball, moving it only a few inches, or I'd skull it, shooting it all the way across the green, past the pin and onto the far fringe. Such performances gave me an ugly feeling in the pit of my stomach.

I remembered a similar sensation when playing tennis as an eleven-year-old in my first tournament. Just before hitting my forehand on a crucial point (especially if the ball hit to me was slow and high and I had time to think about it), my wrist would turn to spaghetti and push the ball way off to the right, onto the adjacent court. Not only was the shot embarrassing, but it was deadly to my confidence. Mistakes like this, whether in tennis or golf, couldn't be attributed to technique. They were definitely caused by a mental lapse, a crisis in nerve.

Hence my first few rounds of golf were humbling, though I was undaunted. I think it was connecting well on a few drives that held the magnetism for me. Those few shots felt so magnificent that not only were my hopes kept alive, but I could feel an appetite growing to keep at the game.

Though I'd heard it was best to start practice with a middle iron, the next day on the driving range I couldn't resist pulling out my driver.

I'd set the ball on the tee. Waggle, *whack*, then reach for another. I teed up balls with an increasing compulsion, as if I was putting another quarter in the slot machine before the wheels had even stopped spinning. When I hit a good one, my spirits soared and I'd want to do it again. When I hit one of my slices, I'd set about to correct the mistake. Before I even thought about using an iron, I'd finished a bucket of a hundred balls.

Here I was, at forty, whacking drives off the rubber tees at the range with the same old "gotta be good" compulsion that had me practicing interminably as a ten-year-old. I'll prove I can do it, I still seemed to be saying myself. *Whack . . . whack . . . whack . . .* "Wow, that last one must have gone forty yards past the two-hundred-yard marker; I murdered it! Let's see if I can do it again . . . Now, how did I bring my arms down on that last swing?"

Suddenly I stopped. I was trying hard to achieve something, and it wasn't working. What was that voice talking to me inside my head, and whom was it talking to? Wasn't it a familiar voice, the same self-appointed expert and critic I had named Self 1 and from whose control I had tried to free my own tennis game as well as those of my students?

This concept that there is an enemy within that is the source of mental interference with our human potential is central to Inner Game theory, and deserves a few pages of elaboration for those not already familiar with it. It is the basis for the strategy of how to learn or to improve in *any* Outer Game, and without understanding it, Inner Game techniques usually have only short-term benefit. It was from remembering how I had decreased similar mental interference in tennis that led me to the first effective Inner Game technique for golfers.

Self 1 and Self 2

A major breakthrough in my understanding of the problem of control of mind and body came when, as a tennis instructor, I became aware of a constant commentary going on inside my head as I played. I realized that my students were subjected to a similar flow of self-instructional thoughts while taking lessons: Come on, get your racket back earlier . . . You hit that one too late again . . . Bend your knee on those volleys . . . Uh-oh, here comes another high backhand like the one you missed last time . . . Make sure you don't miss it again . . . Damn it! you missed it again . . . When are you ever going to hit those things? . . . Watch the ball, watch the ball . . . What am I going to say to my doubles partner if I lose this match?

As I began to take a closer look at the thoughts going through my mind during a tennis match, I found myself asking, Whom am I talking to, and who is doing the talking? I was surprised to discover that there seemed to be at least two identities within me. One was playing tennis; the other was telling him how. I observed that the one doing the talking, whom I named Self 1, thought he knew all about how to play and was supervising Self 2, the one who had to hit the ball. In fact, Self 1 not only gave Self 2 instructions, but criticized him for past errors, warned him of probable future ones, and harangued him whenever he made a mistake. It was easy to see that the primary feeling in the relationship between these two selves was mistrust. Self 1 didn't trust Self 2 to hit the ball, and precisely to the extent that he lacked trust, he would try to force Self 2 to conform to his verbal instructions. I noticed that when I had more confidence in my ability to hit a shot, there was a corresponding decrease in instructions from Self 1, and that Self 2 would perform amazingly well without him. When I was on a streak, there was no talk in my head at all.

Once I became aware of Self 1, it grew increasingly obvious that this judgmental little voice barking away like a drill sergeant inside my head was not the best thing for my tennis game. Self 1 was more of a hindrance than the great help he wanted me to think he was. Thereafter I began looking for ways to decrease the interference of Self 1, and to see what happened if I trusted the potential of Self 2. I found that when I could quiet Self 1 and let Self 2 learn and play without interference, my performance and learning rate improved significantly. My Self 2 was a great deal more competent than Self 1 gave him credit for. Likewise, I found that when, as a teacher, I didn't feed the instruction-hungry Self 1 of a student with a lot of technical information but, instead, trusted in the capacity of *his* Self 2 to learn, the progress of my students was three or four times faster than average, and they learned with much less frustration.

In short, I found that Self 1—the verbalizing, thought-producing self—is a lousy boss when it comes to control of the body's muscle system. When Self 2—the body itself—is allowed control, the quality of performance, the level of enjoyment and the rate of learning are all improved.

Although after a time I realized that Self 1 was really a composite of different ego-personalities that would surface at different times, it was still helpful to group all these elements under the identifying label of Self 1 as the source of our interference with our natural selves. I found that in order to *de*crease interference and *in*crease performance, it wasn't necessary to analyze *why* doubt, fear, judgment and lapses in concentration occurred; it was sufficient to recognize their intrusion, and then concentrate the mind on something real in the immediate environment. From this realization, a number of Inner Game concentration exercises were developed for tennis players.

Some readers of *The Inner Game of Tennis* have associated Self 1 and Self 2 with the popular two-hemisphere brain theory, equating Self 1 with the rational, analytical left hemisphere and Self 2 with the intuitive right hemisphere. I don't make the same association because both right and left hemispheres are part of the human body. I look at Self 2 as the total human organism, the natural entity. Self 1, on the other hand, does not actually have a physical existence; he is a phenomenon of mental self-interference who can and does interfere with both right- and left-hemisphere functions. Self-doubt, for example, can be as crippling in a mathematics test as in a tennis match, on a golf course or in singing a song. But when the mind is concentrated and absorbed in what it is doing, interference is minimized and the brain is able to function closer to its potential.

When Self 1 and Self 2 are clearly defined in this way, the basic premise of the Inner Game can be expressed in a simple equation. The quality of our performance relative to our actual potential is equal to our potential (Self 2) minus the interference with the expression of that potential (Self 1). Or: Performance = Self 2 (potential) minus Self 1 (interference).

Thus, the aim of the Inner Game is not so much to try harder to persuade Self 2 to do what he is capable of doing, but to decrease the Self 1 interferences that prevent Self 2 from expressing himself fully.

Still, I found that like most tyrants, Self 1 didn't like losing control and resisted efforts to minimize his influence. The process of decreasing his control in favor of Self 2 proved to be a challenging one, which required the development of concentration techniques designed to keep Self 1 occupied in noninterfering activity and to consciously allow Self 2 to hit the ball. Once Self 1 was focused in a concentration exercise, his interference with Self 2 decreased significantly, and performance instantly improved.

The Magic of Bounce-Hit

One exercise that found considerable success among tennis players at all levels of proficiency was the bounce-hit technique. In explaining it to the student, I would emphasize at the outset that this technique was primarily for increasing concentration and not for improving results, although improved concentration could only help performance. Then I would ask the student to say the word "Bounce" when the ball bounced on the court and to say "Hit" when it made contact with the racket. The object was simply to keep in visual contact with the ball and to say "Bounce—hit, bounce—hit" aloud with as much accuracy as possible.

After letting go of their concern about results, most students would find even at the beginning stages of this exercise that their concentration was stronger, that they returned many more balls than usual, that they hit balls they normally could not reach, and that in general their tennis was more effortless.

Moreover, the difficulties a person had in performing this exercise accurately told him a great deal about his own mental obstacles. On difficult shots he might say "Hit" considerably after the ball had actually touched the racket; the tension in his voice was audible as he hollered "H-i-i-it," retreated, and took a defensive stab at a deep backhand. If I asked him whether he had said "Bounce" on time he might reply, "I'm not sure, I was too busy trying to get into position," or "I was just trying to hit the ball back." In contrast, on an easy forehand, his "Hit" would be relaxed and on time, indicating a lower level of doubt.

Sometimes I would intervene to remind the student that the only game he need play during this exercise was "bounce-hit"—"Forget about trying to get the ball back over the net, and just play bounce-hit." Gradually it would become obvious to the student, as well as to me, that the more he focused on the concentration exercise and forgot about trying for correct form, the better his tennis became. When the bounce-hit became accurate, the body would move more fluidly and with more coordination; often, to his surprise, the student would see that he was hitting with more power as well. Players were almost always surprised by their experiences: "In order to really get into the bounce-hit accurately, I had to forget about all the things I usually tell myself about how to swing"; "I was just doing bounce-hit, and somehow my body managed to get to the ball and hit it better than I thought I knew how. It was as if someone else were playing tennis while I was playing bounce-hit." This is what is meant by getting out of your own way.

I realized that there were two basic reasons for the success of the bounce-hit exercise. First, it is interesting enough to absorb the attention of Self 1, distracting him from his normal interference patterns with Self 2. Secondly, the added concentration on the ball gave Self 2 better feedback, enabling him to perform his eye-body-coordination task better. Students who practiced the exercise conscientiously attained a state of mind that improved their technique automatically and made their tennis seem effortless. I called this state "relaxed concentration" because the mind was alert and focused, yet not tense, and the body moved with an economy of effort that gave the impression of ease. In this state, tennis players would say that they were playing "out of their minds"—and never "better."

Back-Hit: The Bounce-Hit of Golf

Of course many golfers who were familiar with the Inner Game of tennis were asking me the very question I was asking myself: What is the bounce-hit of golf? What single concentration exercise could keep Self 1 so occupied that he wouldn't interfere with the golf swing? It needed to be interesting enough to absorb Self 1, and at the same time assist Self 2 by giving him increased feedback.

Although I experimented with a number of exercises for focusing attention on the golf ball—such as watching a dimple, the label or a speck of dust—none of these seemed to keep Self 1 quiet for long. The problem was that the darn ball just sat there. My mind would grow easily bored looking at it, and if I forced the exercise, my mind became strained and my swing stiff. The bounce-hit magic seemed to have something to do with the mind's fascination with the movement and rhythm of the tennis ball, and this simply didn't apply to the golf ball. Also, in order to hit the golf ball, Self 2 didn't need moment-to-moment visual feedback; the ball wasn't going to go anywhere until I hit it. The very lack of motion of the golf ball, which gave one so much time to think and grow tense, was exactly what was impeding concentration.

Finally I did find one focus that helped more than the others, and is perhaps worth mentioning. Instead of looking only at the ball, I began looking at the back of the ball *in relation to* one of the blades of grass just below it. By keeping both in focus, I could tell if during the swing there was undue head movement. If the relative position of the ball and the background of grass changed a great deal, it was because I had moved my head a lot. This helped, but it still was not the answer I was looking for.

Finally I came to the conclusion that the primary focus of attention in golf should be *not* the ball but the club head, the critical moving object. The movement was *there*, the feedback needed was *there*, the rhythm that fascinates the mind was *there*—not in the ball. But I couldn't follow the club head with my eyes; if I wished to focus attention on it, I would have to use my sense of feel, and I didn't know how difficult this would be. How much could I actually *feel* the club head moving during my swing? I decided to go out to the driving range to experiment with club-head awareness.

At first I had relatively little sense of where my club was. I found that only if I didn't worry about whether I hit the ball or not, I could feel it better. I tried shutting my eyes and swinging, and found that my awareness of feel increased even more. The movement of the club head was becoming interesting enough to hold my attention throughout the arc of the swing. Whenever I would try simply to *feel* the club head and not to *control* it, the club seemed to swing itself, and I got excellent results—the same kind I had in tennis when my mind became concentrated. But when I split my attention—half to the feel of the club head and the other half to trying to swing—the results weren't so good.

To keep Self 1 focused on the club and away from the process of controlling it, I conceived the following concentration exercise. Keeping my attention on the feel of the club head, I would say the word "back" the instant I felt the club head reach its furthest extension at the completion of the backswing. I would simply sense its position, without worrying at all whether it was accurate. Then I would say the word "hit" the instant the club face met the ball. "Back—hit, back—hit." This exercise kept me in touch with the club head throughout the arc, and was exacting enough that Self 1 couldn't easily do the exercise while issuing commands at the same time. Actually, this drill requires somewhat more concentration than the "bounce-hit" in tennis, and, though it's a little harder to do, it is even more effective.

After only a few minutes' work with this exercise, there were often dramatic improvements in swing technique and results. The only real difficulty was in the tendency to want to control the swing instead of simply doing the exercise. It is natural not to want to give up all of Self 1's control at once. But even with 50 percent of Self 1 occupied in "back-hit," there was significantly less interference with the swing. Then, as confidence grew in Self 2, it was easier to risk focusing more of Self 1 on the exercise and leaving the hitting to Self 2.

It was surprising to many golfers to whom I showed this exercise how unaware they actually had been of their club head. Although most had interesting theories about where it should be at the back of the swing, they were often six to eighteen inches off in their estimate of where it *actually* was. One thing I had learned in tennis was that it is more important to know where your racket *is* than to know where it *should* be. The tennis ball is hardly ever where it should be, but always where it is. I told my students, "Should and is usually miss each other." The same is true in golf. What the body needs to control the path of the club head is not a lot of instructions, but accurate, moment-by-moment feedback about the position of the club head. Back-hit was effective in increasing this input, as well as in quieting Self 1. It took practice and trust, but it paid off in results.

Of course there is nothing magical about the words themselves. One can just as effectively attain the same concentration by saying "One-two" at these moments. I also realized that it was helpful for most players to carry through their awareness of the club head to the completion of the swing, so I began experimenting with "Da, da, da"—the first at the back of the swing, the second at contact, and the third at the end of the follow-through. This three-beat cadence captures the crucial moments in the golf swing and is preferable because it doesn't overemphasize the moment of contact. Some prefer leaving out the contact beat altogether and simply say "Back—stop."

Proof that what was important about the exercise was the relaxed state of mind it induced rather than the words came in a phone call from Mr. Dean Nims, from Des Moines, Iowa. Mr. Nims is the president of a paper company and a devoted but unsuccessful golfer. He explained that though he didn't play tennis he had read both Inner Game tennis books to help his golf game. He was an 18–19 handicap golfer who was "too embarrassed by his game to want to take a lesson from a professional."

"I tried to come up with an exercise that paralleled your bounce-hit in tennis, and finally settled on 'Hit-bounce,' " Mr. Nims told me. "I would say 'Hit' when the club hit the ball and 'Bounce' when the ball landed, wherever it landed. The results were instantaneous and dramatic for me. Playing the McCormick Ranch Golf Course near Scottsdale, Arizona, I shot a 76 for the first time using this drill. It was unbelievable! I could see the ball much better, had much less tension, and didn't turn away from my shots after hitting them as I had before. I'd never broken 85 before. Of course I couldn't help thinking I had the game licked after that and would only use the drill when I thought I was in trouble. Then I'd get better again."

Later Mr. Nims came out to California to take some Inner Game golf lessons from Tom Nordland, and to discuss with me the translation of Inner Game principles to business practices. A few months ago I called Dean and he told me that he was using Inner Game principles in most areas of his life. "I can't say I've won the Game," he said, "but my golf has steadily improved—not only in my scoring but in my general attitude." His handicap had gone down to 8 playing little more than once a week, and he said he was enjoying showing the methods to others.

Dean told me about an eight-year-old girl who was on the range with her father one hot, humid summer day. The father was trying to instruct her, but she was unable to hit the ball in spite of all his help. They were both hot and frustrated when Dean introduced himself to them and showed the girl the "da-da-da" exercise. The girl seemed interested, took a swing singing out "Daddy-da," and hit the first solid ball of her life. She continued to do so the rest of the practice session. Her father told Dean that his daughter had been in a junior golf program and, given the task of playing one hole, had been unable to get off the tee. The next day he called Dean to say that the girl was ecstatic. She had not only gotten off the tee, but had beaten her two competitors, both two years older than she.

But Dean also told me that a lot of adults he'd showed the exercise to had more difficulty.

"What's the problem?" I asked.

"They seem reluctant to really try something new and different, even though they saw what it did to my game. Some say they know they're lousy golfers and didn't expect to get any better, and some don't want to entertain the hope. Others who agreed to do the exercise had a hard time accepting that they were not saying 'Hit' until way after the moment of contact. But when they realized that it was their thinking that kept them from saying 'Hit' on time, and then could let go of Self-One control, they'd experience a significant breakthrough."

As an aside, Dean told me of a salesman of his who hadn't been performing up to what Nims thought was his potential. "Although he wasn't a tennis player or golfer, he agreed to read the Inner Game books and discuss with me their application to sales. The next year he doubled his sales."

The principle behind all the variations of this exercise is the same, and individual preferences will emerge if you choose to experiment with them. The only important thing is to make a commitment to doing purely the concentration exercise. Don't try to add it to another tip or to other forms of swing control. Put your mind totally into the club head and *let Self 2 swing the club*. Then you can find out for yourself what Self 2 can do with less interference from Self-1 thinking and control.

My recommendation is that the exercises be practiced for at least a short time on the driving range and putting green before attempting them on the course. It is difficult enough to let go of conscious control over your swing when in practice; it is almost too much to ask under playing conditions. Once he has found the exercise that works best for quieting his mind, the player should stick with it and give it a chance to work. Eventually it will be difficult not to want to use it in the pressure situations. One can expect, however, that the greater the pressure, the harder it will be to quiet Self 1 and attain the same level of concentration as in practice. But then, that's just when you need it, so persevere.

When first learning how to use these exercises, it is a good idea to say the words out loud, and even to have an observer check your accuracy. When your voice is markedly out of sync with your club position, it will be because your mind has wandered—probably to the task of trying to hit the ball. Most players need some practice with this exercise before developing a concrete feel of the club head.

After a brief period of practicing back-hit or "da-da-da," your concentration will probably improve, and so your swing will be freer and you will get better results. At the first sign of success, be careful! Don't start thinking that these are magic words, and that whenever you say them the ball will go where you wish. Remember that if it works, it's not the words that make it work but improved concentration.

Self 1 will try to reduce the exercise to a magic formula, another superstition. If he succeeds, soon it won't work, like all other gimmicks. Then Self 1 will tell you, "Well, that sure doesn't work—throw it out. This whole thing is nonsense." Don't listen. Just remember that the words were simply an aid to concentration, and that it was the concentration that helped. Every time you succeed in blocking out Self 1 and allow Self 2 to hit the ball, you will get better results. But you have to make the effort *every* time; relaxed concentration is easy, but it has to be constant and continuous. Techniques to help gain that concentration are only as effective as your steady use of them.

The positive effects of back-hit and "da-da-da" were soon very apparent on my own Outer Game. As a result of this concentration exercise, my average score dropped from about 95 to about 88. I had the sense that I was swinging a club instead of hitting away at a ball, that I was a little more like a golfer and less like a tennis player trying to play golf. I also knew that I hadn't attained my capacity; I had a lot to learn about both the inner and the outer games of golf, but an important step had been taken in each.

In *The Inner Game of Tennis* I wrote, "Relaxed concentration is the key to excellence in all things." The mental obstacles of golf are an impressive challenge to the practice of full concentration. This subject will be discussed throughout the book, and in depth in Chapter 6.

At this point it would be useful to take a look at the major Self-1 tendencies that interfere with our ability to concentrate. Chapter 4 deals with self-doubt, the greatest single obstacle to concentration and the cause of more missed golf shots than any other single factor.

To conclude this chapter, I want to present excerpts from an article written in 1929 by Bobby Jones called "The Mental Hazards of Golf," which appeared in *Vanity Fair*. When I read it, I couldn't help being impressed that the Inner Game has been around for a long time, and that at least this great golfer recognized it and had a practical understanding of it.

Bobby Jones's article was subtitled, "Stray Thoughts on Worry, Nerves, Temperament and Lack of Concentration in the Game." Here are some excerpts:

Golf is assuredly a mystifying game. Even the best golfers cannot step onto the first tee with any assurance as to what they are going to do. . . . It would seem that if a person has hit a golf ball correctly a thousand times he should be able to duplicate the performance almost at will. But such is certainly not the case.

The golf swing is a most complicated combination of muscular actions, too complex to be controlled by objective conscious mental [Self 1] effort. Consequently, we must rely a good deal upon the instinctive [Self 2] reactions acquired by long practice. It has been my experience that the more completely we can depend upon this instinct—the more thoroughly we can divest the subjective mind of conscious control— the more perfectly can we execute our shots . . . That intense concentration upon results, to the absolute exclusion of all thoughts as to method, is the secret of a good shot. Few great shots are played when the mind is fixed on the position of the feet, the behavior of the left arm, etc.

In playing a golf shot it always helps if the player can shut out from his mind all worry over the result of the effort, at least while he is in the act of playing the shot . . . After taking the stance, it is too late to worry. The only thing to do then is to hit the ball.

It is not easy, even with the assistance of a first-class teacher, for a man to develop a sound golfing style. But it is possible and practicable for a person to cultivate a mental attitude toward the game which will enable him to get everything possible out of his own capability.

3

OVERTIGHTNESS: THE MOST COMMON CAUSE OF ERROR

The Primary Physical Cause of Error

The single most common physical cause of error in golf, and perhaps in all sports, is overtightness. It is generally understood by golfers with even a little experience that the overtightening of muscles in an effort to produce power is responsible for many poor drives. "Don't try to hit the ball so hard, dummy," is a familiar criticism from Self 1 on the course.

But it is equally true, though less recognized, that tightened muscles cause most slices, hooks, topped balls and fat shots. Overtightening of the shoulders prevents a full backswing and follow-through, and overtightening of the hands turns the putter blade closed or keeps it open at contact, sending the ball off course. Involuntary tightening lies behind the dread "yips" in both chipping and putting.

Commonly, the observation of a beginning golfer watching the pros is, "Wow, they make it look so easy. They don't seem to be swinging hard at all." On almost any driving range the muscled jerkiness of the average golfer's swing is in obvious contrast to the pro's powerful fluidity.

Yet overtightness need not plague even the most inexperienced golfer. The purpose of this chapter is to explore the dynamics of this phenomenon, and to give the reader some tools with which he can significantly reduce overtightness in his swing, whether he is a beginner or an intermediate or advanced player.

Actually, "overtightness" is an inaccurate word when applied to muscles, since no individual muscle unit can be over- or under-contracted. It is either relaxed or flexed. When the muscle fiber is relaxed, it is soft and pliable. When it is contracted, it folds in upon itself and becomes rigid enough to support many times its own weight. Strength is measured in the amount of weight that can be supported by contracted muscles. This is not the same as power. Power is the ability to *use* strength, and requires a very sophisticated cooperative effort between contracting and relaxing muscles. Some muscles pull, while opposing muscles remain relaxed and pliant so as to allow the movement to take place.

What we experience as overtightness in golf is often the contracting of too many muscles—more than are necessary to accomplish the task at hand. For example, if all the muscles in the wrist are tightened before impact with the ball, there may be a lot of strength in the wrists, but little or no power will be generated because the tightness of some muscles will restrict the free movement of others.

Another kind of overtightness occurs when rigid muscles fail to release. For instance, the shoulder muscles involved in moving the club back on the backswing have to release fully to allow for other muscles to produce the forward swing. If they remain contracted because of tension, the muscles that initiate the forward swing have to fight against them in accomplishing their task. This creates a classic case of interference with the expression of power and control.

A third kind of overtightening stems from the mistimed contractions of muscles. If your arms are moving toward the ball and the wrist movement occurs at the optimum timing before contact, the momentum generated by this is added to the momentum of the arm movement and produces power. But if the wrist muscles contract at the top of your swing instead of just before contact, the momentum is lost and the club will not be moving much faster than your arms when you hit the ball.

Different kinds of errors in the swing are caused by overtightening in different parts of the body at different times. A restricted backswing is caused by overtightening in the left shoulder; restricted hip rotation by tightness in the hips; casting and scooping by tightness in the wrist and arms. Most of the subtler errors in the swing can likewise be traced to overtightness in certain parts of the body.

But to attempt to remedy the problem by analyzing each instance of overtightness would be exasperating and self-defeating. Literally thousands of muscle units are involved in the golf swing; their timing and coordination are exquisitely precise, and are simply not accessible to intellectual understanding of Self-1 control. The body coordinates these muscles in response to our general command to produce accuracy and power, but only when the execution of those goals is entrusted to it. The best conscious effort we can make is to be clear about our goal, and to keep from interfering with its execution.

Though some experience of overtightness may be unavoidable in the process of learning the golf swing, by far the greatest amount of it comes from the ways in which we interfere with the workings of our bodies (Self 2) when we attempt to control the swing. This interference can be greatly reduced if we are willing to admit that it is present and notice it when it happens.

Just as instructing your muscles to contract is obviously futile, telling yourself to relax is not a solution. In the first place, literally to relax on the golf course would require lying down. Secondly, the command from someone else or from Self 1 to relax, often spoken as if to an idiot, only causes more tension and tightness. On the other hand, over-relaxing is liable to give you the swing of a wet noodle.

The first step in decreasing overtightness in one's swing is to determine if it is present. This may sound obvious, but trying to cure a flaw without really accepting and experiencing it almost always leads to greater problems. So the first step is to swing while focusing attention on your body as it does so. Don't try to do anything; just swing and see if you notice any overtightness, any lack of fluidity or any forcing. In many cases, simply by paying attention to any restrictions in the flow of movement, you will begin to experience a reduction of overtightness without any conscious effort to loosen up. Ten or fifteen swings may be enough to produce a significant change if you are attentive and don't try to relax.

However, if you have played a good deal of golf, patterns of overtightness may have become so ingrained in your swing that it is hard to notice them. One can grow so accustomed to an overtight swing that it's difficult to feel it, and therefore difficult to change it. The following exercises will help you to detect tightness in your swing as it occurs; once it is brought to your awareness, it can be controlled.

Humming Your Swing

One day, quite by accident, I discovered an exercise that is remarkably effective in reducing overtightness. I was out late one afternoon hitting seven-irons on the driving range while waiting for Tom Nordland, with whom I was going to do an Inner Game practice session. I was not concentrating on anything in particular, simply hitting balls and humming to myself. Suddenly something struck me. I could hear differences in my humming, depending on how I was swinging the club. The experience was such a surprise that I wish everybody could become aware of it as spontaneously as I did. The next time you're on the practice tee, take a few swings and try humming to yourself while swinging. *Listen to the humming.*

I hadn't considered my swing particularly tight, but my humming told me differently. I could actually hear the tightness of my swing in the sound. While going back the sound would be nice and smooth, but during the change of direction my voice would become strained, and at contact my throat would constrict and the humming would increase in volume, pitch and, most noticeably, in tightness. Sometimes, when I really went after the ball, the hum would stop after contact, and I would notice that I had also cut off my follow-through. Using a tape recorder, I later recorded the sound of my practice swing and compared it with a recording of a swing at a ball. The increase in tension was painfully obvious.

This phenomenon turned out to be very practical. I realized that I was amplifying feedback from my body by the use of sound. Overtightness that I previously was not very aware of now became glaringly apparent. The audible alterations in sound while swinging told me a lot about what was happening to my body. What to do? The answer was easy: Simply keep swinging and humming. Use this humming as a biofeedback machine to increase control.

For those who are not familiar with biofeedback methodology, it is a way of hooking up subtle physiological functions—such as blood pressure or even brain waves—to an electronic device that gives you feedback, either in sound frequencies or in visual patterns on a screen, enabling you to perceive slight changes. By simply attending to this feedback it is possible to gain control over bodily functions previously thought to be beyond volitional control. For example, a person can learn to control his own blood pressure or temperature, though he won't know *how* he is doing it.

The sound method works in the same way. The sound amplifies the feedback you are receiving from the overtightening of muscles. By listening to changes in the sound, you can soon gain more control over subtle muscular tightness than you might have thought possible by simply trying to relax, or to hit smoothly—efforts that often impel you to swing too loosely, and with low club-head speed. The best way to use this exercise is to make no effort to swing more smoothly, and to simply keep listening while you hit balls on the range. Automatically, and in specific ways you won't understand—and don't need to understand—your swing will start changing. You will begin to hear less tightness in your humming, will notice that you are making better contact with the ball, and will get more distance while making no conscious effort to get those results. Simply accept them and don't ask too many questions about how they happen. Otherwise you will start thinking you know how to relax and giving yourself instructions about how to do it—which is one of the ways the overtightness was created in the first place. A name for this exercise might be "singing your swing"—or, if you don't mind bad puns, "hum, hum, on the range."

It should be noted that although it is useful to hum loudly enough to make variations in sound easily audible for the sake of giving maximum feedback when first experimenting with the use of "singing your swing," later on I found it sufficient to hum in a voice audible only to myself. Even if the hum is very quiet, overtightness in the swing will usually change the sound. Muscles in the throat constrict with bodily overtightness, and the sound is choked off, giving you the necessary feedback. The principle behind this exercise has nothing to do with sound per se. It is *awareness* that is the curative and controlling factor, a subject discussed more thoroughly in Chapter 5. The sound simply serves as a device to increase awareness of what is happening, just as a biofeedback machine does.

Maximum Tightness

There is one other practical and time-tested method of decreasing overtightness. Paradoxically, it has to do with tightening to the maximum. I first learned of this method in a beginners' class in hatha yoga, and have since learned that it has been used for thousands of years by those whose knowledge of the relation between body and mind is in many ways more sophisticated than our own. *To gain maximum relaxation in the body, first tighten it to the maximum extent, and then let go.* For total body relaxation this exercise can be done on each part of the body from foot to head, holding the muscles in each part as tightly as possible for five or ten seconds before releasing them. In a golfing situation you may not have the time to do all this, but it might help to tighten the stomach muscles and then let go, and perhaps do the same with the arms and shoulders. The tightening will make it easier to relax many muscle units that might otherwise not let go, thereby giving the swing more flexibility and fluidity. An added benefit of this exercise is that it increases circulation of the blood and makes it easier to feel movement. There is one final benefit. When you tighten *before* the swing, you reduce some of your tendency to do so *during* it. A lot of our tightening comes from anger and frustration that build up at an unconscious level. By providing an escape hatch for these emotions, you reduce the chances of letting tension destroy your swing.

As effective as physical techniques may be, they can't be expected to solve the entire problem of overtightness. If they could, golf would be a very easy game and not nearly so interesting. But because it is a game of such precision, it takes the overtightening of only a few muscles at the wrong time to produce a slice or hook. Therefore the more basic causes of tightness must be addressed and reduced.

"When Confronted with the Unknown, Tighten"

In most cases, dealing with causes is more effective than dealing with symptoms. Most players admit readily that golf is largely mental, but when it comes to confronting the mental *cause* of physical error, we become shy. We'd rather stick to the physical symptoms, analyzing one error after another, satisfied if after each bad shot we can point to the technical mistake we made. But since it is so difficult to correct the myriad technical mistakes that can result from a single mental lapse, in the long run this is fatiguing and frustrating.

One becomes a player of the Inner Game only when one is willing to see the existence of mental self-interference. If there were no self-interference with the expression of our potential, there would be no Inner Game. It is only because doubt, fear, poor self-image, lapses in concentration and anger are present in all of us that playing the Inner

Game exists and is played by those who want to excel and to enjoy themselves doing so. Dealing effectively with these mental obstacles need not involve deep introspection or self-analysis. Golfers don't need to lie on the couch or repent their sins; they need only to be open enough to admit to the presence of internal interference, and be willing to employ pragmatic methods to reduce that interference. Once the understanding is there, relatively simple techniques can reduce tension and cure many physical faults simultaneously without your even being aware that this is happening. Such an approach is powerful because it deals with causes rather than symptoms.

Over the past ten years I had done a lot of thinking and exploring on the subject of the mental causes of errors in sports. In tennis it seemed that the primary mental problem was fear of failure; in skiing it was clearly fear of falling. In golf the anxiety and tension seemed related most obviously to fear of failure, and to its brother, fear of success. But the simplicity of golf—just one action at a time—encouraged me to delve further, and I now believe that there is a more basic mental cause of error.

One of the steps that led to the recognition of what I now believe to be the prime mental cause of error in all sports occurred during an informal exchange on the golf range with Archie McGill, who, in his golfing days, played to a scratch handicap, was a student of the Inner Game of tennis and is vice president of business marketing for AT&T. I had been asked by him to speak in New Orleans at AT&T's National Marketing Conference on the subject of improving performance under the pressures of intense competition. After the lecture and demonstration of Inner Game principles and methods using tennis as the medium of expression, Archie offered to spend some time on the golf range to help in the translation of these principles to golf. The brief lesson was a fortuitous one.

I had just hit a few drives when Archie stopped me, asked me to put down my club and to hold his finger as if it were my golf club. I did so. He then asked me to hold his wrist as if it were my tennis racket, and I did so. "Why do you grip the golf club so much tighter than you do the tennis racket?" he asked. Not realizing that I had, I replied, "I don't know. I guess it's because I'm more sure of myself in tennis."

"Right," Archie said. "When confronted with the unknown, tighten." This turned out to be an important moment for me. The words registered and began ringing all the proverbial bells. I looked at Archie, who himself had never made that connection before, and was realizing that he had said something of more than superficial wisdom. "That's close to being a universal principle," I said.

This phrase captures a tendency that applies to many different aspects of human experience. When faced with the unknown or the uncertain—a common condition—human beings tend to enter a state of doubt and to tighten instinctively to protect themselves. When we doubt the sincerity of another person in a close relationship, we tighten our hearts. When confronted with an idea or perspective that seems to run counter to our picture of how things are—or should be—we tighten our minds and are called "closed-minded." When we are confronted by a customer who looks skeptical, our sales presentation tends to become strained. A single disapproving glance from a teacher or parent can evoke a closed response. And on the physical level, when we entertain doubt that we may not achieve the results we want or may "do it wrong," we experience tension in our minds and tightness in our bodies.

I immediately recalled tennis players who tighten their shoulders, forearms and wrists when confronted by a ball that they're not sure they can return. As I thought more about this response, it did seem a common tendency. When we have faith, we stay open. The child is constantly confronted with the unknown but is a sponge for all kinds of experiences until at some age he begins to learn to doubt himself. It is the questioning of whether we can meet a given challenge that seems to trigger the tightening action.

Doubt is the fundamental cause of error in sports. It is self-doubt that causes the skier to tighten to the point of rigidity at the top of the run, and the tennis player to tighten on deep backhands. And it is doubt that causes the stiffness in the putter's arms and body as he tenses over a three-foot putt. It was the problem, I realized, that had caused a lot of my own suffering and worry for a great deal of my life whenever in a challenging situation. In many ways I could see that much of the work I had been doing with the Inner Game up to now had been an attempt to solve the single problem of self-doubt. I had realized that Self 1 didn't trust Self 2, which was why he gave it so many instructions, but I hadn't realized that it was Self 1's doubt of Self 2 that was the cause of the anxiety, stress, frustration and other mental obstacles that the Inner Game had tried to deal with separately. I could see that if I did nothing more in the Inner Game as applied to golf than teach myself and others to reduce the obstacle of self-doubt, I would have done enough.

I tried out this idea on Archie. "Would you think it fair to say that self-doubt is the prime cause of error in golf?" Archie paused and reflected. "Absolutely," he answered. "And I do not know of a single golfer who can say that he has overcome it." Just about every playing or teaching professional I asked about this agreed that self-doubt is his biggest enemy, and that it inflicts itself without warning not only on the weekend player but even on the seasoned tour player.

The next chapter explores the anatomy of self-doubt and the techniques for reducing its negative influence on one's golf swing.

4

SELF-DOUBT AND THE TRYING MODE

The Dynamics of Self-Doubt

Little has been written on the subject of doubt as a cause of human error; yet it is, I believe, a more basic one than the much studied phenomena of anxiety, tension and fear of failure. But since doubt is so near the root of the problem, it's not an easy subject to grasp. However, if we can understand more about it and take practical steps toward decreasing its influence, there will be a significant increase in both our performance and enjoyment.

What is doubt? My dictionary defines it as "a lack of certainty about the truth or reliability of something." For the golfer, it means a basic questioning of the reliability of his competence to hit the ball where he wants it to go. It is not a questioning of his ability to do something that is clearly beyond his physical or mental capabilities—for example, hitting a four-hundred-yard drive—but a lack of trust in his capacity to perform actions (such as sinking a four-foot putt) that are well within the scope of his ability.

Self-doubt is a negative quality that is uniquely human. It is a needless questioning of one's potential to know, to learn, to be or to do, and is the main cause of the gap that exists between what a man is capable of doing and what he does do.

The problem can best be understood in relation to natural faith. All human action is based on an innate faith in the body's ability. One cannot take a step toward something without the conviction that he can take the next. To walk down a flight of stairs, the body flings itself out into space, taking fully for granted that one leg and then the other will move forward and support it. This faith does not function at a conscious level in the sense that we choose to have it or not have it; rather, it is an essential part of continuous movement.

If you began to doubt that your legs could move correctly to carry you downstairs, hesitancy would ruin the natural continuity of the action. Then you might start thinking about *how* you walk downstairs. As doubt eats away at the fabric of faith the smooth and efficient interconnectedness between the different elements of behavior deteriorates. Actions begin to look mechanical and self-conscious; and in extreme cases they become so halting that they cannot take place at all. For example, stuttering is probably the result of a form of self-doubt that overtightens the vocal cords and blocks the natural flow of air and words.

One of the reasons why doubt has not been more closely studied is that it is easy to confuse with anxiety or fear of failure. Doubt and fear are definitely friends, perhaps even relatives, but they are not identical twins. We often experience fear in the presence of a real or imagined danger—that is, when we are vulnerable to harm, or imagine that we are. But self-doubt relates neither to our vulnerability nor to external danger, but to our *competence* to avoid or neutralize the danger. No matter how much pressure is riding on a given putt, we do not feel anxiety if we do not first doubt our ability to sink it. If the putt were only one inch long, we would have no doubt and therefore no anxiety. Anxiety increases not only with the perception of danger, but also as our sense of our competence *decreases*. Therefore if we can lessen our self-doubt, our anxiety automatically wanes.

The power of doubt lies in its self-fulfilling nature. When we entertain a lack of faith that we can sink a short putt, for example, we usually tighten, increasing the likelihood of missing the putt. When we fail, our self-doubt is confirmed; Self 1 says, "See, I told you so, you can't sink three-foot putts." Next time the doubt is stronger and its inhibiting influence on our true capabilities more pronounced.

Every kind of performance that I know of is severely impeded by this invisible enemy. On the course, as the golfer confronts the ball sitting still before him, doubt knocks sharply at the door of his mind, and he opens up to it. In a whisper so quiet that it's below the level of conscious thought, Self 1 says, "I just want to remind you that it's very possible you might mis-hit this shot; you've done so in similar situations in the past, so it might happen again." This suggestion produces fear and tension. The voice of doubt sounds so logical, even helpful, that we reply, "Thank you very much for warning me," and immediately begin compensating to prevent—and to ensure—failure.

Once we ever open the door to doubt, our crucial mistake is to believe its logic that if you've flubbed similar shots in the past, it's likely to happen again. It is better to put your trust in Self 2 than in the past. You have the power to do what you can do; there's no need to let memories limit that power. Listening to doubt, we feel the need to begin telling our bodies how to hit the ball, and in doing so, make it more difficult for Self 2 to do its nonverbal task of coordinating muscle movement. The only truth in the doubt is that you may flub the shot if you believe that you might.

The effects of self-doubt can be minimized if we attempt to see what it is. One of its characteristics is that it tends to strengthen as the challenge increases or as it represents increasing risk. For the golfer, progressing from low to higher challenges in the following imaginary sequence increases doubt:

1. Chipping in your backyard.
2. Driving at the driving range.
3. Hitting a drive to a wide fairway on the first tee of your club in a $5 Nassau with your arch rivals.
4. Narrow fairway, trees on left, OB on right; eighteenth hole; par needed to win club championship; your competitor's drive has landed in the middle of the fairway two hundred fifty yards out.
5. You have a five-foot breaking putt to be the dark-horse winner of the U.S. Open; national television cameras are focused; thousands are watching in hushed silence; you've never won a tour championship; you've been putting well all day, but choked on the seventeenth green, leaving a ten-foot putt short by three feet.

The first physical symptom of doubt is weakness. When a golfer stands over a crucial putt, he experiences weakness in his knees and wrists, light-headedness, a general loss of feel and of muscle memory. In short, he loses command of his own resources. There are two common ways of reacting to this sensation: one is to give in to it, the other to resist it. Giving in to the challenge, or avoiding it, decreases effort, motivation and concentration, and produces what I call "the unconscious mode," a state of mind characterized by inattentiveness, lack of motivation, lassitude and sloppy performance. When this response to doubt becomes habitual both on and off the course, one's life becomes one of underachievement.

In our culture the more common reaction to self-doubt is to "try harder." Since our culture values achievement and censures laziness, most of us are encouraged by parents, teachers or employers to overcome our shortcomings. "When in doubt, try harder," we are exhorted. In other words, we learn to compensate for doubt by exerting increased Self-1 control over ourselves. Although the "trying mode" could be considered a better solution than the "unconscious mode" (since trying tends to produce greater alertness of mind and stronger will to overcome obstacles), it nonetheless produces significant interference with the expression of our potential. Since you never try to prove what is certain, trying to prove oneself is, in effect, a mode based on doubt. It always creates mental tension and conflict, which are reflected on the physical level as overtightness; in turn, this restricts fluid coordination of muscles and thus limits the quality of our performance.

In many ways golf is a perfect vehicle for the trying mode. The challenge is so clear and the demarcation between success and failure so distinct that it is hard not to overcontrol. In tennis a double fault by a professional is not as big a failure as a topped ball or shank by a professional golfer. At every level of the game the difference between one's worst and one's best is embarrassingly large. When I am standing over a chip shot and entertain doubt about hitting a decent shot, I try harder for control, tighten in doing so, and to that extent make it harder for Self 2 to execute the shot. But when I don't doubt myself on a putt, I don't *try*; I simply putt in a spontaneous and natural way. The natural Self-2 effort expresses itself without overtightness, as when you walk down a flight of stairs or put food in your mouth— actions that don't generally call forth doubt but still require considerable coordination.

In short, "trying" is essentially compensation for mistrust in ourselves, and generally leads to poor performance. Fritz Perls, the father of Gestalt therapy, observed that human beings are the only living species with the capacity to interfere significantly with their own growth. How? Mostly, Perls said, by *trying* to be something we're not. Perls was fond of remarking succinctly, "Trying fails."

Five Common Types of Trying in Golf

Basically there are five kinds of trying too hard in golf. All of them are compensations for a present or long-standing doubt, and involve an overtightening of muscles that interferes with your swing. Once doubt is identified, practical steps can be taken to eliminate its influence.

Trying to Hit the Ball

As a beginning golfer I experienced the same doubt as almost every novice: doubt that I would hit the ball at all. Most golfers remember their initial experience of failure. We stood far above a small white ball that we were supposed to strike with a long, unfamiliar club in such a way that the ball would travel a long distance. Both the ball and the club face seemed very small, and the chances of the two making contact seemed remote. Taking the club back further and further from the ball, we aimed, swung hard, and missed the ball entirely—an embarrassing and frustrating experience. This first association of failure remains with many throughout their golfing careers. Somewhere deep inside is that memory of missing the ball and thinking that it's really hard to hit. From this doubt comes some of our overtightening on the downswing, and our tendency to *try* to hit the ball, instead of letting Self 2 swing the club.

I still find it remarkable to observe the difference in the swing of most golfers when the ball is not actually in front of them. An amateur who was having a tough time playing in a foursome including Sam Snead during a pro-am tournament at Rancho Canada Golf Course finally asked him for help. Snead replied, "The only thing wrong with your swing is what's wrong with most amateurs'; you don't hit the ball with your practice swing." Something about the presence of the ball invites doubt.

Trying to Hit the Ball Up into the Air

After the beginner has managed to make contact with enough balls, his focus often shifts to trying to hit them up into the air. It appears doubtful to him that swinging down on the ball will make it go up. Trying to lift the ball up by scooping under it is one of the most common causes of error cited by professionals.

On a round with a teaching pro, I bladed an approach shot over the green. What's happening? I asked myself. As if I'd spoken aloud, the pro said, "You're trying to lift the ball up into the air. You actually elevate your body as you hit the ball. *Don't try to lift the ball; let the club do it*."

Trying to Hit the Ball Far

There has never been a golfer who has not once succumbed to the temptation to try too hard to hit the ball far. During my first month on the driving range my favorite club was the driver! I had an almost compulsive urge to see if I could knock each ball past the last marker. Of course I couldn't, so I tried harder and fell into a familiar pattern: trying to muscle the ball to get maximum distance.

Equating power with physical strength, and physical strength with the tightening of muscles, I would whale away, using, in particular, the muscles of my right arm, which had been developed through thirty years of playing tennis. Every once in a while I would connect and send the ball what seemed to be a mile. This would whet my appetite, and my over-efforts would continue. But you can't be around the game for very long before you hear the platitude "Swing easy." I had to admit that the pros on TV didn't seem to be using as much effort as I did. The interferences caused by trying to hit with more power actually inhibit power. If you try to be strong, you only get in your own way.

The way to achieve power *without trying* is discussed further in Chapter 8.

Trying to Hit the Ball Straight

The closer we get to the pin, the greater our doubts about hitting the ball straight. This results in the kind of trying often called "steering." This is the kind of overcontrol that doesn't work any better in golf than it does in tennis, football, basketball or baseball. When I try to steer a putt into the hole, I seem to flub it in the very act of trying to make sure it gets there. Sometimes after the putt I can feel the tightness that comes from the steering, and realize that it corresponds exactly to the degree of doubt I had in my mind before putting. In the same "Mental Hazards" article quoted in Chapter 2, Bobby Jones described how he once hit one of his worst golf shots at a golf course called Brae Burn:

> The seventeenth hole is 255 yards and requires a very accurate brassie shot. The more serious difficulty there lies to the right, and this was the side I determined to avoid. But, as I addressed the ball, I was thinking more about keeping away from the danger on the right than about driving to the green, and, as I hit the ball, I did something—Heaven knows what—that sent the ball an inconceivable distance into the very woods I was trying to avoid. I was very lucky to get out of that scrap with a four. This desire to *guide* the shot is the most difficult fault in golf to overcome.

Trying to Hit the Ball "Right"

Although the first four kinds of trying cause overtightness and introduce error into the swing, they are self-induced and relatively simple compared with the fifth kind of doubt. When trying hard to hit the ball far and straight fails, as it inevitably will, the golfer turns to trying to hit the ball "right," and in so doing involves himself in a web of such complexity that it is almost impossible to extricate himself from it. Once a player starts "taking apart" his swing and analyzing its mechanical elements, he not only lets himself in for endless self-criticism, doubt and trying too hard, but handicaps himself in putting it together again. Every "shouldn't" invites mistakes and every "should" challenges both our memory and ability to make our bodies conform. Chapter 5 explains in greater detail this major pitfall of traditional golf instruction.

Many golf pros are aware of the difficulties imposed on students who are overtight, and the "shoulds" and "shouldn'ts" of the golf swing. One professional poked fun at his own profession with the following satirical piece about how easy it is to play golf:

> IT'S AN EASY GAME: Everyone can learn to play golf. Once a player has mastered the grip and stance, all he has to bear in mind, in the brief

two-second interval it takes to swing, is to keep his left elbow pointed in toward the left hip and his right arm loose and closer to the body than the left . . . and take the club head past his right knee . . . and then break the wrists at just the right instant while the left arm is still travelling straight back from the ball and the right arm stays glued to the body . . . and the hips come around in a perfect circle; and meanwhile, the weight must be 60 percent on the left foot and 40 percent on the right foot at the start . . . and at just the right point in the turn the left heel bends in towards the right in a dragging motion until the left heel comes off the ground . . . but not too far . . . and be sure the hands are over the right foot, but not on the toe more than the heel . . . and be sure the hands at the top of the swing are high and the shaft points along a line parallel with the ground . . . and pause at the top of the swing and count one, then pull the left arm straight down, and don't uncock the wrist too soon. Pull the left hip around in a circle . . . but don't let the shoulders turn with the hips. Now transfer the weight 60 percent to the left foot and 40 percent to the right . . . and tilt the left foot so the right side of it is straight . . . watch out for the left hand, it's supposed to be extended . . . but not too still or the shot won't go anywhere . . . and don't let it get loose or you'll smother the shot . . . and don't break too soon but keep your head down . . . then hit the ball. That's all there is to it!

Technical instructions are easy to give, but not so easy to execute. Because Self 1 is not designed to translate complex instructions into actions, doubt is incurred when he receives them and is expected to be able to make Self 2 perform them.

"Whatever You're Trying to Do, Don't"

Once during an Inner Golf clinic I walked down the golfing range asking the participants what they were trying to do on their swing. There were varied answers: "I'm trying to keep from slicing"; "I'm trying to make sure I follow through"; "I'm trying to swing from inside out"; "I'm trying to keep my left arm straight"; "I'm trying to swing easy." And, of course, there was a beginner who said, "I just want to lift the ball off the tee!"

To each person I gave the same simple instruction: "Whatever you're trying to do, *don't*. Don't try to do it and don't try *not* to do it. Simply don't try at all and see what happens."

What happened was that each person improved—without trying to. The slicer sliced less, the left arm stayed straight all by itself, and the beginner was so exuberant over hitting every ball up in the air that she kept jumping up and down, saying, "This is easy, this is easy."

The less the golfer *tries*, the more fluid his swing will be and the easier it is for Self 2 to achieve the optimum coordination and timing that produces the true golf swing.

The very nature of Self 1 is to doubt Self 2. Self 2's attributes of spontaneity, sincerity, natural intelligence and desire to learn are beyond Self 1's ability to conceptualize. Instead, he says that they don't really exist, and programs his computer with beliefs and concepts about the way you are in order to take Self 2's place. The self-image Self 1 creates is a cheap imitation of the living, limitless real you, the you whose capabilities and attributes surpass anything that Self 1 can conceive with his thinking mind.

The Limitations of the Trying Mode

Many people are perplexed at the suggestion that trying hard is a questionable virtue. Over and over in our culture we've been told, "When at first you don't succeed, try, try again." Hence, for many of us the word "try" means to succeed, and not to try has come to mean accepting failure. But the point of this chapter is that success comes easier when we make an *effort* but don't *try*.

Part of the difficulty of this concept is semantic. I use the word "try" to refer to the kind of Self-1 effort that is a response to self-doubt. "Effort" is the necessary energy expended by Self 2 in order to complete an act successfully, and is based on faith, or self-trust. Faith is the natural underpinning of all successful acts, and it doesn't have to be learned. Babies don't *try* to learn to walk or talk, but they do make an effort. They don't overtighten when grasping your finger firmly; only the necessary muscles are used. (By the way, this would be a good image to keep in mind when gripping your golf club: hold it with the kind of firmness with which a baby grips your finger.)

When we realize that Self 1, having introduced doubt, attempts to take control over our acts himself, we are near the heart of the matter. Having weakened faith in Self 2, he makes his bid to take over as much as we will allow him to. His first ploy is to set himself up as your internal judge, to judge your actions as good or bad, and then to judge *you*. After bad shots, he tells you what you did wrong, and what you should do next time to avoid the error again. After a good shot (which probably happened when you weren't thinking about any instructions) he wants to tell you how you did it so that you can do it again—but next time it almost never works.

Self 1's control is essentially coercive. He praises you and punishes you. He is a sergeant who wants to run the show and thinks that the private (Self 2) is stupid. He uses concern over results to entice you to depend on him. The natural outcome is that Self 2, who knew how to succeed all the time (or could easily learn), is so overridden that failure follows. No matter how familiar we may be with it, and no matter how far we've progressed in spite of Self 1, the fact is that control through self-judgment—that is, *trying*, with ego reward and punishment—is neither effective nor very satisfying.

Golf is traditionally a game played in silence. Few players will tolerate another person saying a word to them once they have addressed the ball. Then why are we so tolerant of Self 1's distracting voice chattering within our own head? If another person in the foursome were to remark, "You'd better watch out for that sand trap in front of the green," we'd probably accuse him of trying to psych us, and try to ignore him. But if Self 1 whispers the same sentence in our heads, we listen as if he were a trusted friend, and may even reply, "Thanks for reminding me: I'll try hard to avoid it." Of course disaster in one form or another usually follows. My own best golf is played when everything is quiet inside as well as out.

There is a state of mind more conducive to excellence than either the *trying mode* or the *unconscious mode*. The true professional in every field performs from a base of solid faith in his potential to act successfully, and to learn to do what he hasn't yet achieved. He keeps his goals high, without letting himself become so emotionally attached to them that he fears failure. His sense of his own value is independent of external results. He doesn't listen to self-doubt, nor does he perform by rote. He dances to the tune of his Self-2 intuitions. In this state of mind his attentiveness to detail is sharp and selective. He sees each situation as it is, not as he would have liked it to be, and nonjudgmentally he perceives in each situation opportunities to propel him toward his goal. Though he gets more done than most, his acts seem relatively effortless. What appears difficult to accomplish in the trying mode seems easy to him. This state of mind—what I call the *awareness mode*—is conducive to optimum performance, and is a subject that will be discussed at greater length in the next two chapters.

The Doctrine of the Easy

Obviously, golfers experience self-doubt and start trying hard when they look at the game as difficult. Part of this sense of difficulty is, of course, inherent in the exacting requirements for precision and power in the game. On the other hand, it is within almost everyone's experience that when we hit our best shots they seem easy, in comparison with the difficulty so often experienced during our worst shots. Some experts say that the golf swing is a natural movement. Others assert the opposite—that golf is difficult because the swing is so unnatural and contrary to instinct. This issue is worth some examination, because it is the sense of difficulty of the game that is responsible for much of our mental tension and our despair about significantly improving.

In his introduction to *Power Golf*, Ben Hogan took the position that golf was a tough game to learn:

> In order to develop a golf swing your thoughts must run in the right direction. Otherwise it will be impossible. Perhaps you will understand me better when I say that when you grip a golf club to take your first swing at a golf ball every natural instinct you have to accomplish that objective is wrong, absolutely wrong.
>
> Reverse every natural instinct you have and do just the opposite of what you are inclined to do and you will probably come very close to having a perfect golf swing. However, every golfer, even the so-called "natural player," learns the hard way. Some are just a little more fortunate than others in being able to learn a little quicker, that's all . . .
>
> My approach to golf in this book will be positive rather than negative. In other words, you will not read anything in this book which will make you self-conscious and frighten you by emphasizing all of the faults you can acquire in trying to develop a golf swing . . .

At the other extreme is Ernest Jones, called on the book's jacket "America's foremost golf teacher," in a book called *Swing the Club-head*. In the first chapter, entitled "Good Golf Is Easy," there appears a sequence of pictures of Diane Wilson swinging a wood with near-perfect form at the age of five. The caption reads: "At her age Diane can swing so beautifully because she does not let her imagination interfere with the feel of the clubhead. She has shot a 71 for nine holes, and her father, a well-known professional, is now entering her in junior tournaments. Diane makes golf look easy because it is easy." Mr. Jones writes:

> If a five-year-old child can learn to swing, there is no reason on earth why you cannot. All you need to do is to repeat the action of that child. She was not distracted in her swing. Her mind was not cluttered by the countless don'ts which fill the air whenever people talk golf. She merely took the club as it should be taken, in her two hands, and did with it what comes naturally. She swung.

So who's right? Is golf easy or hard, natural or unnatural? Tennis professional Vic Braden, my friend and occasional critic, has stated that one flaw in the Inner Game approach to teaching tennis is that it assumes that tennis is as natural as walking or talking, and that in fact it isn't. Since tennis calls for movements that are not instinctual or "natural," he contends that tennis strokes must be learned through close analysis of patterns based on the law of physics.

My own belief is that Hogan, Jones and Braden are all correct. Golf and tennis are both difficult *and* easy. On the one hand, it is probably true that our genes do not carry instinctual information about the most effective way to hit a golf ball. It is also true that the most effective way to hit the ball is opposite to what you might at first think. For example, students need to learn that hitting down on the ball makes it go up, and that tightening muscles don't necessarily produce power. But whether the golf swing is natural or not, it is exacting enough to call for our full attentiveness in learning it. The true issue is not whether golf is *natural*; the point is that learning is natural. Even what might be called unnatural can be learned naturally. Natural learning is easy, but being taught something *un*naturally can make it very hard. Speaking, for example, would be virtually impossible if you tried to learn how to pronounce words by studying the necessary tongue positions. So however difficult golf actually is, we can make it harder or easier by the way we learn or are taught the game.

There is one other way in which we make the game harder for ourselves. What does "harder" mean? In this context it means close to the limit of our capabilities to learn. Hence, the lower the image we hold of our innate capabilities to learn or perform, the more difficult a particular task seems. When we assume too readily that poor performance is based on a lack of innate capability—that is, when we blame Self 2 for our failures—we automatically make the game seem harder. The main point of this chapter has been to establish that the more probable cause of error is Self-1 interference rather than Self-2 deficiency. Self 1 usually prefers to blame the difficulty of the game, Self 2 or various external causes, and it is this very perception of Self 1 that something is harder than it is that sets the self-doubt cycle in motion. The doubt produces "trying," which produces tightness, which produces error, which produces more self-doubt.

The "doctrine of the easy" states that acts done well are done easily and that that which seems hard is usually not being done well. Since it is always hard to perform with the interference of doubt, the difficulty of golf lies not so much in the precision required by the Outer Game, but in the task of circumventing the tension that results from thinking how tough it is.

Of course we think golf is hard because most of us make frequent errors. Since we have failed more often than we've succeeded in our attempts to hit almost every kind of shot, we are likely to entertain doubt about how we will do on the shot confronting us. Some degree of mental tension is apt to be present even if our past failures are not remembered consciously.

Below is a description of a technique that, with practice, can reduce or entirely circumvent this kind of tension. I call the technique "association with the easy." It works to relax the mind in the same way as associating with past failures works to produce tension. The technique is simply to remember or associate with a seemingly difficult task (in this case the golf shot) some action that is simple, preferably one that has never failed. For example, when addressing a ten-foot putt, you might remember the action of simply picking up a ball out of the hole. By vividly associating with this easy act there is no room left in the mind to associate the upcoming putt with failure. Therefore there will be less tension and less trying.

The first time this technique occurred to me I hit ten golf balls out of ten into a target across the carpet in my office ten feet away. What amazed me was that after doing so it didn't seem remarkable. It was easy to pick up ten balls.

Before trying the technique again I asked Molly, an Inner Game assistant, to experiment with it. First I asked her to make ten putts toward another golf ball about fifteen feet away. Measuring, I determined that her average putt landed about nine inches from the target. Then I said, "This time, Molly, I want you to think to yourself that all you are doing is reaching out and picking up that golf ball. Mentally I want you to associate these next putts with that simple action, not with the harder task of putting."

Molly got the idea, and hit ten putts very close to the target ball—an average of only four inches away. Afterward she said, "The target ball somehow seemed more in my immediate world, not something out there. I had no doubt that I could reach out and touch it." Her stroke looked different too; it was not consciously controlled, yet it was authoritative and followed through in a much less tentative manner. This technique uses a trick of Self 1 against himself. If doubt is engendered by association of a present action with past failure, why can't confidence be engendered by associating with an act you never fail at? I reasoned that it wasn't necessary, as it is sometimes suggested, to remember past successful golf shots; it would be more productive to associate with actions that you have *never* doubted you can do. Each time I succeeded in totally immersing myself in this concept, there was not a trace of doubt in my mind about sinking the putt, and Self 1 seemed to be entirely fooled. He didn't even become excited over shots better than my expectations; anyone can reach out and touch an object, and there's no need to congratulate oneself for that. And because the putt seemed easier, my stroke was easier, with no tendency to overcontrol.

This technique is easily adaptable to any part of your game. When I next had a chance to go out to the driving range I asked Molly to come along.

I looked out at the yardage marker a hundred and fifty yards away, a six-iron in my hand. It just didn't feel right to associate hitting a shot that far with reaching out and touching it. Realizing that I was searching for something, Molly asked, "Well, what could you do in relation to that sign?" I thought for a moment. "Well, I know I could throw a tennis ball pretty close to it."

"Okay, you're just throwing a tennis ball to your student, who is right at the one-hundred-fifty-yard marker."

This association had the same magical effect for me. I held in my mind the memory of tossing a tennis ball and felt so comfortable inside that I didn't steer. Ball after ball went straight toward the marker. Only when I got sloppy with my technique or started thinking about my swing would accuracy desert me.

Then I asked Molly to try the same association. At first there was no noticeable improvement. I realized that she hadn't thrown a tennis ball much, so we tossed balls back and forth for a few minutes so that she could experience how easy it was. Her next shots were not only significantly straighter, but were more cleanly hit and had better distance. "It may be hard to play golf, but it's easy to toss balls," she said, grinning.

When I started experimenting with drives, fairway woods and the longer irons, I found it natural to associate with throwing a baseball. Projecting a fairway to exist between two trees about thirty yards apart on the range, I would have thought that my chances of driving a ball into that opening were about fifty-fifty. There definitely would have been some doubt that I could do it consistently. But I had no doubt that I could throw a ball into a thirty-yard-wide opening, and neither would anyone else who has ever spent much time throwing. This association seemed to make it easy for me to let power out in the swing without fearing that I was losing control; I knew I could throw the ball hard and still keep it within the opening. The effect this had on the consistency of my drives was even more surprising than in the irons. There were no severe slices or hooks, simply straight balls, gentle fades and a few slight draws—all in the fairway.

What excited me about all this was that I wasn't getting excited. This may not seem to make sense, but it was important to me. I had played enough to know that whenever I became aware that I was playing particularly well, the wave I was riding on would soon crash.

When I experimented with this technique on the putting green, I found I had the best results by associating mentally with reaching in the hole and picking up the ball. Another association I liked was that of threading a needle. Remembering that action not only relaxed my mind but concentrated it, and automatically put in me a state of mind conducive to precise action. For chipping, I liked thinking about the simple action of taking the stick out of the hole.

Although there are other ways of circumventing self-doubt, this one is simplest to learn, for both the beginner and the advanced golfer. There are just three guidelines I found useful for successful association. First, the associated action should in some way include the target; that is, putting your hand in the hole is a better association than picking a daisy in a field. Second, the associated action should be not only a simple one but also one that you have actually done frequently. Details such as distance are not important; it didn't matter to me that my tennis students had never been one hundred and fifty yards away, or that I had never thrown a baseball two hundred and forty yards. Third, it seemed to help if the action was generically similar to the one you were doing, but not so close that you might try to physically substitute one for the other. The technique is *not* to swing a golf club the way you toss a ball. The association signals the mind to relax, but does not tell the body how to swing. It is effective in inducing a state of mind that is optimal for performing a physical action.

This technique is effective and simple, but it is not a panacea; don't expect it to make your ball go where you want it to every time. But when done with concentration and not as a gimmick, it can reduce the elements of self-doubt and tension that interfere with performance. Especially when you are prone to associate a particular golf shot with past failure, I recommend using this technique as a kind of shield to to block out doubt. After a while you won't have the negative association any longer, and you can put away the shield.

It is likely that if you succeed in convincing Self 1 that golf isn't difficult, he may start thinking that the game is easier than it really is. You'll know this is happening when, instead of getting overly tense, you grow too casual and sloppy. This is not a bad sign. Be thankful of being rid of your tension and make one adjustment: *Do the easy with full attentiveness.* For example, it is easy to pick up a golf ball out of a hole, but it requires effort and concentration to do it with maximum attentiveness. In this case, you might think of picking up the ball as if it were a valuable diamond you wanted to examine, or performing the act with maximum grace, care and coordination. Since it is easy, you have no fear of failure, but since you want to do it well, it requires concentration. A commitment to attentiveness will result in the best from both worlds: you step closer to that state of mind in which performance is optimized, while avoiding the tension associated with past failure.

5

LEARNING GOLF IN THE AWARENESS MODE

Something's Gone Wrong with the Way We Learn

During my entire forty-two years I have been involved in the process of education offered by our culture—as student and teacher, child and parent, athlete and coach, and recently as a corporate trainer as well as trainee. If I can draw one conclusion from my experiences, it is that something is out of balance in the way we go about learning and teaching. The scope of this book does not allow for elaborating extensively on this view, but I do want to address briefly the problem of learning and teaching golf within the context of education in the culture at large.

If asked to state the imbalance concisely, I would say that institutional education has overemphasized conceptual learning to such a degree that the value in, and trust of, the natural process of learning directly from experience has been seriously undermined.

Based on the assumption that the mind is an empty receptacle that develops as it is filled with facts, conceptual learning is concerned primarily with the accumulation and ordering of concepts and theoretical information. Experiential learning has more to do with the development of innate potentialities and skills. The word "education" comes from the Latin *educare*, meaning "to lead out," and indicates that the potential intelligence sought already exists within us, and needs to be drawn out. This drawing out by a teacher, system or environment is the primary function of true education. Thus, talking, for example, is not a skill imposed on the child from without; rather, it develops from an innate capacity encouraged and supported by parents and the youngster's experience of his environment.

Balanced education requires a proper relationship between cognitive and experiential knowledge, but in the teaching of physical skills, learning through direct experience should take priority over learning through formal instruction in concepts. In golf, small but important steps have recently been taken in the direction of experiential learning. Bob Toski's book *The Touch System for Better Golf* attempts to establish the primacy of feel and muscle memory in the swing, and former PGA educator Gary Wiren's work *The New Golf Mind* attempts to clarify and separate the function of analytical "left brain" thinking from the intuitive, nonverbal "right brain" functions.

Obviously, the difference between conceptual learning and experiential learning lies in the difference between a concept and an experience. A concept is a thought or an idea, but it is not the reality it refers to. As such it has its value: it can point the way to a desirable experience, or can warn against an undesirable one. But when any educational process becomes more involved in concepts than in the realities behind them, serious imbalance results.

The following is a description of the downswing by Ben Hogan, one of the greatest golfers of all time:

> Just before the hands and arms come into play, the body should be set for the hit. By that I mean that 90 percent of the weight should be on the left foot and the right arm should be very close to the body.
>
> All tension should be released from the right leg and hip. The right knee should break in toward the left knee. The wrists uncock, the right arm straightens and then turns over going forward over the left shoulder. This all takes place in that sequence and you will find that it will bring you to the complete finish.

Are you confident that after reading this you could reproduce the action the author is describing? I couldn't, especially if I thought about it, but I am confident that with study I could get 100 percent on a multiple-choice test given on the material. I learned how to do that in college. Even if I went over the elements of the instruction one by one and tried to repeat the actions I thought were being called for, I'm sure that no matter how technically correct the resulting movement might be, I would feel extremely awkward and disjointed.

The problem is that there is a limited amount that Self 2 can learn from concepts; it learns primarily from experience. In easy acts words work fine. If I say, "Raise your hand," and don't specify how high, how fast or in what manner, the student will probably not experience self-doubt and will have no trouble obeying the instruction. But the minute I make the demands complex, or give a lot of even simple instructions at the same time, circuits blow, self-doubt enters, and both learning and performance suffer.

The Essence of Experiential Learning

I sometimes wonder what man's fate would have been if in the development process he taught himself to understand language before he learned how to walk. No doubt parents would have coached us when to shift our weight from left foot to right, and we would have spent a lot of time on the floor analyzing the causes for falling down again. Undoubtedly, many of us would have developed negative self-images about our motor skills and would still be tripping over our own feet.

Instead we learned from experience as a natural process, just as kids teach themselves how to balance on bicycles and skateboards. It is a process that engages one's complete attention and is enjoyable. Although the desired results are not always reached overnight, the process is easy.

On the golf range, one sees few examples of natural learning taking place. Instead, a lot of interference with natural learning can be seen. People are working harder than necessary for results and few seem to be enjoying the process. Faces are contorted in frowns of self-contempt and frustration. Each shot is judged, and each "bad" one is analyzed for the mechanical causes of error; then more strain goes into forcing the body to "do it right" on the next shot. Tightness and awkwardness are more the rule than the exception, and soon seem normal to the average golfer. If it were not for the lure of the game itself, learning golf would be no more popular than most classroom learning is for high school students.

Psychologists confirm that most of us learn more in our first five years than in all the rest of our lives. Yet small children don't go through this torturous process of self-evaluation, analysis and trying to do it *right*. They don't have to *try* to learn; they simply do so. Until adults teach them otherwise, learning is so natural for children that they don't even know it's happening, and in contrast with the experience of most adults, they have fun doing it. The talent to learn is one that we adults still possess, and if we can let go just a little of our attachment to conceptualization, it can be used and developed to great advantage.

Experiential learning is a function of *awareness*. That word makes some people uncomfortable; it has ethereal connotations associated with the vague, the impractical and the downright weird. It deserves more respect. Without awareness, or consciousness, there is no such thing as learning—or more fundamentally, no such thing as life. The entire evolution of life, from the single cell to the complex arrangement of cells called the human body, is based on the power of the living organism to be aware of external and internal stimuli, and to respond selectively to them. Yet throughout my education I heard almost nothing about the power and necessity of awareness.

Stated simply, the first principle of the Inner Game approach to learning is that whatever increases the quality of awareness in an individual also increases the quality of learning, performance and enjoyment. Conversely, whatever interferes with or distorts awareness of things as they are detracts from learning, performance and enjoyment. Inner Game learning involves three steps: first, to increase awareness of what *is* (and decrease interferences that distort perception); second, to increase awareness of our goal or purpose (and decrease interferences with clarification of goals); third, to trust the natural learning process. In this book, these principles are, of course, applied specifically to golf, but they are applicable anywhere else.

A Critique of the Do-Instruction

Perhaps the primary tool used in conceptual teaching of physical performance is what I call the do-instruction. It is an order from the mind of one person (the teacher) to the body of another (the student), who is supposed to comply with the command by translating the instruction into the appropriate physical behavior.

There are two kinds of problems with the do-instruction. One is that of authority and power. Most of us don't like being told what to do, unless we have given consent willingly to the teacher because of trust and respect. Even then, do-commands often produce unconscious resistance because we associate them with being manipulated by orders in past circumstances where the trust, respect and consent were absent. I've often met students who were so sensitive to being "taught" that if I simply asked them to notice an aspect of their swing they would ask defensively, "What am I doing wrong?" (Incidentally, I have observed that "trying too hard" to comply is one of the most common forms of resistance to do-instructions. The trying shows good intention while frustrating the teacher because it results in failure. Most children learn this way to retaliate against parents who insist on showing them how to do everything.)

Even when there is no ego resistance to do-instructions, they cause problems for the student, and it is my contention that their misuse is a primary cause of self-doubt. So common is this teaching practice that the consequent interference with the learning process, and thus with performance, is generally taken to be an inevitable part of "the difficulty of learning." But self-doubt is *not* an inevitable part of learning, and encouraging it, to say nothing of introducing it, defeats learning.

How do do-instructions incur doubt? How do you write your name? How do you tie your shoe? How do you walk down a flight of stairs? Think about one of these actions and see if you can come up with a set of instructions about how to perform it. Then try to do the action by following your own instructions. It's not easy if you described the action in any detail, but why?

The primary difficulty lies in our inability to translate any but the simplest verbal command into a bodily action. When asked to do more, we invite self-doubt because the brain cannot consciously control the body with words; that part of the brain that analyzes, conceptualizes and instructs us verbally is incapable of moving a muscle, and has only a limited capacity to communicate to the part of the brain that does control our physical behavior.

Besides the general tendency of the ego to resist being told what to do, there are five basic ways in which do-instructions engender doubt.

The first is the communication gap between teacher and student. The student doubts that he even intellectually understands what the instructor means. Teachers are notorious for developing their own jargon and assuming that everyone speaks the same language. For example, I'm still not sure exactly what the famous golf instruction "Pronate the wrists" means. Not knowing the meaning of the instruction obviously invites doubt that I can follow it.

The second is the internal communication problem with the student. Intellectually the student may understand, but his body doesn't. This is the most prevalent gap, and a universal invitation to doubt. Because the mind understands, the student assumes that he should be able to make his body conform. He also knows that his teacher expects conformity. But unless the body can associate that instruction with an already familiar action, it can't conform. Without *muscle knowledge* of the instruction, the student finds himself unable to meet his own or his teacher's expectations, and doubt increases.

Third, the student may understand intellectually and his body may understand, but the action called for is outside his present capability. For example, it was some time before my body was ready to deal with the subtleties of leg motion at the outset of the downswing. It's easier for instructors to see what's wrong in a person's movement than to know which particular correction should be focused on in a given development process. Doubt increases as the student is asked to do something out of line with his natural learning progression; this reinforces his "I can't do it" self-image.

Fourth, in many cases do-instructions given by teachers to students and by students to themselves are just plain incorrect. Trying to follow commands that do not conform to the mechanics of golf or to the physiology of the body obviously causes doubt.

Fifth, there *are* do-instructions that are understood intellectually and in body language, and are correct, are within the natural progression of learning and are easy to accomplish. Such do-instructions need not cause doubt, and can aid learning in some cases. But doubt arises when one tries to conform to too many of these at a time. Almost every time we receive a "should" instruction, there is a spoken or implied "shouldn't," which leads to another and then another, until the mind is clogged with more instructions than it can handle.

Much of modern physical-skill teaching relies heavily on do-instructions in spite of their inherent limitations and general misuse. Students knowing of no other form of instruction take them for granted, disguise their resistance and suffer doubts because they don't know of another way to learn. In fact, most golf students feel cheated if the instructor doesn't tell them what they're doing wrong and what they should be doing. But it is this process that we have become so accustomed to that actually cheats us of recognizing our potential as learners. It persuades us subliminally to mistrust ourselves. Educationally the cost is high, and the resulting gap between our performance and our potential is proportionately large. Unfortunately, we learn from our teachers how to teach ourselves, and soon we all develop a Self 1 who continues to sow seeds of self-mistrust whenever we listen to him, whether or not we are taking lessons from a pro. To redress this problem is, in my opinion, one of the most important challenges before education in general, and it would be interesting if sports teaching could lead the way.

Before addressing the alternative to the do-instruction in the teaching of golf, I should point out that there are excellent instructors of every sport who understand the limitations of do-instructions, and who have developed the art of speaking a language that the body can understand. The best teachers have always used image-rich language that invokes not an abstract description of a movement but a concrete picture or "feelmage" associated with acts already familiar to the body. Bob Toski, for example, suggests that your swing should feel like a canoe building up momentum and then going over the falls, and that "The left wrist should feel as firm through impact as it would if you were backhanding a rug-beater." Gary Wiren in *The New Golf Mind* points out that Sam Snead used to think of the word "oily" as he swung, thus engaging his right-brain hemisphere and avoiding the pitfalls of conceptual left-brain thinking. Unfortunately, as Ben Hogan pointed out, the golf swing is not easily associated with other common movements, so most of us do not have many useful analogies in our muscle memories.

The Awareness Instruction

Fundamental to the Inner Game approach to teaching is a workable alternative to the do-instruction, one that engages the student in learning from experience and increases his self-trust. I call it the awareness instruction. Simply defined, it is a command to the *attention* of the student rather than to his body. Instead of saying, "See if you can do this or that," it says, "See if you can *see, feel* or *hear* what is happening right now and right here." For example, "Pay attention to the direction of the downswing." The back-hit exercise introduced in Chapter 2 involves an awareness instruction that requests that the student focus on the club, with special emphasis on its position at the back of the swing and at its completion. None of these call for a change in *behavior*, but simply for heightened awareness of what is happening.

"See if you can *feel* whether the blade of your club is open, closed or square at impact" is also an awareness instruction, circumventing the doubt about *doing it right* by involving the pupil's mind in the process of simply noticing what is happening. The instructor might ask the student to shut his eyes, then arrange the club in different positions—open, square and closed—until he can feel the difference in his hands while the club is motionless. The next step is the challenge to the student to see if he can feel the angle of the face at the moment of impact when the club is moving at normal speed. If the student thinks that this is a gimmick to help him to hit the ball square, he is apt to *try* to do it right, and to be caught in the same trying mode as if he were simply told to make sure that his club was square at impact. But if he takes the awareness instruction for what it is—simply a request that he attempt to feel what is happening with the face, no matter what it is—then there is no question of right and wrong, the mind focuses on the experience, and soon experiential learning will take place as he learns to differentiate the sensations of the different angles of the club face.

Awareness instructions are radically different from do-instructions, and tend to put the student in another frame of mind entirely. They engender a mode of learning that is free of doubt, frustration and discouragement. They induce a natural state of learning, which, once rediscovered, progresses organically and rapidly. Most important, they strengthen the student's faith in his own capacity to learn from experience; the instructor's role is only to help him in focusing on the most relevant parts of his experience.

Let me add that when a student has been helped by an Inner Game teacher to regain trust in his ability to learn from experience, certain do-instructions *can* be given at appropriate moments in such a way that they neither cause doubt about their achievement nor undermine the student's basic trust in his own learning capacity. But so conducive are awareness instructions to learning that I use them 95 percent of the time, and employ do-instructions only for simple tasks or when a high degree of trust for Self 2 and the teacher has been established.

Most do-instructions can be better framed as awareness instructions, and their translation becomes easy after a little practice. When I first heard the tip "On the downswing swing from the inside out," I was confused. Even after I understood the instruction intellectually, I had little confidence that I could do it, so of course I *tried*. I didn't get it right, so I tried again, and, of course, only became tighter. A couple of times my friend Tom Nordland said, "That time you got it," but I couldn't feel the difference between those "right" swings and all the others.

The translation of this doubt-producing do-instruction into an awareness instruction might sound like this: "Just swing the club without trying to do anything, but feel whether, on the downswing, it's moving from outside the ball—that is, further away from your body—to inside—closer to your body—or the other way around." Before beginning, the instructor might move the arms of the student from outside to inside and then from inside to outside to give him a *feel* of the difference. As soon as he can distinguish between these two broad categories of movement while actually swinging, the student can be asked to distinguish more subtle changes. He might be asked, for example, to see if he can tell after each swing whether it was more or less inside out than the last. In this case, in order to pinpoint his focus more subtly on the swing, awareness can be heightened by the use of a rating scale. If a downswing that is square to the target line is O, a swing that is slightly inside out could be called a +1; more inside out, +2 or +3. Likewise, outside in downswings would be rated −1, −2 and −3. (With advanced golfers, the scale can be refined indefinitely to focus on smaller and smaller fractions of differentiation.) This fine-tuning of the student's attention creates more refined differentiation in feel, and allows learning to take place. By experimenting, Self 2 discovers which stroke feels and works best for his body at his level of development.

Sometimes a golfer's swing becomes stuck in a groove, and despite focusing on the downswing it remains stuck. If the student feels that his normal swing is a −2, the instructor might say, "Why don't you see what a minus 3 feels like? . . . Now try a plus 3, a plus 2, a plus 1." After he has broken out of his rut by experiencing different swings, he can go back to swinging without trying, and if he sincerely doesn't *try* to swing "right" but sticks to awareness exercises, his body will automatically select the swing that feels and works best. Through such a natural learning process the student can groove his new swing without *thinking* about it but by concretely *feeling* it.

Here are some examples of translating do-instructions into awareness instructions. As you read them, try to imagine the difference in the way you might react to each instruction.

1. Keep your head still throughout the swing. It's imperative to keep it still. Keep working at it until you get it.

1. See if you sense any movement in your head during the swing. Notice whether there is more or less movement on each succeeding swing.

2. Early in the downswing, the right elbow should return to the right side. (Sam Snead)

2. During the next few swings, pay attention to your right elbow. Don't try to change it in any

3. Keep your left arm straight.

3. Notice whether your left arm is straight or whether is bends on each swing, and scale the amount on a scale from 1 to 5.

4. The most common fault of the inexperienced player during the downswing is hurrying into the downswing before the backswing is completed, rushing the right shoulder around before the club head reaches the hitting area, and turning the upper body into the shot too quickly. (Ben Hogan)

4. On the next twenty shots, pay attention to your body and see if you can detect any rushing during the swing. If so, tell me how you rushed—that is, which muscles you used to rush and when. Don't try to avoid rushing; just notice what you are doing, and any changes in degree.

5. Try to be certain the back of your left hand faces down the target line as you strike the ball. (Arnold Palmer)

5. Take a few swings paying attention to the back of your left hand. Notice if it is square, open or closed in relation to the target line.

6. It is the consensus of *Golf Digest*'s professional teaching panel and advisory staff that the ideal position of the club shaft at the top is parallel to the intended line of flight. (*Golf Digest* magazine)

6. Without looking, sense whether the shaft of your club is parallel to the target line, inside the line or outside it. It might help if you shut your eyes during the swing to increase your sense of feel.

In each of these examples one difference between the two kinds of instructions is consistent. The do-instruction asks the golfer to achieve a certain result that he may or may not feel he can produce. Because there is a potential for success or failure, he is likely to be over-concerned with getting results and thus be open to doubt and to straining. Even if he succeeds, he will think that he has to remember that tip every time he wants the same results—along with all the other instructions already in his head. The awareness instruction, on the other hand, asks only one thing of the conscious mind: pay attention to what is happening. There is no doubt because there is no right way or wrong way, and there is no fear of failure because there is no externally implied standard for success. Yet the body learns because it is now free to focus on what feels good and to see for itself what works.

One of the primary characteristics of the awareness instruction is that it is nonjudgmental. Awareness simply sees and accepts what is; it doesn't place a positive or negative value on the result. Some instructors who have tried to make awareness instructions work for them fall into the use of quasi-awareness instructions, such as "Are you aware that you're taking your swing back incorrectly?" or "Be aware that you're not turning." But it's impossible to be aware of *not* doing something because awareness can focus only on what *is* happening. What's not happening is a concept based on a judgment about what you think *should* be happening.

The most difficult thing about awareness instructions is to realize that they work, when all your life you've believed only in do-instructions. It's not hard to see that they circumvent self-doubt and frustrations, but perhaps it's not so easy to believe that they get results. If it's any comfort, I have the same problem; even though they improve learning and performance whenever used, each time I am surprised. It blows my mind that changes for the better can take place so effortlessly. It is not always the change I anticipated, but that only makes it more interesting. Nothing but my repeated experience that awareness instructions do work has given me the confidence to rely so heavily on them. It is results, not theory, that warrants their use. Therefore I don't suggest that you make a heroic effort to forget about results, or to convince yourself that your score is really not important. What I do suggest is that you experiment with awareness instructions long enough and sincerely enough to discover their effects for yourself.

Introducing Al Geiberger to the Inner Game

Ever since I heard of Al Geiberger's score of 59 at the Colonial Country Club in Memphis, I had wanted to meet him and talk with him about what he had done in the inner game to achieve such outer-game success. When I called him, we made a date to meet at a private club in Santa Barbara.

I arrived at the club first and went to the pro shop to meet the club pro with whom Geiberger had arranged to use the putting green and range. When I introduced myself, he expressed some curiosity about what I intended to do with Mr. Gieberger on the range. "You're not going to do anything that looks like teaching, are you?" he asked somewhat threateningly. I asked him what he felt would look like teaching.

"Well, I just don't want you showing him how to swing a golf club, or him standing over you showing you how to address the ball or anything like that." I couldn't help being amused at the prospect of teaching Geiberger *anything* about how to swing a golf club, and though I knew that he was certainly competent to teach me, I didn't want to learn that way. "No, I can assure you that what we do won't resemble that kind of teaching," I answered.

When Al arrived his bearing and manner reminded me immediately of Jimmy Stewart. He told me that he'd been interested in the mental side of golf for some time and that he was particularly open at this point; he had just had a disastrous time trying to learn the hows and how-not-tos of the parallel turn from a skiing instructor who'd made him dizzy with instructions. "Finally I said, 'To hell with all this,' just skied down the hill and began to get the hang of it."

I asked Al about his inner-game experiences in golf. He recalled that several times when he was practicing putting before a tournament and someone came up to talk to him, he would continue putting and be surprised that it would improve while he was engaged in casual conversation. When the interruption ended, he would say to himself, Now I'll get back to some serious putting—only to find that his performance would drop off significantly. "From this and other experiences," Al said, "I've come to realize that I perform best when I'm letting my subconscious mind hit the ball and my conscious mind is otherwise occupied. Is that what you're talking about in the Inner Game?"

"That's a part of it," I replied, "but it's possible to use the conscious mind in a productive way while still allowing what you call the subconscious mind, part of what I call Self 2, control the hitting of the ball. You don't have to distract the conscious mind away from golf; you can involve it in a task that helps Self 2 in his task."

I offered to give Al an example of one way this might work in putting, and began by telling him that I had found that one of the greatest single obstacles to performance among tennis players was in trying too hard for results. "The same seems to be true in putting, where the goal desired is within immediate reach. The overconcern with results produces tension, tightening and consequent loss of touch, which makes achieving the goal more difficult. So the key to increasing one's putting feel is to switch games—to change from the game called 'trying to get the ball in the hole' to an awareness game called 'see if you can *feel* where your ball goes in relation to the hole.' " The hole would still be the target, but the primary object of the game wasn't to drop the putt, but to be able to tell, without looking, where the ball stopped in relation to the hole. Only by focusing on the feel of the swing can you make an accurate guess.

At first Al had a hard time really letting go of trying to sink the ball. He would putt and guess, then look up to see where the ball had actually gone. If he had missed by what seemed to him too wide a margin, he would shake his head in mild disappointment. Finally I insisted, "Al, don't try to get the ball into the hole. That isn't the game right now. Pretend that we're betting a hundred dollars a putt that you can come within six inches of telling me exactly where your ball comes to a stop."

"You don't *want* me to try to sink it? Should I try to miss it?"

"No, don't try to sink it and don't try to miss it. Just putt toward the hole and see if you can tell by feel alone where it goes."

This time Al prepared to putt with much less tension in his face. Instead of looking at the hole two or three times, he looked once, shut his eyes and stroked the ball right into the cup. I caught it before it could make a sound and asked him where it had landed. "It was pretty good," Al said. His eyes were still closed, but there was more certainty in his voice. "Maybe it went three inches past the hole on the right edge."

"Nope, you're off a little. It went directly into the hole, though it probably would have rolled a few inches past if you'd missed. See if you can do better next time," I challenged. Al was beginning to see what this drill was about, but the surprise to him was that he was putting considerably better when he was sincerely playing the awareness game than when he was trying for results.

Thereafter Al became absorbed in the awareness game, and I could tell from the diminished tension on his face, both during his setup and after the putt, that he had let go of some of his concern about results. Most of his focus was now concentrated on increasing his feel in order to be more accurate in his guesses, and within a few minutes he significantly improved his ability to tell where the ball stopped. Simultaneously, his putting stroke became smoother and slightly less deliberate. Instead of looking at the ball, then back at the hole three or four times, he would sight once, close his eyes, putt, and then, even before the ball stopped, guess.

"How can you tell whether the ball went right or left of the hole?" I asked.

"I don't know for sure, but I can feel it."

"Putt a few more and see if you can discover what gives you the most accurate feedback about the direction of the ball," I suggested.

After three more putts Al decided that he could feel the direction by paying attention to the points on the thumb and forefinger of his right hand where they touched the leather of the putter handle. When I asked him to focus his attention on those points, he was able to tell me with amazing precision just how far to the right or left his putts went. As the accuracy of this feedback process increased, so did the accuracy of his putts, and soon they were considerably more consistent in their direction. Then I asked the same kind of question about how he could best determine the length of his putts. Although there were several factors here, by focusing on what seemed the most reliable feel he was able to increase the accuracy of his guesses, and automatically the accuracy of the length of the putts themselves increased.

As happens with almost everyone I have taught, after Al noticed the improved results he was getting during this awareness exercise, he would sometimes lapse into trying to repeat the "good results" by a conscious effort to control the putter. Inevitably the results would be worse. "Can you feel the difference when you try?" I would ask. "Yes, I tried to sink that last one," he'd say. Then he would return to awareness-putting for a while until he couldn't seem to help trying again to sink the putt. There wasn't much for me to do, since his own experience was teaching him that trying for results instead of simply focusing on the feel of the stroke was giving him worse results. The fact that he could physically detect the difference, depending on which "game" he was playing, fascinated him. He seemed about to discover something important, but was a little afraid to accept the full implications of what he was learning.

"This might be really hard to do during a tournament," Al finally remarked after sinking three twenty-foot putts in a row.

"It's always hard to let go of long-standing patterns," I replied, "but the fact that it works makes it easier. I suggest you don't try it in a tournament until you have spent more time with the exercise on the practice green. Even if you don't radically change your approach to putting in tournaments, doing this exercise ten or fifteen minutes every time you practice putting can't help improving your feel for length and direction."

"That's the crux of putting—just feel of length and direction," Al agreed. I could see that he was wrestling with himself about his experience. Somehow he couldn't quite bring himself to trust not trying to control the putter and sink the ball, in spite of his clear experience that he putted best when his Self 2 was engaged. On the other hand, he had experienced such surprising results that he couldn't dismiss the difference.

"Let's go to the driving range," Al suggested. There we started with an exercise similar to awareness-putting. I asked him to swing without looking where the ball went, and then see if he could describe its trajectory. At first Al was surprised that this exercise was so difficult. He said that he was in the habit of looking at the ball in flight to determine what, if anything, he had done wrong on his swing. I knew that this was a traditional method, but suggested to Al that perhaps there was a better one. "What if you could actually *feel* the first tendency of the swing to leave its groove? Then wouldn't it be possible for correction to take place even before the ball was hit? I don't know much about the mechanics of the golf swing, but I feel confident that if I could feel the difference between a hook and a slice or even between a draw and a fade, I could then control which kind of shot I produce. On the other hand, I'm not sure that even if I correctly analyze a given error, I will succeed in trying to correct it on the next swing."

Al agreed that during a tournament round most pros don't attempt to make mechanical corrections, though perhaps they might modify their address to the ball if something seemed wrong there. "We save mechanical corrections for the practice range," he said.

So with renewed motivation we began the awareness game, beginning with an eight-iron and then moving on toward the longer clubs. As with putting, after he had developed by feel a general awareness of where the ball went, I asked Al to try to be more specific. "What part of your body is most reliable in telling you whether you're getting a fade or a draw? And how can you tell the height of the trajectory?" These questions piqued Al's curiosity. He had never really tried to locate what cues from his body gave him this feedback, since he had relied primarily on his eyes and analytical mind to figure out what his swing was doing. As time passed he became more accurate and confident in his descriptions of his trajectories, and it was easy to tell that he was more aware of his swing. Increased control was inevitable. "I think you're on to something here, Tim," he said, "but what about the fundamentals? Surely you have to teach the fundamentals."

I answered that of course I felt the fundamentals were important for advanced players as well as for beginners, but that before we discussed how to deal with them, I wanted him to give *me* an Inner Game lesson. Al agreed, and I told him of a simple awareness process that I had used in both tennis and skiing. It seemed to me that in golf, too, it would be useful in correcting errors and reinforcing strength.

"First you ask the student to forget about results and simply focus on the kinesthetic sensations of his body while swinging the club. When you see that the student is not trying to hit the ball but is simply focusing on the feel of his body, ask him if he is more aware of any particular part of it. My experience is that if there is an important flaw in the swing, the part of the body that is critically related to that error will draw itself to the student's attention. On the other hand, if there isn't an error, generally the part of the body that is critical in controlling the optimum swing will receive the student's focus and be reinforced. When the student locates the part of his body that is in the foreground of his attention, he can then be asked exactly *what* he is feeling there. For example, if he is most aware of his right shoulder, he may answer that he feels a little tightness or jerkiness there during the swing. At that point the coach may ask him to take a few more swings while focusing his attention on his shoulder and see if he can locate the exact moment in the swing in which the tightness occurs. It's important that the coach not give the student the impression that the tightness is 'bad' and should be eliminated, only that it is there and that we want to find out more about it. Perhaps after a few swings the student determines that the tightening occurs just at the beginning of his downswing. At this point his feel has progressed from general body awareness to a specific 'where,' then to a specific 'what' and finally to an exact '*when*.' The final step in the process is to discriminate the *degree* to which the action is occurring. To help the student do this, the coach might say, 'I want you to take a few more swings paying attention to whatever is happening in your right shoulder at the moment your downswing begins, and specify the degree of tightness you feel. If you feel the same tightness as on the last few swings, call it a five; if there's more, give it a number from six to ten, depending on how much; if there is less, number the degree of tightness from four to zero.' By helping the student differentiate between degrees of tightness, his body unthinkingly starts to select the kinesthetic sensation that feels and works the best."

"So you never try to help him actually make the correction even if you can see what's wrong?" Al asked.

"No, because the whole point of the exercise is to help the student recognize that his body has the inherent capability of correcting itself. It's not that a novice golfer can't benefit from outside instruction; of course he can. But most of us have become so reliant on external authority to correct ourselves that we've lost confidence in the extremely sophisticated mechanism we have within us for self-correction. This process is designed to strengthen that confidence, and it also allows the student to gain more from external instruction at those times when it is useful."

After this explanation, Al watched me take a few swings with a seven-iron and then began to give me an Inner Game lesson.

After five swings Al asked me if I was particularly aware of one part of my body, and I answered that I seemed to focus on my right hand. I also remarked that my shots seemed to lack consistency, and that I really couldn't tell if they were going to go straight, draw or fade. "Don't worry about that," Al said, "just tell me what you are noticing about your right hand." I said that its grip seemed a little loose, and he asked me exactly which part of the hand. After a few more swings I said that I could actually feel my fourth and fifth fingers leave the club handle. "When does that happen?" Al asked. "At the back of the swing, before coming down," I answered. Of course I realized that this was probably a flaw in my swing, but sticking to the process I'd outlined, Al said, "Don't try to hold the club any tighter; just keep swinging and give me a number that indicates how loose you hand is on the club at the back of the swing. Zero will mean that your fingers didn't leave the club at all, and a plus figure means the degree of firmness of your grip."

I took about ten shots, calling out numbers after each one: "Three, two, three, zero, one, zero, minus one, minus one, minus one, minus one." "The last four shots were the best I've seen you hit," Al said. "They felt more secure somehow," I replied, "but it also felt as if I was getting less power." "It may have felt that way," said Al, "but in fact they were a good five to eight yards past the others."

Al was not surprised that keeping my hand on the club produced better results; in fact, he said, the standard instruction to combat this common error is, "Keep the last two fingers of your right hand firm on the grip." But he admitted that while watching my swing he hadn't picked up the fact that my fingers were coming free, and that the Inner Game method had been an effective way of detecting the error.

"What if you had seen the error and given me the traditional instruction, and I had asked you *how* firm I should hold my fingers?"

"Yes, I see what you mean; the numbers do make it more precise."

"Not only that, but the big difference is that now I don't have to try to remember to do something right, and therefore won't tighten up or become frustrated about my fingers. All I have to do is to feel what's happening and get feedback from the results. This state of mind is very different, even though the technical correction may be the same, and it will help me maintain poise and self-control."

Al remembered a lesson he had recently given his son, and how frustrating it had been when the boy couldn't seem to master a particular mechanical detail. "I threw his whole swing off by trying to get him to do one simple thing right. Finally I told him to forget about it and just swing the club, and his rhythm began to return. Maybe the Inner Game approach wouldn't tie him up in knots the way I did."

"I find with tennis players and skiers the method is almost frustration-free because there is never any right or wrong put in the student's mind. It's just a process of helping him to learn naturally from his experience, without having to grow involved in the shoulds and shouldn'ts of mechanics. Yet, as you can see, the process is quite technical because it guides me to the ability to differentiate between a plus-four and a minus-one degree of tightness in two fingers at a specific moment of my swing. That's a lot more precise than what I could have achieved through most verbal descriptions of correct mechanics."

"I'm beginning to get the point," Al remarked, "but I'm still not sure how you'd go about teaching the fundamentals. Good players can swing the golf club somewhat differently, but the laws of physics require that certain fundamentals be obeyed. I know this is true in tennis and skiing as well, and if your theory doesn't include the fundamentals, it will be only partially useful and easily criticized."

I felt that Al was pinning me to the wall a bit, but I knew that he was doing it for constructive reasons, because he felt that there was something valuable in the Inner Game approach and didn't want to see it shot down.

I admitted to Al that even though I had included a chapter on fundamentals in my first book, *The Inner Game of Tennis*, some traditional teaching pros had criticized my approach as impractical because it didn't spell out the mechanical fundamentals of the major strokes in tennis. On the other hand, the criticism came from those who hadn't tried the method. Over and over again, my experience has shown me that by using simple awareness techniques a beginner who has never held a racket before can usually learn the proper footwork, swing, and grip changes for the forehand, backhand, serve and volley in a one-hour lesson, and be playing tennis with never a worry about "doing it right." When I was being taught the fundamentals more than thirty years ago, it had taken me six months to learn a simple change of grip from forehand to backhand before I could do it unthinkingly. Inner Game students were doing it—usually without even knowing it—within the first fifteen minutes of the lesson. Moreover, I found that if I brought it to their attention that they had learned to change grips all by themselves, they then often tried to do it consciously, and soon lost all the natural coordination they had previously enjoyed. So my only possible answer to the question of fundamentals is: Yes, they do need to be *learned*; and no, for the most part they do not have to be *taught*.

At this moment Jeff, the tennis pro from the country club, came over to say hello. I introduced him to Al, who immediately asked him if he had ever played golf. When Jeff said that he had not, we persuaded him to be the guinea pig for an Inner Game lesson demonstrating how fundamentals can be learned without being taught.

In the half hour we spent working with Jeff he learned many of the fundamentals of grip, stance, rhythm, balance and tempo. Of course, he didn't master them all, and there was still room for improvement in his swing. Every once in a while Al would say to me, "It's amazing how fast he is learning without being told any of the hows, but I keep seeing things he's doing wrong and I itch to tell him. But I don't, and pretty soon the very flaw I was wanting to fix starts to correct itself." Within that half hour Jeff was definitely on his way to becoming a golfer.

The next chapter discusses what I believe to be the true fundamentals of the game of golf and how they can be learned, practiced and taught.

6

THE ART OF RELAXED CONCENTRATION AND THE PERFORMANCE TRIANGLE

Sports and the Mind

In the last decade there has been significantly greater attention directed toward the relation between mind, body and spirit in sports, with the purpose of tapping hidden potential to heighten performance and experience. Notable books dealing with the subject include George Leonard's *The Ultimate Athlete* (1975), Michael Murphy's *Golf in the Kingdom* (1974) and *The Psychic Side of Sports* (1978), and Thomas A. Tutko and Umberto Tosi's *Sports Psyching* (1976), as well as a lesser-known book by Laurence Korwin called *You Can Be Good at Sports* (1980).

I'd heard for a long time that Iron Curtain countries were exploring the possibilities of extending physical capabilities by practicing mental disciplines that are still considered exotic in our culture. A psychologist on the U.S. Olympic Sports Psychology Committee said recently in an interview with the Los Angeles *Times*: "At the Moscow games, the Soviets expect to triumph, and to ascribe it to mental training."

When last in England I was invited to speak to the British Davis Cup team, which responded—though guardedly—to my suggestion that the key to success in sports lies in higher states of concentration. (Two days later they upset Australia.) But the British Olympic pentathlon coach actively sought me out and beseeched me to help train his team in riding, swimming, running, shooting and especially fencing, none of which I had ever played competitively. Why was he so eager? Because in the past few years his fencing team had been losing ground to the Czechs, who had suddenly made a quantum leap, and he attributed this to "new psychological techniques" they were reputed to be using. Even though I was an American and the coach knew I had no experience in fencing, he wanted me to conduct an Inner Game training program for the team. I was amazed at how a little international rivalry could open minds to ideas that previously had been shunned.

Most of the fruits of the study of the mind-body relation in sports have been focused on professional and Olympic competitors, the majority of whom now play the Inner Game, using a wide array of mental techniques and procedures. But relatively little work has been done to help the average sportsman, although it is generally accepted that the state of one's mind significantly affects the quality of one's game. Chapter 4 explored the reasons why the mental states I call the *trying mode* and the *unconscious mode* are not the ideal states for fulfilling one's potential.

How can you gain more control over your state of mind when playing golf? My name for this optimum state of mind for performance is the *awareness mode,* and the remainder of this chapter explores how we can enter it, as well as the inner skills that can be developed to sustain it for longer periods of time.

The Awareness Mode

Everyone has experienced the awareness mode at one time or another during moments of peak performance or experience. In those spontaneous but all too elusive moments of heightened alertness and perception, actions seem artlessly excellent and life simple and whole. Even in complicated, demanding situations the effort needed is clear, and actions flow out of us that are uncannily appropriate. Golf shots are made as if they were the easiest imaginable, and we wonder what we ever thought was difficult about the game.

What is going on in your mind during your best performance, during a peak learning experience or during a moment of total enjoyment? How does this state compare with your normal frame of mind during average or less-than-average performances? I made my initial observations about this on the tennis court, and found that when playing badly my students' minds were filled with (1) a lot of self-instruction; (2) self-judgment; (3) various thoughts and feelings stemming from doubt and fear of failure. Yet when they were playing at their best, they reported that their minds were relaxed, absorbed and quiet, free of these tensions. Often they would say that they weren't thinking at all, and that their bodies seemed to know without conscious thought how to hit the ball.

Athletes often call this experience "playing out of one's mind," a phrase that indicates an absence of mental interference. I have interviewed many athletes who reported that when they are at their best they are not thinking; the mind is clear and very much aware. Ted Williams said that in such moments he could see the baseball so well "that sometimes it almost stands still for me." Arthur Ashe calls this state "playing in the zone." Eastern martial arts disciples have known for centuries this fundamental equation between mind and body; the less conscious thought in the mind, the better the chances for pure and precise action. "A single conscious thought through the mind diverts the arrow from its course towards the target," says the Zen archery master (*Zen in the Art of Archery*).

People who have just experienced heightened performance in this state of mind are often surprisingly humble about their achievement, attributing the credit not so much to themselves as to the amazing capabilities of the body and mind when working harmoniously. There seems to be less room for ego (Self 1) in the awareness mode, and when it does intrude the magic of the experience usually vanishes. Self 1 demands that the magic return, but it seldom obeys.

The objective of the Inner Game is to learn how to get out of the boredom of the unconscious mode (where we often are when unchallenged), and out of the stress of the trying mode (where we often are when challenged) so that we can reach the state of relaxed concentration of the awareness mode, where performance and quality of experience are optimal. We want to learn how to enter into the awareness mode at will, and then how to stay in it for longer periods of time. The key to doing this lies in learning the art of relaxed concentration.

Concentration in Golf

Golfers are pretty unanimous in recognizing the value of concentration, but few are clear about exactly what it is and how to achieve it. Recently when I conducted an Inner Game clinic for twenty-five LPGA touring pros, I asked how many of them believed that concentration was the single most important mental attribute in golf. Twenty-three raised their hands. When I asked how many of them had been taught anything about what concentration is and how to increase it, only two raised their hands.

What Is Concentration?

Concentration is *the* most important skill both for outer and inner games. Nothing of excellence is achieved without it. It is the primary ingredient of the learning process and the foundation of all true enjoyment. Yet it is one of the least studied and understood of all our innate capabilities.

Concentration is the flow of conscious energy that makes it possible to be aware of what is going on around you. The word "awareness" has a bad press; it has an unpragmatic ring to it in the minds of many result-oriented individuals. But I can assure you that it is *most* practical. Without it we would not be able to know or to do anything; when it is heightened, all is seen better and done easier. Awareness is the internal energy that makes it possible to see through our eyes, hear through our ears, feel our feelings, think our thoughts, and understand what we understand. It is like a light that makes our experience *knowable*. To some extent we have control over our focus of awareness through a function called attention, a primary tool of natural learning.

Imagine a light in a dark forest that illumines equally all objects within its range. If, by use of reflectors, that light is focused into a beam, the objects in the line of that beam will be seen in much sharper detail than previously, while those lying outside it will become less distinct. The relationship between awareness and attention is analogous. A human being's range of experience is made knowable by the light of his awareness, and is heightened selectively by the choices he makes in focusing his attention. That which we attend to we come to know. If we want to know something more closely— because we want to gain a greater measure of control or simply to appreciate it more—we need to shed more light on it by focusing our attention.

Concentration is nothing more than focusing our complete and undivided attention upon the objects of our choice. Focusing your awareness always involves choice. We shine more light on some objects in order to see them better, simultaneously blocking out less relevant details and events.

At this point we might question how much control we actually do have over our attention. Can we keep our awareness focused where we want to? Pick anything in your present experience and concentrate your attention on it: the feeling of your body against the chair, your breath going in and out, anything within your sight that you find interesting. Let your attention make as full contact with it as possible. See to what extent you can attend only to this one experience and to nothing else. How long is this possible before your attention shifts because you get tired or bored?

It's impossible to learn about concentration without practicing it, and it is not until you start practicing it that you become aware of what it is, what its benefits are, and perhaps how unconcentrated you have been. Control over one's attention is a fundamental freedom. I was shocked to find how little of that control I consciously exercised. To me learning this art is perhaps the most important thing in life; to the extent that I learn it and discover how and where to focus my awareness, my life will be truly experienced.

For this reason, I don't write only about how concentration will help your golf game. It is more to the point to discuss how your golf game might help your concentration. Proficiency in golf is far less important an achievement than proficiency in the art of concentration, whether you are seeking achievement or pleasure. So though I speak about concentration in connection with golf, and in the remainder of the book will offer techniques for heightening it specifically while playing the game, my recommendation is that you use these exercises and golf itself as a medium for learning the master skill of relaxed concentration, through which you can raise the quality of performance and experience in *any* activity.

Many people don't even like the word "concentration" because they associate it with strain, as in "trying to concentrate" for a final exam. But *trying* can't produce concentration. When a pupil is told he must concentrate in class, he seldom does, and is often accused of not being able to. Examples of concentration might include a baby fascinated by a multicolored mobile, a cat playing with a ball of string, a hawk flying over hills watching for a field mouse, or even a kid playing after school with an electronic toy. Concentration is natural, and thus the best examples are generally close to nature. You can't make it happen any more than you can make sleep happen. It occurs when you *allow*—not force—yourself to become interested in something.

Steps in Concentration

Discipline. The first step is to make an effort to switch your attention from wherever it is and place it where you want it. Doing the simple back-hit awareness exercise requires such discipline. Your attention may want to fly away into thoughts about how to hit the ball or what will happen if you miss. One purpose of the exercise—indeed, of all the exercises in this book—is to provide a focus for your attention on something specific *here and now*, away from the interferences of past, future, should, shouldn't, and what might have been. Here and now the mind can begin to quiet itself, and the quieter it grows, the more feedback it gives Self 2 about what's happening.

Imagine that the mind is like a lake. When its surface is calm, reflections of trees, clouds, birds, etc., can be seen clearly and in rich detail, as can whatever is in its depths. But when the surface is ruffled by the wind, it does not reflect clearly. Objects look darker, less distinct, even distorted. Likewise, the mind that is restless or agitated cannot make clear contact with reality, and then we have a difficult time dealing with our surroundings. Hence quieting the mind is the first step to the first level of concentration.

Interest. Concentration reaches a deeper level when the mind becomes interested in its focus. It is difficult to keep your attention on something in which there is little interest. When there is discipline but no interest, it takes so much effort just to keep the mind still that concentration is generally superficial and of short duration. This is why tennis players find it hard to obey the command, "Watch the ball, watch the ball," but much easier to keep their eyes on it when it is suggested that they focus on the subtle patterns made by its spinning seams. Likewise, the golfer can practice increasing awareness of the club, ball, body and target by attending to details of increasing degrees of subtlety.

Each individual needs to find his own focus of interest. Any of the awareness exercises described thus far or in the next two chapters are only meant to serve as initial suggestions. Interest increases as you get into the subtleties; details are always more interesting than vague impressions. The path to this state of interest is to become ever more receptive to experience and to sustain your effort to make contact with what you are focusing on. If you try to force interest, it will evade you.

Absorption. A third level of concentration could be called absorption. It is a deepening of interest to the point where you begin to lose yourself in what you are attending to. When a person becomes so absorbed that he is close to full concentration, he is hard to distract. A golf professional absorbed in addressing an important shot won't hear people near him talking, or be aware of cameras or his competitors, because they are not relevant to his immediate task. This level of concentration is pleasurable as well as being conducive to excellence, for you literally leave worries, doubts and troubles behind by losing touch with your Self 1. Most great athletic performances are accomplished in this state, where even the most strenuous action somehow seems effortless. There is no room for anxiety because your mind is so concentrated that you don't even hear doubt knocking at your door.

In an interview, Jane Blalock described the experience of absorption vividly: "It doesn't happen all the time, but when I'm playing well sometimes it's as if my eyes change. I can feel it. I just feel like Dr. Jekyll and Mr. Hyde—a transformation happens, I'm a totally different human being. I don't hear anybody, I don't see anybody, nothing bothers me, nothing is going to interfere with what I'm about to do."

In this state we experience an intensified contact with reality. Relevant details are seen more clearly: golf balls and holes seem larger than usual, and actions flow with little or no consciousness of thought. You seem to simply know the best thing to do with each change in the situation.

Oneness. This is a fourth level of concentration I have experienced only a few times in my life. It could be called "oneness." It's almost impossible to describe the experience because it's like falling asleep; you don't really know you did it until after you've waked up. Only in looking back do you realize that you were in a different state of consciousness.

Oneness can happen in any activity, but only when you give yourself totally to what you are doing. It may sound mystical, but at the time the experience seems quite natural: you totally lose yourself only when you totally give yourself. I believe that this is one of the primary reasons that athletes make the great effort they do. Of course, there are also ego reasons, but there is a matchless feeling of exhilaration when we have made a total effort and somehow in the process lost all traces of Self 1. To accomplish this even for only a few moments is enough to prove that it is possible to survive perfectly well without Self 1 around to help you, and it gives us a goal to shoot for.

My own experience and the descriptions of others who have performed in an optimal state of mind seem to indicate that there are three essential characteristics of relaxed concentration: (1) heightened awareness, or perception; (2) heightened trust in potential and an absence of self-doubt; (3) strong and undivided desire, or will. Awareness, trust and will are not merely ingredients but skills that can be developed by practice. They become doors to the awareness mode and to its ever-escalating levels. As such, I see them as primary Inner Game skills that automatically increase performance, learning and enjoyment in any activity.

Awareness skills increase our ability to focus our minds nonjudgmentally in the present moment, on details relevant to our purpose. *Trust skills* decrease doubt and give us confidence in our true potential. They involve learning to count on what is reliable for a particular end, and to let go of dependence on what is not reliable. In Inner Game terminology, this means that the golfer learns to trust Self 2 (the body) to hit the ball rather than Self 1 (the ego mind). *Will skills* develop our ability to clarify goals, both short-term and long-range, and to find the energy and determination to overcome the inner and outer obstacles in order to achieve what we really want. They involve learning what your true goal is, and making the effort to trust and be aware.

From this description it is easy to see that the three skills are interrelated. None can exist without the others, and a heightening of any one will automatically heighten the other two. However, the concentration produced by their combination is only as strong as the weakest link in the triad.

Awareness Skills

The essence of awareness skills is learning to see things as they are— that is, nonjudgmentally. When a golfer sees his swing in terms of "good" or "bad" he will not have a clear picture of it as it *is*. Awareness never judges; only Self 1 does. True awareness is like a flawless mirror; this principle is basic to Inner Game understanding. Awareness is curative only when there is no judgment; and when it is combined with purpose, effective action and learning can take place.

If the game of golf has to do with the controlling of a ball and a club with a body, and we understand that better control is accomplished by increasing awareness, then the priorities for one's attention are narrowed to the ball, the club, the body, the course, and the target. Since the course, target and ball (before contact) are immobile, they do not require the greatest concentration of the player's mind. Nevertheless, they should be observed, but not in a judgmental way. Your lie is not "bad," nor are the lake and the OB posts; nor are the trees you went into on your last round. Neither are they good. They are best observed without attributing positive or negative values to them. Your lie is the way it is: in a divot, in the rough, buried in the sand or sitting up smartly in the fairway. It's important to see the situation in clear detail, and judging it either negatively or positively will warp your ability to see this detail clearly. Negative judgments tend to obscure your vision of what you wish wasn't there, and to cause doubt and tightening. Positive judgments tend to make you feel it's unnecessary to see details, and you become too casual.

Clearly, the most important focus for attention in golf is the body and the club. It is a game in which the sense of feeling is far more important than the sense of sight. For example, there are a number of very good blind golfers. But a person who could not feel his bodily movements simply could not play golf.

I can't resist telling a story about a blind golfer whose lifelong dream was to play a round with Arnold Palmer, his idol. Finally, after a tournament he had the courage to introduce himself and ask Palmer. Understandably, Arnie was noncommittal. "Well, sure, sometime that would be fun," he answered, and then began talking to someone else. But the blind man would not be dissuaded so easily. Again he asked and again he was put off politely. Finally he made one more try, and with a number of people standing around he challenged Arnie: "Mr. Palmer, I know you're not the type to turn down a fair challenge. I have ten thousand dollars I'd like to wager on a single eighteen-hole medal-play match with you. Will you accept my challenge?"

"Sir, with all due respect," Palmer answered, "I don't want to take that money from you. Thanks anyway."

"Mr. Palmer, I'm not kidding. If you don't accept my wager, I'll feel justified in letting it be known that you weren't sure you could beat me."

Arnold Palmer has never been criticized for being uncompetitive. People were looking on, he was slightly annoyed by the persistence of the stranger, so finally he agreed. "Okay, if that's the way you want it, I'll play. Ten thousand dollars. You name the course and the time, and I'll be there."

"Very well," said the blind man. "I'm delighted to finally have the chance to play with you. Let's meet on the first tee of this course tomorrow at *midnight*."

According to the story, which may or may not be true, Arnie blushed, smiled and capitulated. The blind man withdrew his wager, and they played a friendly daytime match.

Most individuals in this culture are accustomed to being asked to look or listen closely, but often are uncomfortable if asked to *feel* something closely, whether it's an emotion or a physical sensation. Often when I ask a tennis student to become aware of his body, he'll respond, "What do you want me to try to do?" or, "What do you want me to think about?" But if I ask him simply to look at the ball, he doesn't ask what he should think about; he knows he is being asked only to look.

This cultural blind spot is a primary reason why many average athletes do not play better; they avoid feeling their body sensations clearly. To a great extent, excellence in golf is a function of how aware you are of the sensations of your body during the setup and swing. The much discussed benefits of muscle memory are not derived so much from "good memories" as from vivid muscle experiences. To control your body, you have to feel it. To control movement effectively you have to feel it vividly. Feel in golf comes from sensing how your muscles move. For example, how sharply can you detect the difference between a draw and a fade, or even between a slice and a hook? Do you *see* the results and then guess what happened to produce them? If you can learn to *feel* the difference, it then becomes much easier to control that difference. If you can't, it seems very hard. No one can "keep the feel" unless he keeps feeling. My experience, both with myself and with students, is that the primary skill needed to increase control is whatever will increase awareness of the feel of one's body during its swing.

To some extent everyone feels, or else he couldn't move. When your leg goes to sleep, you have almost no control over it. As sensation starts to return, there is increasing control over the leg's movement. To achieve higher degrees of control in golf, we need to increase our kinesthetic awareness by focusing our attention. In short, we need to become more in tune with our bodies.

Teaching the Fundamentals of Putting with Awareness Skills

Let's invent a student named John and assume that he has never played golf. How might he learn the fundamentals of putting using the principle of maximizing body awareness? The following set of awareness instructions demonstrates how one of the fundamentals of the Outer Game of golf can be learned through the inner skill of focusing attention.

After explaining to John the Inner Game approach, I might hand him a putter and ask him to find a grip that would give him the best feel of the club. I might even say, "The objective in putting is to develop a feel for the distance and direction that the putter imparts to the ball. You're going to need a grip that will give you the best touch for the club face, so put a lot of flesh on the leather and find a grip that will allow your hands to work as one. You don't have to find the 'right grip'; there is no such thing. Just experiment and you'll find the best grip for you at this moment; if you keep in mind the goal of maximum feel, the grip will adjust itself with practice over time."

With this instruction, most novices will come close to a workable grip suited to their hand size and individual body characteristics.

"Now I want you to familiarize yourself with the putter by moving it around, first with your eyes open and then with them closed, and see if you can feel where the putter head is by the sensation in your hands. The goal here is to get to the point where the putter feels like an extension of your body, not an alien instrument."

At this point John is probably feeling relatively relaxed because nothing has yet challenged his competence. There are no rights and wrongs yet, no dos and don'ts—only concentration on feeling, and since the teacher can't really tell if he's doing a good job of that, it's really between the student and himself.

When it's time to introduce the putting stroke, I could demonstrate it if I like, but if I do, I should do so subtly, so that John won't think that he should do it in exactly the same way. I might lay a yardstick or string along the green, stroke the putter a few times, and ask John to look at its face relative to the line of the yardstick. Showing him what open, closed and square faces look like, I might ask him to tell me with each of my swings whether my face was open, closed or square. Then I might ask him to swing himself, and call out the same on his own swing (which probably would have unconsciously picked up certain basic elements of mine).

"Now close your eyes and swing, and see if you can tell whether the face is open, closed or square simply by paying attention to your hands. Try to sense the direction of the putter blade through your fingers. It doesn't matter which; just see if you can tell accurately. Don't guess;

feel. If you can't tell, say so, and I'll tell you the way I saw it, which will make it easier for you to identify it correctly the next time."

Pretty soon John has learned his first golfing fundamental: feel of the club-face angle. He will need this skill his entire golfing life, and will have to develop it to the point where he can sense the angle when his woods and irons are moving at much higher speeds. That's one good reason to start learning golf with putting; it's easier to develop awareness when something is moving slowly.

Similar exercises could be given to John to increase his awareness of the direction and length of his putting stroke. For example, with the aid of a yardstick, he could be asked to sense, with eyes closed, whether his swing was going to the left or right of the yardstick pointed in the direction of the hole. If the instructor gives correct feedback about the actual direction, John will soon be able to feel the difference between outside to in, inside to out, and a straight stroke. Control is developed as a natural consequence of this ability to sense accurately the difference in direction.

Likewise, a sense for the length of the stroke can be heightened by placing a yardstick behind the ball and telling John the number of inches his backswing extends on succeeding putts. Soon he himself will be able to accurately gauge differing lengths and obtain another important element of control.

All these awareness games are challenging enough to be interesting, but they create no doubt because there is no "right" or "wrong" and therefore no fear of failure. By the end of these three exercises John has a rudimentary sense of feel of the club-face angle, swing direction and swing length. Before actually striking some balls, I would probably ask John to do an exercise to increase awareness of the height of the putter above the green as he swung. Then we would repeat the exercises while hitting balls along the green at no target.

There are many similar exercises to accomplish these same ends. What is important is the essence of each of them: nonjudgmental awareness of what *is.* Through simple focusing of attention on physical sensations, John has learned to discriminate different feels without judging them as good or bad, and learning is taking place automatically. The central strategy in introducing him to golf in this way is to circumvent the anxiety and doubt that would normally prevail in learning something new. By presenting him at first with only the smallest challenges, none of which will conjure up the possibility of failure in his mind, and by giving instructions that lead him gently into the awareness mode, he can learn to trust his innate ability to learn and avoid the trying mode.

Practicing Movement Awareness

The best way to learn to increase awareness of bodily movement is to focus attention on ordinary movements that you make automatically and unconsciously during the day. Attending to certain actions, not for the sake of improving them but merely for the sake of experiencing them, is a skill that when applied to your golf swing will enhance the quality of both performance and enjoyment. You can pay attention to your movements while walking up or down stairs, sitting down in a chair, walking, eating, brushing teeth or driving a car. One thing you may notice is how complex some of these acts are, and yet how effortlessly Self 2 performs them without help from Self 1. Attending to movements without consciously trying to control them is a primary goal of Inner Game learning and is much easier to practice with actions that don't challenge your competence. Having observed the capability of Self 2 in these activities, it becomes easier to try increasing your awareness of movements that present a greater challenge.

The twin keys to heightened awareness in golf are (1) keeping your mind receptive and focused; (2) making a commitment to awareness instead of trying to get results. This is where trust comes in. You have to let go of concern about results to attain heightened awareness, trusting that it is the heightened awareness that will eventually give you the control. The instant you make this decision you leave the trying mode and enter the awareness mode. As a consequence, tension decreases and alertness increases, doubt and fear of failure subside, and overtightened muscles relax.

In this way we can relearn how to feel movement in the natural way we learned as children—which, by the way, was very well and very fast.

Specific awareness exercises for putting and swinging are described in the next two chapters. Any one of them can give you a focus for getting into the awareness mode. Before practicing them on the range, it might be helpful to practice movement awareness of your swing and putting without a ball, perhaps in your living room or backyard. See how much you can increase your feel for tension and relaxation by simple attentiveness.

Trust Skills

Concentration is impossible without trust. Doubt disrupts attentiveness. We cannot really keep our mind focused on the club head or on the target if we doubt that our swing is "correct." The doubt will make the mind jump to trying to take control of the action instead of simply attending to it. I learned this lesson over and over in my own golf experience. When you're trying for control, you lose awareness, and when you lose awareness you lose control! When I was chipping in my backyard, I would feel almost at one with the club. I could hear the ball come off the face, and my accuracy was excellent. But on the course, where it counted more, I would somehow try to control the shot more, and then I didn't feel that oneness with the club or hear the sound of the ball at contact.

Learning that *gaining* Self-2 control requires letting go of Self-1 control is probably the most difficult lesson to be learned in the Inner Game. "Trust and let go" have become bywords; we even began printing the words on tees to remind ourselves. But merely saying the words doesn't do it; *you* have to do it.

The reason why concentration requires trust is that focusing energy in one place involves taking it away from someplace else. To concentrate on the club head, you have to abandon your favorite thoughts. To be one with your action, you can't be thinking about how to execute it; you have to trust that it will be done. Of course, we couldn't accomplish the simplest action without trust; the hard part is to have that trust while doing something "difficult" or something that seems important to us. But that's exactly when concentration is most necessary.

Here it should be pointed out that trust isn't something to be given blindly. Letting go isn't necessarily a virtue. Before you let go, it's wise to question what you are putting your trust in. The virtue is in learning to trust what is trustworthy. Everyone has to find this out for himself. Is it a virtue to trust a three-year-old to drive the family car? Or to trust yourself to hit your drive three hundred yards over the widest part of the lake? Over- and under-confidence, which often coexist in the same person, are usually not the result of too much or too little trust, but of the misplacement of trust. Ask yourself, What am I trusting and for what purpose?

Imagine a golfer on the seventeenth tee, looking at a small green a hundred and eighty yards away. A lake guards the green, and he remembers hitting into it last time with a three-iron. He thinks, You'd better take a three-wood and play it safe; remember what happened last time. Then he notices that his opponent, who hits a little shorter than he as a rule, has a three-iron in his hand. He remembers his club pro telling him, "Don't try to be a hero; hit with the club you know will keep you out of trouble." Then he recalls a Scottish saying: "Hit the value of the club." He thinks, Usually I can hit a three-iron a hundred eighty or a hundred ninety yards if I make decent contact. He remembers Arnold Palmer saying that the secret to good contact is a still head. Then another voice is heard: "You should have confidence . . . Think positive . . . Of course you can do it if you believe you can . . ." Nervously he thinks, What about a four-wood? Just then his opponent says, "What are you gonna take, Tommy, a four-iron?"

Whom is Tommy going to trust? Should he believe his club pro, the Scottish adage, Arnold Palmer, his opponent or one of the voices in his head? I can't answer that question for him, but I can say that in his present state of mind Tommy is not likely to get over the lake with any club.

The best thing Tommy could do at this moment would be to quit all this analysis, relax as much as he can, step up to his bag and let Self 2 pick out the club he wants, knowing that, at worst, he'll learn from the experience.

I have a good friend whose father tried to teach him a lesson about trust early in life. One day in the course of a little carefree play the father lifted the child up onto a table and told him, "Jump and I'll catch you." The laughing child leaped from the table toward his father's outstretched arms without a thought. But at that instant the father dropped his hands to his sides and stepped aside, and the astonished child fell flat on his face on the rug. My friend remembers feeling stunned and hurt as he looked up at his father uncomprehendingly. "That will teach you," admonished his father. "Never trust anybody or anything in this world."

I don't know what my friend learned from this experience, but I do know what my reaction to the story was: Why should I trust the statement of a man who just let me fall?

Human beings have no choice but to trust in something. In golf, where trust is linked to control of the body, the question becomes whether to rely on Self 1 or Self 2.

The purpose of driving ranges and practice putting greens is to provide a place for experimentation. They are ideal low-risk situations in which you can experiment about how to swing the club— or, even better, how to swing without any ideas at all. Let the body show you how it would like to do it if it didn't have to obey all your theories on how it should be done. What will happen? Will it be totally wild? Try it and see. It's possible that in experiencing your initial freedom from restraint, a part of you that simply wants to whale away at the ball may take over. Do just that until you get it out of your system. But keep on swinging the way you really want to. My experience is that changes begin to take place. I find that the body knows a lot more than I thought it did, and that it learns very fast when I give it free rein. It's also a very exhilarating experience to let go. As a result, I started gaining a true respect for what my body is and what it can do, and to wonder why I've been bossing it around all this time.

But Self 1 will always try to sneak back. No sooner will I hit a great shot than I'll hear a little whisper in my head: "Wow, you really came through the ball that time; you had a much fuller turn. Why don't you try that again?" Self 1 steals most of his information from Self 2, then uses it to try to control Self 2. Why should I listen to him? Couldn't Self 2 do it again on his own if I let him?

In short, the only way to build trust in your potential is to let go and do it. Try it little by little if you like, and in practice before you do it on the course. Of course, it's there that you really need to trust yourself, but it's also in the heat of competition that we're usually too timid to do it. But that's what games are for. Learning how to perform in simulated realities prepares us to perform at our best under real pressure.

To heighten concentration before every approach and putt, and every tee shot, let go of control! Learn to not worry about results. As you do, you will feel your mind relax and your awareness of feel pick up immediately. To repeat: *trust and feel go hand in hand; you don't get one without the other.*

But remember, relaxed concentration can't be forced. If you think you *must* concentrate to make a good shot, you'll probably try to force it and almost certainly fail to gain much concentration. Remember the child's concentration or the cat's; there's no "I have to concentrate" attitude with them.

Practicing Trust on the Range and Green

All of the Inner Golf exercises described in this book require trust, especially some of the putting exercises in the next chapter, in which Self 2 makes decisions about the break of the green, where to aim and how hard to hit. Right now I would like to mention some exercises designed to explore the capabilities of your Self 2 in practice situations.

Let Go of Trying. On the range or putting green, practice losing all conscious effort. Pick a target, but make no conscious effort to swing "right." Let go of all control and let Self 2 hit the ball to the target any way he wants to.

Setting Up Wrong. After you have gained some confidence in Self 2 from the above exercise, give him a harder challenge. Set yourself a goal—for example, hitting a six-iron to the hundred-fifty-yard marker. But instead of taking your usual stance, assume a position that is either too open or too closed. The task you're giving Self 2 is to get the ball to the target handicapped from a "wrong" position. Don't let Self 1 help by making any conscious compensations. Trust Self 2 to do it. If you really let go, you will see that Self 2 can hit a ball to a target even from the wrong stance. It may be easier with a correct setup, but Self 2 has enough control to compensate for mistakes without conscious thought. This exercise helps increase trust in Self 2 and decrease fear of mistakes. It's nice to know that Self 2 can compensate for some errors.

Stretching Self 2's Limits. Having experimented with the above exercise, set some goals for Self 2 that explore his limits. For example if you never draw the ball, you might try to have Self 2 learn to hit draws. Don't think about how to do it. Give Self 2 *no* help; simply let him learn by experience. Watch each result carefully, then let him hit again, allowing him to guide you out of your normal swing.

Next, set a goal for Self 2 that he can't possibly reach—for example, hitting your six-iron two hundred yards. When I tried this, I couldn't conceive how to do it, so I had no option but to let go. I still don't know how Self 2 managed it, but I felt my legs coming through the ball at impact more than I ever had before, and the ball flew off the club with the trajectory of a three-iron and went one hundred eighty yards, a good twenty-five yards further than what I usually hit a six-iron Next, I asked Self 2 to hit the six-iron to the hundred-yard marker. He did so with an entirely different swing.

I was excited about being able to break rules and hit clubs in different ways; I felt as if I were just *playing*, not working at golf. I also believe that I acquired skills that I wouldn't have learned if I'd stayed within the bounds of normal practice. Most important, I increased my trust in my Self 2.

The Balance of Awareness and Letting Go

When a golfer begins practicing letting go of his conscious Self-1 control over his swing, he sometimes does so without paying much attention to what he's doing. He tends to merely set his goal and let 'er rip. This is fine for breaking out of mechanical and overtight swing patterns, but it won't necessarily produce consistency. In the Inner Game approach, consistency is a function of awareness, so a balancing is necessary. First let go, then slowly put more and more awareness into the swing. It is not always easy to not care about results when you are being attentive, but excellence is a function of both skills working together. The aim of inner swinging is to focus on the swing without consciously controlling it. If you are aware, but still trying for results, the swing will be tight and controlled. If there is letting go but little awareness, the swing will tend to be fluid but inconsistent. The optimum balance comes easiest when these skills are practiced separately before you try putting them together.

Taking Your Trust in Self 2 from the Practice Range to the Course

At some point you have to take the plunge and trust Self 2 under pressure. It always feels a bit risky when we let go, but to do so under pressure feels downright dangerous. It is also more exhilarating. The only way I can make myself let go is by recalling the exhilaration that comes from taking the risk of truly trusting myself. Of course, there are occasional poor results, but mostly I experience these when I chicken out at the last moment and allow Self 1 to take over control of the swing. It may also be helpful to remember that what you are experimenting with is not just a gimmick to improve your golf game but an exploration in increasing your self-control. If you find that Self 2 really does exist and can be relied upon, you have discovered something very valuable—well worth the risk of dropping a few strokes.

Self-2 Satisfaction versus Self-1 Satisfaction

One final word about trust skills. Relying on Self 2 to hit a golf ball, solve a problem or carry on a conversation is a delightful and amazing experience. It feels good immediately when Self 2 hits the ball without interference, but it's a very different feeling from the kind of ego-satisfaction that Self 1 is looking for. There's no way around this. Self-1 control offers another kind of reward, and we have to make our choice according to which we prefer.

One tennis player I know chose Self-1 control even after a lesson in which he'd freed himself from doubt and Self 2 had changed his serve from a tight, powerless one into a strong and fluid one. He returned the next week with his old stroke, saying, "I know the serve I learned last week was much more powerful and accurate, but I really didn't like it because I never felt I knew what I was doing. This one doesn't go in the court so much, but at least I feel I'm in control." A very clearly stated choice!

Will Skills

Will is inseparable from concentration. We only attend to what we have a desire to attend to. If our goals are scattered in several directions, our attention will be too. Will is like a force; it has both direction and strength. If we have the desire to hit the golf ball, this conviction will direct our attention to the relevant components of the intended action—the ball, body, club and target. The strength of our desire will determine the quality of our concentration. If it is weak, concentration will be easily distracted; if strong, it will overcome both external and internal obstacles to reach its goal.

Without desire, there is no goal and no action. You can be very much aware of the ball sitting on the tee, but unless you have the impetus you won't hit it. Developing will skills has to do with the two aspects of this force: (1) goal clarification; (2) the strengthening of will through its exercise. Goal clarification is perhaps the more important because it is primarily in this process that energy can be shifted from conflicting desires and directed toward the desired object of attention.

Poor concentration can usually be traced to divergent desires. If a golfer has difficulty in concentrating, the problem probably lies in the fact that he wants too many things at the same time. Perhaps on the one hand he wants to achieve a low score; on the other hand, he doesn't want his handicap to get much lower because he won't have the same advantage in handicap tournaments, to say nothing of his bets with fellow players. This obvious example of conflict in will can only result in poor concentration. Fear of failure also weakens one's will to win. If a player is overly anxious about hitting out-of-bounds or into a lake, he diverts energy from the single-minded will to hit toward the target. The other side of this coin is the fear of succeeding, the problem of raising expectations—a subject that will be discussed in Chapter 9.

If you look at will as a force vector in physics, it is easy to see how it works. If one force tugs in one direction at a given strength and others pull in other directions at other strengths, the resulting acceleration is far slower than the sum of all the forces, and is directed somewhere in between them all. Thus, force of will is strengthened when some of our desires can be surrendered, or else channeled into a single direction. Then you are doing what you *really* want to do, and excellence follows as a matter of course. To the extent that this happens, concentration is easy. As soon as a child is allowed to do what he really wishes to, he begins to concentrate and to exhibit qualities that were previously not apparent.

The effort I must make when taking an Inner Game approach is to (1) be clear about my goals; (2) focus my attention in the present; (3) trust Self 2. No matter what my Outer Game situation may be, if I make an effort in these three areas, everything works out well for me. It's when I start thinking about how to correct my swing, worrying about the score, or trying to impress the people I'm playing with that I get in trouble.

Strengthening the Will

The will to focus attention and to trust has been discussed in the last two sections. Here I simply want to underscore that it is *an issue of will*: you have to actually *choose* to let go and to practice attentiveness. Merely to stick to one simple awareness exercise, such as back-hit, for three holes without forgetting is a will-strengthening practice. Will is strengthened when we decide to do something and then do it; it weakens when we decide to do something and then don't. It's not until we attempt to discipline our attention that we find that it requires a continuing effort—and perseverance, not force.

The more one practices awareness and trust, the more the will is strengthened. It is because golf requires such precision and deep concentration that the game has unique value. It calls on the golfer to face up to the depth of his concentration and will, and challenges him to strengthen it.

Overconcern about Results

It has been implied earlier that one of the greatest obstacles to relaxed concentration is overconcern about results. Again this is essentially a will problem, an issue of goal clarification. When a person thinks that his goal is to achieve an external result, there is usually a will conflict that will interfere with his attaining it. This is not always easy to understand in a culture that has valued external success as single-mindedly as ours has, but it's true nonetheless.

How does the conflict work? First, precisely because they are external, achieving external goals is not entirely within our own control. Wanting something we may not get produces anxiety, which interferes with our concentration of effort to reach the goal. Second, because of the uncertainly of success, in order to heighten the probability of success a person tends to set his sights lower than what he might actually be able to achieve. If you really want to break 80, put everything you have into it, and then fail, it hurts. So our tendency is either to aim at an easier goal or to simply not make the effort. Then we can console ourselves by saying, "Well, I could have broken eighty if I'd really gone for it, but I didn't. If it weren't for the OB and those two three-putt greens I'd have done it, so it just shows that I *could* do it." These may be comfortable ways out of the dilemma of the uncertainty of external results, but they are not conducive to maximum performance.

What is the alternative? It is to set both Outer Game and Inner Game goals. If my Outer Game goal is to break 80, my Inner Game goal might be to develop strength of will and to overcome my tendency to be casual and undisciplined. Putting the two goals together, I commit myself to making a maximum effort to break 80. The emphasis is not merely on breaking 80, but even more on the rewards that will come to me by making a maximum effort—the exhilaration that comes from committing myself totally and exercising my relaxed concentration. The score is only the *direction* of my effort. The difference is that, this way, my effort *is* within my control. Nothing can keep me from making a maximum effort, and success in that part of my objective is not conditional on outside circumstances.

The last time I set this goal I arrived at the par-three eighteenth hole of Los Robles with a 78; thus, I needed a hole in one on this uphill 185-yard hole to break 80. To my Self 1 it seemed absurd, but I went for it, making my best effort to score a hole in one on a hole where I usually miss the green more often than I hit it. I took a two-iron—not my favorite club—out of the bag and let Self 2 have his way. I couldn't believe my shot. It was probably the straightest two-iron I'd ever hit. Everyone in the foursome watched. At first it seemed it was going left of the pin, then it seemed to go right; as it came down, it looked as if it was right for the stick. Because the green was raised, none of us could see where it came to rest. "That might be in the hole," said one of my partners. I couldn't resist telling him that I'd gone for it, that I really had allowed myself to want a hole in one. As we walked up the hill, one of my opponents said to me, "It couldn't be any more than three feet away." All the way up to the green I held my expectations in check. But when we reached the edge, I couldn't believe it; there was no ball near the hole, though there was one at the back of the green. For one lovely moment I thought that mine had gone in the hole, and that this ball belonged to my partner. Then I realized that it had to be mine. It had hit the summer green hard six feet directly in front of the pin and rolled twenty feet past. Nevertheless, I had reached my Inner Game goal on that hole. I had gone for it; I had concentrated my energies; I had let go, and it felt wonderful. The disappointment of not getting the ace was not even very strong; I had accomplished what I *really* wanted. In this situation I valued making a quality effort more than getting a score, and in the long run I knew that this would benefit me more.

When I was asked recently what I felt was the most important fundamental in golf, I skipped grip, stance, swing and even what has been called—erroneously I believe—the one unarguable golf fundamental, the still head. I also had to omit the master skill of relaxed concentration. To me, the most important and most basic fundamental of golf is *to know why you play the game.* You are alive and are choosing to spend a good part of that life playing golf. To what end? This question focuses attention on the difference between the goal of the game of golf and that of the golfer, a difference that is too often overlooked.

The Outer Game goal of golf is clear: to get the ball into eighteen consecutive holes with the minimum number of strokes. But is that the reason the golfer plays? Is it because those eighteen holes need to have white balls rolled into them and then picked up again? If it were, there would be better instruments to use than a bag of sticks. A golf course is a huge expanse of carefully prepared terrain covering many acres, sometimes in the midst of city real estate worth hundreds of thousands of dollars per acre. It was not laid out so that balls could be hit into holes, nor that the player could make a low score and feel good about himself—in fact the course is designed in many ways to frustrate one's chances of low scores. The real purpose for laying out a golf course is to provide certain benefits for the golfer that transcend the mere mechanics of the game.

When I ask golfers why they play, the most common answers are "For the fun of it," "For the camaraderie and competition" or "For the exercise." Still, I sense that they aren't really clear about their purpose in playing. Tennis players, for example, often tell me that they play because they like to win. "Then why do you usually try to match yourself with players better than you?" I ask. Anyone whose goal was simply to win could do so every time by choosing much less experienced players to play against. The fact is that the tennis player knows that he can somehow benefit himself by playing against stiff competition, and can gain that benefit even if he loses. Golfers sometimes experience the same confusion. They choose to play a really challenging course, and then complain when the par-fours are long, or when they are left with a fifty-foot putt that breaks in three directions. When we go out to compete we want a challenge, but in the midst of the game we often change our minds because of confusion about goals. We don't want the challenge anymore; we simply want to win.

The Performance Triangle

Clarifying goals always involves employing a little philosophy. A person has to consider what is valuable to him in light of his overall purpose, and to discriminate how that value can be achieved in a given situation. Golfers are generally at home with philosophy because the very nature of the game almost compels it. The golfer who makes a sincere effort to understand his goals can benefit more from what the game truly has to offer.

Essentially, any human activity offers three different kinds of benefits: the rewards that come from *performance*, or the external results of the action; those produced by the *experience* of performing the activity; and the *learning* or growth that takes place during the action. For example, a person may eat food in order to nourish his body, or to savor the taste, or in order to learn something about foods—to find out which foods are easy or hard to digest, or seem to satisfy a particular hunger.

Generally a person focuses on only one of these three benefits in any given activity. We tend to work at our jobs for the rewards promised by successful *performance*; we play more for the *experience*; we read a book or take a class for the sake of *learning*. But any activity offers all three kinds of satisfaction, and if we focus on only one we are shortchanging ourselves and are bound to be somewhat dissatisfied.

If we examine the particular activity called golf, it therefore makes sense to ask not only what we can get from good performance—that is, results—but what we can learn, and what enjoyment we can find. If you really want to gain all three benefits, you should ask yourself whether you are getting them.

If you feel that golf is a goal-oriented game and that what you want primarily is good results—a low score—then to attain your desire, you have to take another step. What benefit will come from achieving good results? Excluding the professional who gains obvious financial benefits, you should mull over this question until you get to the bottom line for yourself.

Next you could ask what kind of experience you now receive from golf, and what is possible. Although Self 1 may assert that my experience depends entirely on my score, and that therefore I should simply strive for the lowest possible one, my own experience shows me differently. Generally speaking, scratch players don't seem to have much more fun than those who shoot in the 80's. Both groups think wistfully that they'd be happy if only they could break through the next score barrier, but would they? Admittedly, I generally enjoy playing well more than I do playing poorly, but it's also true that I have had some wonderful times on days that I had a relatively high score. One question I sometimes ask tennis players is, "When does the enjoyment happen in tennis—after you've won, or during the course of play?" Or along the same lines, "When do you actually feel the pleasure of a good tennis shot—as you hit it, or after you've seen where it goes?" Some only look for pleasure in results and miss the joy of the shot itself. Clearly, there is satisfaction in each. Many golfers say they play the game for the fun of it, but not so many actually have fun. To really enjoy golf, you have to focus on the fun of it, and you'll find that you play very differently from the way you do when you are concerned only with results.

Finally, the golfer should ask himself what benefits in learning or growth he can get from the game. This may not sound like an appealing goal, but it is a large part of what games were designed for. There is more to learn from playing the game than golf itself. Much of this book has been concerned with the value of learning the art of relaxed concentration, developing awareness, trust and will skills, decreasing self-doubt and learning directly from experience—all while hitting a ball around the course. The number of strokes I take stays on the scorecard, but what I learn stays with me and can be used to benefit my life.

At this point one might well ask if it's really worth the effort to consider all these points. Why is it so important to know why you want to play, beyond the obvious reasons that take one out to the course? The answer is that success in both outer and inner games depends on one's state of mind and on one's ability to achieve relaxed concentration. When your motives are not clear or when desires are pulling you in different directions, concentration can't be sustained and you don't attain the satisfaction that you're looking for.

I have found the effort it takes to clarify goals, even in recreational activities, is most beneficial when it is an ongoing process. Thirty years of playing the Self-1 game, "Let's see how good I become," ended up in boredom for me. Self-1 desires tend to vacillate between the dullness of the unconscious mode and the stress and strain of the trying mode. Relaxed concentration is infrequent when Self 1 dominates, for his desires are usually mutually exclusive and tend to split the force of will.

On the other hand, Self-2 desires harmonize with one another. He likes to express himself in performance when he is allowed to do his best, he enjoys himself, and he is an insatiable student who likes to learn from experience. These desires do not divide the will but strengthen it. When a person learns, he performs better, and his enjoyment automatically increases. The heightening of any one of these aspects of action reinforces the other two. When this kind of mutually reinforcing effect occurs, Self 2 grows in strength, effectiveness and well-being.

But when an imbalance occurs—perhaps because of Self 1's overemphasis on one aspect of action at the cost of neglecting the other two —the triangle tends to collapse. For example, when learning becomes the only goal, you tend to develop the ivory-tower syndrome: lots of knowledge but ineffective action and a lack of enjoyment. When enjoyment is sought and excellence forgotten, boredom eventually results. When performance alone is the goal, and learning and enjoyment are neglected, it isn't long before performance itself evens off or sometimes declines. The last is the most prevalent imbalance in our goal-oriented society.

Many large corporations are now facing the consequences of an overemphasis on valuing external results. (Some still don't perceive this imbalance, and are worse off because they aren't taking steps to redress it.) Some companies now talk a lot about what is called QWL, the Quality of Work Life. When this idea is taken seriously and sincerely, it has revolutionary results. When the employee is considered to be more important than his work, it's not surprising that the quality of his work rises. The same paradox holds true for the golfer; he is more important than his golf. When he surrenders his tight grip on the importance of results, he increases his ability to get those results— but in the process he also achieves more than the results he was seeking!

All of us must strive for a balance between the three kinds of satisfaction possible from human activity. For the golfer to attain this balance, he may need to consciously choose to experiment with different priorities. On a given day he might want to stress enjoyment. How difficult would it be for your Self 1 to give up his desire for the best possible score, and to hit each shot in a way that maximized pleasure? It might be hard, but it could be exhilarating. Obviously, you would still aim at the target, but you would swing for the fun of it and would use the clubs that you most enjoy. In short, you would literally be *playing*. If a golfer does this without undue expectations about results, if he can truly free himself from caring about his score, he may be very pleasantly surprised.

One could do the same for learning and for performance. Then, having experienced giving your priority solely to each, it should be easier to find your proper balance for a particular day. At that point it might be a good idea to set specific goals for each aspect. You might choose to set a performance goal of breaking 85 or of hitting twelve greens in regulation; an enjoyment goal that focused on the beauty of the day or the pleasure of the company of the people you are playing with; and a learning goal to practice relaxed concentration or any of the exercises offered throughout this book.

If you set goals you truly want to achieve, you gain a heightened experience. But goals are always easier to set than to remember and implement, especially in golf. The game and its players have a momentum of their own, and I know how easy it is for me to fall back into my Self-1 patterns of trying to prove myself. It helps when I'm with another golfer who's also playing the Inner Game; then we can remind each other and reinforce our mutual commitments. But I also find that I like playing with strangers. It's a challenge for me to follow my own will, to dance to my own inner drummer while others may be marching to very different beats. It's not always easy, but I find that it helps to make a brief note of my goals on the scorecard, and to refer to it from time to time. It gives me a chance to renew my efforts, to notice where I am in respect to my intentions, and to make adjustments if necessary.

7
INNER PUTTING
AND INNER CHIPPING

Toward an Inner Game Technology for Golfers

The word "technology" may sound antithetical to your concept of the Inner Game and what is natural. But nature *is* technical. What is *un*natural is the use of technique to replace what is natural. When technical information undermines trust in ourselves and interferes with our awareness, it is detrimental to natural learning and to performance. Throughout this book my objection has been to the use of technical information about the golf swing replacing and interfering with the body's natural ability to learn. Technique is most useful when it *supports* natural learning.

Inner Game technology is designed to increase awareness of what *is*, and to encourage trust in Self 2's potential to learn, perform and enjoy. Each technique discussed in this chapter can help the golfer to get out of the trying mode and into the awareness mode. This transition requires a basic trust—trust that if "I" stop trying to control my golf swing, there will be something or somebody at least as effective to take over. In other words, it requires trust in the existence and ability of Self 2. Inner Game exercises are designed to help the golfer shift the means of internal control from a Self-1 base to a Self-2 base.

Trying any Outer Game technique picked up from a golf book, a friend or a pro is not particularly difficult. That is, it may be hard to *do*, but it isn't hard to *try*, because it doesn't require risking the current acceptable approach to the game. Conversely, Inner Game techniques are easy to do, but deciding to adopt them involves risk: the surrender of a familiar means of control in favor of something relatively unknown. Trusting the unfamiliar is always frightening at first, but experience will prove that relinquishing ego control is a matter not of giving up something but of shifting to a control system that is infinitely more sophisticated and capable. Very few people find they can free themselves of ego control all at once. Although theoretically there is no reason why we can't give up swinging according to a concept or trying to repeat a good shot by analyzing how we did it, for most of us the process of letting go is a gradual one. Depending on Self-1 control is second nature; because it's a habit, it seems normal, and breaking habits always feels unnatural.

But it's not. Self 2 is spontaneous and wants to break through the barriers of this so-called second nature. Self 2 *is* nature, first and last. Shifting from normal to natural is a risk to the ego; yet to the extent that I surrender that ego, each shot is an adventure. If I am able to concentrate my mind and let go, something new happens every time I swing. The swing seems to occur by itself.

Outer Game techniques are easily tested: we try them no matter how awkward they may feel because someone says they'll produce results, and the ball may or may not go where we want it to. Inner Game techniques don't work in the same way; they never guarantee instant results. They are part of a continual process of focusing concentration and encouraging trust. Concentration and trust *do* work; in fact, they are the only functions that continue to work over any length of time. If you put effort into developing these inner skills, your Outer Game *has* to improve.

Putting

Putting is an easy and exciting place to start the practice of the Inner Game. Here our physical limitations are virtually no factor. Control of the mind is what counts; awareness and trust make the putt. I doubt if many eighty-year-old ladies can hit a drive two hundred yards, but they definitely have the physical ability to sink a thirty-foot putt. On the other hand, if a pro hit his drive only two hundred yards, he'd be disappointed, but he would be delighted about sinking a thirty-footer.

The Outer Game objective in putting is the simplest and most precise of all golf strokes: to get the ball into the hole. How? Expect no tips from me regarding the stance and stroke that's best for your body. Enough—perhaps too much—has been written on the subject of putting mechanics by professionals more competent than I. The remainder of this chapter describes awareness exercises that have helped my own and others' performance and experience on the putting green. Use these exercises to discover which ones will allow your body to perform at its best, and adopt the ones suitable for your present potential.

All Inner Game techniques deal with increasing awareness of what is—that is, the factors in the here and now that are relevant to your objective. In every golf shot the essential objects of awareness are the body, the club, the course, the target and the ball. In putting, awareness of the green and hole is obviously important.

Increasing Awareness of the Putting Surface

Almost all golfers could make a significant improvement in their putting by *seeing* the putting surface more clearly. The most common mistake is to look too hard and think too long about the line of the putt. Near the hole, the final target, tension tends to increase; we know that a small error can add a stroke to our score, so we tend to strain as we look back and forth between the hole and the ball trying to fix the line in our minds.

But this isn't how to see something well. The eyes work best when they are relaxed. As in other tryings, "*trying* to see" fails. Even a slight tension in the mind can cause a tightening of the muscles that regulate the shape of the lens. In effect this means that staring or tensing the eyes will actually make the hole appear either farther away or closer than it actually is. Tension can also make the hole look smaller and distort the slope of the green. The eyes don't need help to see; you don't have to squint or stare. What we see comes to our eyes, not the other way around. The best way to look at a green is as a picture coming to you as a gift; simply relax and receive it. In this state it is natural for our eyes to move around; trying to hold them still prevents them from absorbing information. Only when you are relaxed and receptive does the light reflected from external objects fall on the most sensitive part of the eye, and only then are details seen in full clarity.

Thinking and analyzing while you are seeing doesn't really help; in fact, thinking *hinders* the seeing process. Most golfers feel that they should be figuring the break when they line up a putt. "Let's see, it's a downhill lie, so I should hit it soft, maybe with a longer, smoother swing . . . There's a break to the right, so I guess I should aim about six inches above the hole . . . But I left the last putt like this short, so I don't want to hit it too soft . . . I wonder what the effect of the grain will be . . ." This kind of thinking interferes with seeing.

It's not your intellect that needs to analyze the putt, because, as I hope you now believe, it is not your intellect that can direct your putter to hit the ball effectively. You can see the slope of the green and distance to the hole without saying to yourself, "It's eight feet downhill, with a break to the right." To translate the situation into words invites intellectual analysis and Self-1 interference with your stroke.

Allow your mind to rest in a quiet and relaxed manner on the object of awareness. Let it notice the slope of the green between the ball and the hole without thinking about it. Simply observe it, noticing the grain and texture of the green without consciously calculating its effect. From behind the ball, focus on the distance between it and the hole. To increase your awareness of the distance, you can divide the distance into equal parts in your mind's eye. On a short putt, notice the halfway point to the cup; on a longer one, you may want to divide the putt into thirds or quarters. Don't try to estimate the distance in feet. The exercise of dividing the distance will simply encourage you to sense it more accurately. I find that when I do this exercise on breaking putts, my eye does not pick out a straight line to the cup, but automatically picks out a breaking one.

On the practice green another way to increase distance awareness is to close your eyes, hold your putter by the club head, walk toward the hole and try to stick the handle of the club into the hole. Start with shorter distances—say, just over eight feet—until you begin to trust the exercise, then experiment from fifteen or twenty feet.

Relaxed seeing without calculating will put the clearest image of the green in your mind with all the detail you allow yourself to receive: the more relaxed your mind, the clearer the image recorded on it. Green-reading is a skill that develops over time as Self 2 constructs a storehouse of memories. A vivid image will help you not only on this putt, but in reading future greens with accuracy.

When slopes have a lot of contour, it is easy to be nervous because the putt looks too hard for Self 1 to figure out. Wishing you didn't have such a difficult putt will hinder clear vision of what is. Try not to judge what you are seeing; simply absorb the whole picture with interest and let Self 2 do the figuring. Does the angle of the curve change any closer to the hole? Grading slopes and contours on a scale of 1 to 5 will help your awareness, as well as increase interest in difficult greens.

Having recorded a clear image of the putt, there's no need to *think* about how to hit it. Let Self 2 absorb the picture, compute a solution and execute it. If you become responsive to Self 2, you will know when he is ready to putt. This is where trust comes in. Do you believe that Self 2 will stroke softly on a downhill putt if you don't tell him to? Try him and see; you may be surprised.

Though this may sound radical, I also recommend that you experiment with ignoring any conscious thought you may have about where you should aim to allow for the break. Self 2 is also better at that.

Self 2 already has in his computer bank all the information he needs to make the putt. Translating this information into words not only is unnecessary, but reduces accuracy dramatically. First, it shifts control to Self 1, who knows little about muscle coordination; second, verbalizing involves subtle forms of interpretation; third, words are not accurate enough for the precision demanded in putting. Putting without thinking shortcuts the mind and eliminates one of the prime causes of error: the loss of accuracy that results from translating images into words.

If you doubt this, think about how accurate a frog's tongue is when catching flies. It may miss its prey a few times, but it won't be because the frog was thinking about it. Shortcutting the verbalization process doesn't guarantee that you'll sink the putt, but when perceptions are fed directly into muscle responses without interpretation, accuracy will be greater.

I don't expect you to trust in Self 2 on my say-so; trust will have to come from your own experience. Try it for ten or fifteen minutes on the practice green, and I think you'll be surprised at what Self 2 can do without consultation. Using the back-hit exercise during your swing will also help decrease the effects of doubt. My father was extremely skeptical when he tried this approach to putting, but later he said that though the experience was somewhat frightening at first, the results were uncanny.

One of the greatest advantages of not consciously calculating the line of the putt is that there is much less tendency to steer your stroke. Steering is a major symptom of "trying" in putting, and is a compensation for lack of trust in Self 2.

Going to School on Other Golfers' Putts

It is commonly felt that you can learn a lot about the contour of a particular putt if one of your opponents has a line similar to yours and is putting first. But it is to your advantage to go to school on *every* putt both before and after your own. If you do this exercise, it will not only sharpen your awareness of the speed of this particular green, but give Self 2 further information that will help you in the future. Estimate the length and slope of each player's putt; then, before the putt is halfway to the hole, decide whether the ball is going to stop short or beyond the hole, and by how much. This gives Self 2 valuable practice in reading greens, as well as precise information about the relationship between the speed of the ball and how far it travels. I find it's also more fun than just standing around pretending to be interested when I'm not, and keeps me from analyzing my last putt or worrying about what will happen when it's my turn.

Body and Club Awareness

Feel is widely recognized to be a prerequisite for control in putting. In his book *Golf My Way* Jack Nicklaus says, "Such is putting! 2% technique, 98% inspiration or confidence or touch . . . the only thing great putters have in common is touch, and that's the critical ingredient . . . none of them found it through mechanizing a stroke, nor do I believe they could maintain it that way."

To me, perhaps the most important focus for attention on the club in putting is the angle of the putter face relative to the target. It doesn't matter what the angle is at the outset; if you are aware by feel and sight of the angle of the face, Self 2 can compute this information along with the mental picture it took of the green and adjust the line of the swing with great accuracy.

Your grip is your point of contact with the putter and should allow for maximum feel. Don't try to hold it "right" according to some theory; experiment to maximize your feel. Don't try consciously to adjust the firmness of your grip; if you focus on it you'll notice fluctuations of tightness during the swing.

Find the stance that provides the most comfort and balance for *your* body. No one else can tell you what that is. Get as comfortable as you can. You can experiment with this by noticing degrees of comfort and discomfort.

Don't be afraid to experiment with different grips and stances. Often a change will increase your sensitivity to the feel of your body. Similarly, changing putters can often increase your awareness by helping you to absorb different putting sensations. This is one reason why golfers often putt better for a short time after switching putters.

Probably the most important focus for body awareness during the putt is movement. Don't *try* to stay still; you'll become too tight. But don't try *not* to stay still either. Simply notice any movements in your body, and especially your head, during the putt, and observe whether your eyes are over, in front of or behind the ball. If you do this, all unnecessary movement will tend to decrease and eventually to disappear without conscious control. Advanced golfers who do not think that they can detect slight movements and imbalances will discover them and then find that they disappear with a little practice in this awareness exercise.

A Holistic Solution to a Complex Problem

For any putt that has a complex slope or texture, there are always several possible solutions. The ball can be struck with more force to allow less for the break, or it can be struck softer so that more break will occur. Many different swings will give a good result. The more complex the problem, the greater our conviction that it needs thinking about, but quite the opposite is true. The more complex the problem, the more Self 1 should stay out of it. Self 1 likes to assert himself when the situation looks difficult, but in doing so he only makes matters worse. When I'm putting in the awareness mode, I let my Self 2 gather a clear picture of the putt, stand over the ball and let him decide the solution.

Increasing Awareness of Any Technical Aspect of Putting

Once you understand and trust the basic principle of the control-through-increasing-awareness process, it is not difficult to devise exercises that will increase your control over any technical aspect of putting. Here are the basic steps and an example of the process:

1. Focus your attention *without judging* on the part of your body that gives you the best feedback about the particular aspect of the putting stroke over which you want to increase Self-2 control. (Example: Suppose you are erratic in your direction—sometimes left, sometimes right—and conclude that it is the angle of the face at contact that is not consistent. You notice that it is the back of your left hand that gives you the best indication of the direction of the face.)

2. Locate the moment that feedback occurs, and try to receive it at the earliest possible moment. (In the example above, you might notice that the earliest possible moment occurs at the point that your swing changes direction.)

3. Scale the feedback on successive strokes. Don't try to change it; just absorb it and putt again. This allows the differentiating and self-selecting powers of Self 2 to store up information. (The scale might be a zero if the back of the left hand is square to the target, $+1$ to $+5$ if the hand has turned clockwise and opened the putter head, -1 to -5 if it has turned counterclockwise and closed the putter head. Simply putt and mentally note the numbers.)

4. When the changes stop, groove the improved stroke by continuing to focus on the feedback area until you are confident that the change will hold up even when you are not attending to that specific part of your body. By merely observing without trying to change or correct, you will increase natural learning. Your body will learn what works by its experience.

Once a golfer understands the relationship between simple awareness and control of his swing, it is simple to create awareness exercises of his own. Devising awareness games that develop external skill is one of the most enjoyable aspects of the Inner Game. Furthermore, the practice of those exercises is far more effective in the long run than trying to conform to a list of technical instructions imposed from outside. Below are several components of the putting stroke for which awareness exercises could be easily invented by any golfer who wished to:

—awareness of putter head speed
—awareness of direction of the path of the putter head
—awareness of the length of the swing
—awareness of the angle of the club face before and after contact
—awareness of the height of the putter over the green
—awareness of the spin imparted to the ball

More Awareness Exercises for the Practice Green

Every golfer knows that mental control is nowhere more elusive than in putting. The pressure for results mounts with each stroke that brings you closer to the hole and reaches its peak in the putting green, where the demand for precision is high. For this reason I have included a few awareness exercises devised for the practice green that have the twin goals of improving performance and increasing trust in Self 2 in a low-risk situation. In time you may want to incorporate those that work well for you into your game.

Putting with Eyes Shut. Your sense of feel of all golf strokes can be increased by closing your eyes. With all of your attention focused on the movement of your body, sensations become more distinct and touch improves. This exercise can help increase feel with any club in practice situations; however, only in putting could this be a practical technique to use when stroking the ball. After some practice, I found that not only did my sense of feel increase, but results were surprisingly accurate. Self 2 could remember very well where both ball and target were. I know some putters who, after trying the exercise on the practice green for a few days, began experimenting with it during play on the course and have stuck with it ever since. One great advantage to it is that it gives you confidence that Self 2 can learn to hit the ball squarely without looking at it with his eyes. You start to "see" the ball with your hands. Blind putting has great value in increasing feel and trust, and in improving your ability to putt the ball solidly without looking at it. This will help you take a step toward the goal of fully trusting looking at the hole while putting.

Looking at the Hole. During the time I was experimenting with the technique of "association with the easy" (see Chapter 4), I began to look at the hole while putting instead of at the ball. This worked marvelously for me during practice. After all, if I were merely picking a ball out of the hole, I would look at the hole, not at my hand. Focusing on the hole made it seem more easily within my reach, and I didn't feel I had to remember where it was. Once out on the course, however, I did hit a few balls off center, and it wasn't until I had spent some time on the practice green with my eyes shut that I developed the ability and confidence to "see" the ball with my hands and make solid contact with it. This gave me the best of both worlds; I could "see" both targets at once. I had the confidence of an archer looking at the target or a bowler looking at the headpin. The goal was in my immediate vision.

A second advantage of this method is that it helps keep your head still during the swing. You don't look up to see where the ball is going because your eyes are already on the target. Because the putting stroke is so short, looking at the hole does not restrict your body movement.

A third advantage is that this technique helps overcome fear of the ball and the unconscious tendencies to steer, break or yip. When this method is used in conjunction with *the doctrine of the easy*—imagining that putting is as easy as picking up a ball—it can have wonderful effects. The mind is relaxed and yet concentrated on its target while the body is trusted to do the action. The experience can be as natural as picking up a glass—or perhaps more aptly, as threading a needle. Let me repeat, however, that I don't recommend trying this under pressure until you have done it often enough with your eyes closed to build sufficient trust that you can make solid contact without watching the ball.

The Black Hole of the Universe

Recently I had a conversation with a doctor named Janet Goodrich who does valuable and innovative research in the field of vision correction. She said she had never played golf, but when I asked her what advice she would give a golfer on the putting green, she didn't hesitate to make a specific recommendation. "The most important thing is to relax and to stay present; don't think either about the past or about the future. The way to do this is to use your imagination. Imagination is stronger than intellect in fending off tension. And colors should be noticed; colors are very important. For example," she said, "imagine the grass as a green magnetic field and the hole as a black hole in the universe. Nowadays everybody knows about black holes; they suck in everything that comes near them. Just look at the black hole and let it swallow the white ball. The movement of the body during the putting stroke is only a physical action as natural as any other natural phenomenon—like a bird flying or a blade of grass bending in a light breeze."

I took Janet's suggestion to the practice green. It helped my concentration to see a black hole in the universe instead of a mundane one in the green, and it increased my confidence to imagine that this little hole had the property of attracting my little white ball. Still, I felt that this fantasy might sound a little too weird for the average golfer. To my surprise the very next day I saw an article in a golfing newspaper by Parker Smith, who wrote: "Our perception of a golf ball, a hole, a green, is the only perception that counts. They become what we define them in our mind's eye. The four-plus inch cup can be a black hole of gigantic proportions possessing unlimited gravity (thereby pulling all putts straight into its bottom), or it can be a pinhead lost in a sea of wildly uneven green grass."

Of course, the issue isn't so much whether you see the cup as a black hole or not as whether you can use your imagination enough to focus on it. The more vividly you see the hole, the more your mind is allowed to become interested in it, the more steady your vision will be and the higher your perception will become, as there will be less room in your mind for doubts, fears and interfering thoughts.

Seeing the Hole Vividly. Whether or not you are ready to make such a revolutionary change as looking at the hole while putting, it's important to "make contact" with it. Especially if you putt looking at the ball, you want your mental attention to stay on the hole so that the movement of your body will follow your attention. Therefore, when you look at the hole, try to find something interesting about this one in particular. It may sound strange, but a fundamental law of concentration is that you can only really fasten your awareness on something that interests you. Although the hole doesn't move, you can always find something to engage your specific interest. Perhaps it is light reflecting off several blades of grass, the hole's oval shape or the richness of the dirt at the back of the cup. Of course, what may interest one player may not attract the attention of another, but unless you want the hole to scare you because of its associations with past failure, it's wise to let it attract your attention by some other means. To repeat: the ball will follow your body, and your body will tend to follow your attention.

After you have found your point of interest, retain it in your mind while looking at the ball. The moment this image seems most *vivid*, putt. At that instant your mind is relaxed and you will have less interference from Self 1.

One-Handed Putting

One way to notice the effect of doubt on performance is to putt one-handed. First take a few strokes and ask a friend to notice if your hand wobbles. Then putt a ball toward the hole. If there is no wobble, it's not a bad way to putt. Try it in competition on the course. Any wobble? Doubt has a greater effect on our small muscles, and with no left hand to steady them, their movements become more obvious.

Now that you have a clear feedback system, you can work to decrease the effect of doubt. Keep putting and simply observe the wobble with detached interest, noticing everything about it without trying to suppress the doubt or curb its effects. If you can do this, the wobble will diminish by itself. The doubt will have no fuel; you will realize that doubt doesn't have to be fought, and that it will go away if you don't resist it but stay focused on what *is*.

Listening

Hearing can be more of an asset than it is generally given credit for in golf. It can give you input that you don't get from other senses, especially about the contact you are making with the club. By listening to the sound of the ball as it is struck, you can learn to discriminate whether it is being hit inside, outside or directly on the sweet spot. As this awareness increases, so does the percentage of solid putts.

This exercise reminds me of the blind golfer who was playing in a foursome and was being ribbed by the other players. After one of his opponents left a sixteen-foot putt five feet short, he remarked, "That has to be the worst putt I've ever heard!"

Reducing Unnecessary Head and Body Movements

Unnecessary head and body movements are said to be one of the greatest causes of error in putting. The following awareness exercise will help build the habit of a naturally still body and head without causing the stiffness that often comes from forcing stillness upon yourself. The golfer simply putts in his usual style and determines if he can detect any movement in his head or body. He might ask a friend to observe in case he can't feel the movement that he has been told is there. After locating where the movement is, and without making any effort to change it, he should try to notice exactly when the movement begins and when it stops. After he is certain that he is focusing on the movement directly with relaxed attention, he can rate its degree on each succeeding putt. If this is done without consciously trying to decrease the movement, it will reduce itself to a level that is effective for the individual at that point. Soon it will feel more natural to move less, and large movements will come to his attention instantly.

Actually, Self 2 is perfectly capable of sinking a lot of putts even if you do move your head. It just makes it harder for him because he has more variables to plug into his calculations. So unless golf is becoming too easy for you, it's wise to find a comfortable but relatively motionless putting posture that will allow all Self 2's effort and attention to focus on feeling and direction.

Awareness versus Fear of Failure

Awareness is not a phenomenon that switches on or off; it is quantitative. Just as a 300-watt light bulb shines more light on an object than a 50-watt one, awareness is greater or smaller depending on one's attentiveness. In golf, as in other goal-oriented activities, our degree of awareness tends to decrease as the fear of failure increases. This is nowhere more evident than on the putting green, where the hole, the final target, confronts us with the immediacy of success or failure. The nearer the golfer gets to his goal, the greater the tendency toward tension and loss of awareness. The art of putting depends on maintaining a high degree of feel in circumstances of increasing pressure.

Prentiss Uchida and I went to the practice green one afternoon to explore this relationship between feel and tension. We started with a no-pressure situation and moved toward increasing it while attempting to keep awareness at its highest possible point. At first we did a simple exercise of increasing our feel of the putting motion without a club in hand. With palms against each other and moving our arms along an even path, we tried to become as aware as possible of the subtle sensations of this movement. In less than a minute we both could feel our degree of awareness rise to almost double that of our first movements.

Next we put putters in our hands and practiced the same movement. Immediately awareness decreased, then slowly built up again as we continued to focus. Putting a ball in front of the putter was the next step, and had the same effect of lowering awareness. It was surprising how the simple act of hitting a ball tended to take our attention away from the movement itself. We practiced putting without any target for a few minutes, making our only goal the maximum feel of the swing. Before long we were highly conscious not only of the swing but of the sound of the ball at contact with the putter.

Then we added the element of a target, but not the hole. We continued hitting balls, guessing where each would land in relation to the last. Soon we could tell by the sound of the contact and the vibration in our hands exactly where on the face of the club the ball had made contact. Finally we hit toward a hole. The first few putts again produced a marked decrease in feel. Both of us realized that the *ping* sound, which had seemed so noticeable when there was no target, seemed absent. But when we shut our eyes and didn't try to sink the putt, our awareness picked up and more balls went in the hole.

Of course by this time the relationship between concern for results and awareness was obvious to us in principle; still, each time we got nearer to "putting that counted" the degree of feel would decrease. But by just gradually increasing the stakes we were able to rebuild the degree of awareness before taking the next step. Nevertheless, it took us over an hour to achieve the same degree of awareness while putting the ball toward a hole as when we did so without a target.

We ended the afternoon by playing a competitive putting game for a quarter a hole, and awareness fell off by about 20 percent from the highest level achieved earlier. So did results.

Yet there was a significant overall gain in awareness and control as a result of the afternoon's effort. It was easy to see that by increasing the pressure in small increments, it was possible to break through the negative effects of pressure on awareness—and, in fact, to turn pressure to our advantage. If a golfer could end this progression by being fully aware of the feel, sight and sound of a six-footer on the eighteenth hole of a nationally televised tournament, he would have taken a significant step toward winning the Inner Game.

Inner Putting on the Course

On the course it is almost always the performance leg of the performance triangle that has priority. Many of the awareness exercises already described in this chapter are more appropriate for the practice green because they are suited to a learning situation or require too much time to practice in the midst of a game. But there are a couple of awareness exercises I've discovered that will not interfere with the pace of the game and will help to keep Self 1 quiet as well as give Self 2 more accurate information when you putt.

Rehearsing the Putt

I always used to putt only after a practice swing, but as I began to trust myself more I found my putting improved when I didn't take a practice stroke. The same was true of chipping. Often my practice swing seemed smooth and authoritative, but the real one turned out to be hesitant. I did better when I just read the green, set up and putted.

However, I have now found a way to rehearse that seems to help me. The crucial difference is that I take a practice stroke in the awareness mode instead of the trying one. I crouch behind the ball and read the green, then straighten up and, looking at the length of the putt, take a few practice swings, letting Self 2 translate what it is seeing into a putting "solution." There will be a little variation in length of stroke and acceleration until the solution clicks and I can tell that Self 2 feels comfortable with it. Then when I set up over the ball, I let Self 2 fine-tune my stroke and pay close attention to its feel. I don't try to control; I just let go and experience it. Self 2 has just rehearsed several times and has no doubt about the general parameters of the swing. All that remains is the fine-tuning. Self 1 feels more confident because Self 2 has already demonstrated that he knows what to do; the feel of putting is fresh in his memory. As a result, there is less doubt and more accuracy.

Rehearsal does not help when it is a response to self-doubt and interferes with the spontaneity of the actual swing. But when the rehearsal itself is spontaneous and is an attempt to achieve a greater freedom of expression during the moment that counts, it can be useful. In a sense, all games, including golf, are rehearsals for the "real thing." What is important is not to try to *repeat* the rehearsed swing. Self 2 will repeat it if he wants to, or he may alter it slightly. Whichever he does, I have faith that he is recognizing a better solution.

Another use of rehearsal swings is to lessen tension and increase feel. Jack Nicklaus describes his use of practice swings to increase his feel of distance:

> During a round, I pay a good deal of attention to touch, on all putts. If I have an 8-footer, for example, on my practice stroke I don't simply swing the putter through—I try to simulate the feel of an 8-foot putt. A 15-footer or a 45-footer, same thing: I try to tailor the practice stroke to the putt coming up.

If you have left the last three putts short of the hole, giving yourself no chance for a birdie, you don't want to fall into the pattern of putting short; conversely, you don't want to overcompensate and hit the ball six feet beyond the hole. Let Self 2 swing much too long and then much too short to dispel any tension about "getting it right." These swings will also give you the opportunity to correct any erroneous grooves you may be developing.

Chipping

Chipping is like putting in that it requires only a short swing, with at least part of the shot rolling along the putting surface. I recommend the same "seeing without thinking" exercises. Let your computer do its work without interference; you don't need to think. In chipping, feel is all-important. Don't become involved in rights and wrongs; they cut down on feel and increase tension.

The greatest physical cause of error in my own chipping—and which didn't occur in putting—was mis-hit balls. I tended to be a little tense and either to skull the top of the ball or to hit into the grass behind it. I found the back-hit exercise the most helpful in giving my mind a focus that freed me from self-doubt; at the same time it increased my awareness of the club head, giving me more feel for distance and accuracy.

For greater concentration on the back-hit in chipping, I focused on the leading edge of the club, which is the crucial factor in giving direction to the ball. The moment I felt the leading edge was at the back of my swing, I would say "Back," following with a staccato "Hit" at the precise moment of contact. Narrowing my focus to one edge of the club head forced me to concentrate more deeply and consequently gave me more accuracy. I could easily feel any change of direction in the leading edge that might tend to send the ball off course. Either back-hit or "da-da-da" can also be effectively used in conjunction with this exercise.

Again a reminder about deep concentration: "deep" does not mean "hard." Trying hard to concentrate doesn't work any better than trying hard to do anything else. Light, relaxed concentration grows deeper as the object of it absorbs more of our attention.

A lot of people try to figure out how much of the chip shot will be in the air and how much will roll along the ground: "Where should my shot land on the green?" I suggest that you don't try to figure this out, but do become aware of it. There are many different combinations possible with the club. Line up your shot; then guess what its height will be and where a shot of that height should land to make it to the hole. But don't *try* to get that result. Simply let Self 2 do it, then watch the loft, where the ball lands and how it rolls.

As on all other shots, this is the most important thing to remember: *Whatever you normally try to do, don't.* Don't try. Enjoy the uniqueness of each chip shot. Enjoy its rhythm and feel its feel. If you detect some stiffness, focus on it. If you feel the ball glancing off the face of the club, focus on that. Let Self 2 correct these flaws. The practice of the Inner Game is a never-ending challenge to trust Self 2 with any and all functions formerly controlled by Self 1.

No matter how poor a golfer you are, the aim of the chip shot is to hit the ball into the hole. You are close enough to do it. Of course, there are more variables than on most putts, and perhaps more luck involved, but Self 2 can do it. If you go for it, you will automatically become more aware of the line and distance. Go for the bull's-eye and accept what you get. Self 1 will try to talk you into coming close enough to the hole to get down in one putt because you're "not good enough" to sink a shot from off the green. Well, if you're not good enough, that's all the more reason to go for the hole; if you miss, you will still be closer than if you miss a larger target of ten feet in diameter around the hole. Inexperience is no excuse for not aiming at the target.

Thinking

As in any shot, any thought about what may go wrong in the midst of a chip shot is apt to introduce error. Your mind needs to be quiet and concentrated enough that there is no room for thought or doubt. Concentration on something interesting is the best defense against doubt. Don't fight the yips; that only encourages them. If when addressing the ball you start remembering previous yips, you're only increasing your chances of yipping this time. Even a lot of practice swings won't help. I used to take four perfectly smooth practice swings, and then yip on the fifth when I was actually hitting the ball. My best counsel, based on my own experience with the yipping syndrome, is this: Don't resist. Resisting doubt strengthens it; I've seen it happen not only in people's games but in their lives. Better than resisting is ignoring, and the best way to ignore doubt is to become absorbed in something else. If "da-da-da" or back-hit doesn't do the trick, create an awareness exercise for yourself that does work. If you can't find any exercise strong enough to keep the yips from barking at your door, as a last resort you can do what I did: welcome them.

Welcoming the Yips

Like all manifestations of Self 1, yips hate the light of awareness. Much of the time a yip won't even work its tricks if you are focusing on it. Most of our errors happen only in the dim light of semiconsciousness. We think that what we're doing is so bad that we don't want to really look at it. We don't like to see ourselves falling prey to something so embarrassing and stupid as a yip. The way to get over them is to see through them. Fearing yips perpetuates them; awareness of them reduces our fear and weakens them. Welcoming yips, I say to them, Okay, if you want to yip, go ahead and yip; I'd like to see how you do it. Yip as much as you like—I'll be right here watching and feeling exactly what happens. In effect I'm saying, You can't scare me.

What to Do When You Lose the Feel

Nowhere is feel more crucial than in putting and chipping. Everyone experiences days when the club feels like an extension of the body and control seems simple, and everyone has times when the feel just isn't there—especially when playing under pressure.

The greatest cause of loss of feel is self-doubt, usually brought on by missed putts. Using the doctrine of the easy can help by taking your mind off negative associations with past putts and bringing positive associations into your swing.

But the basic strategy for increasing feel is to consciously switch games from a game of results to one of awareness. Usually it is overconcern with results that leads to overcontrol and decreased feel, so change your goal to increasing awareness. Pick any awareness technique and increase your focus on whatever feel is there. Don't judge it as good or bad; merely observe it. Feel will pick up immediately and improved results will follow as a matter of course.

Another reason for losing feel is boredom. When a player becomes bored, awareness declines, and although his swing may be so grooved that it achieves satisfactory results for a while, he will soon stop learning, and shortly thereafter performance will drop off. Boredom is best combated by taking conscious risks and concentrating on enjoyment. Experiment with a radically different putting stroke, or even change putters. It doesn't have to be a *better* stroke or putter, just a different one; it is the change that will increase awareness and decrease the boredom.

Equally effective is putting for pure fun. Playing the results game without ever giving yourself a break is dull, and ironically leads to a decline in results. Take a break. Do whatever's necessary to introduce pleasure and excitement into your putting. Use your imagination; risk a few failures. An increase in feel is the inevitable result of increase in the quality of your experience. Results will inevitably follow.

Tips and Gimmicks

Tips are Self 1's favorite weapon against the awareness progression, and there is no harder task than to rid ourselves of the hunger for tips. Self 1 constantly offers hope that there is some one thing he can do that will work.

Perhaps I hit a putt while thinking about something specific, and the ball goes into the hole. "That's it!" says Self 1. "You thought that thought and the ball went in! It works!" If you think the same thought on the next hole and sink the putt again, you're really in for trouble. You'll be sure you have The Answer, and will probably start telling other people about it too.

Of course there isn't any such tip; there is no thought, no technique, no theory, in either the Inner or the Outer Game, that is going to make the ball go in the hole. A tip is really nothing more than a superstition, and it carries the implication of a superstition that if you *don't* do it, something terrible will happen.

The human body and the energy that moves it make the ball go in the hole, and we have no choice but to rely on them. All we have to learn is to concentrate the mind and keep ourselves out of the way of the body so it can either do its job or *learn* to do it better than it now can.

8
INNER SWINGING

The technical requirements of the golf swing are precise and complex. The demands of power and accuracy accentuate the central problem, control of the body. As early chapters have noted, this control is contingent upon the extent to which we can quiet our minds, and Self 1's conceptual control is inferior to Self 2's more natural and sophisticated predominance through awareness.

Therefore this chapter will give you no "do-instructions" with which you can take apart your golf swing and try to put it back together again. Rather, it will show you how to increase awareness of the feel of key elements of the swing, and how to practice golf in a way that will be less confusing and frustrating and yet can lead to a technically more sound swing. Awareness is more technical than words, just as we can see subtler shades of color than we can name. The art of relaxed concentration will allow you to discern more and more subtle bits of information provided by your body and thus heighten your control. By following its criteria of what feels good—that is, the quality of your body's experience—and what works, Self 2 will automatically differentiate between feelings and select the most appropriate solution.

The natural learning process of Self 2 has one other key advantage for the average golfer with a limited time to practice: it cuts down significantly on learning time. Give Self 2 enough balls to hit and a clear objective, and with a little trust he can quickly learn to hit them. Tennis players using Inner Game techniques generally learn in one half or one third less time than they do with conventional instruction. How fast you learn depends on how well you are able to concentrate and block out mental interferences, and on how much trust you are able to invest.

In an interview with the *Boston Globe*, PGA teaching professional Tom Shea related how he had developed and used Inner Golf techniques with his students from watching the Inner Tennis television series and reading the Inner Game books. "I was absolutely amazed at the results," he said. "I have pupils who have advanced as much in twenty minutes as they probably did in twenty years. It has made a definite improvement in my own game." Tom's enthusiasm is not unique. When a teacher is able to guide his students into the awareness mode, a certain magic happens that instills confidence no matter what kind of drill is used. Once the confidence in Self 2 is implanted, learning occurs very quickly. But teachers who try to use the technique without really inspiring the student's confidence in his Self 2 will meet resistance and a decreased learning rate.

The exercises in this chapter are designed as catalysts for this natural learning process; with a willingness to experiment and to trust Self 2 the process can become self-generating.

Of course, valuable things can be learned from conventional golf instruction, and at the end of this chapter I'll offer my views on how to benefit from the extensive experience of teaching professionals.

It doesn't take a pro to see that among the crucial elements of the golf swing are balance, rhythm, tempo, power and accuracy. Most pros understand the mechanics of these components far better than I, but I believe that it is most valuable to learn about these elements of the swing from our *own* experience. For a start, it's not a bad idea to forget all that we *think* we know about the golf swing. This is the secret of children's success in learning: *they don't think they know.*

Balance

How does a child learn to balance himself on a bicycle? Not by reading a book, and not by being told how. He learns by experiencing the difference between balance and imbalance, and by unconsciously selecting the kinesthetic behavior that promotes balance. He understands that this is his goal, and if his trust in his potential is intact, all he has to do is pay attention to his body. First he may fall a few times, but by focusing on slight degrees of imbalance, he can gain control in a surprisingly short time. You can learn balance in the golf swing in much the same way—by attending to balance, first by noticing extreme examples of imbalance, and then by fine-tuning.

The first step is to take a few swings on the range, or even indoors without a ball, paying attention only to balance. Your goal is simply to be aware of whatever balance exists, so simply swing as you normally do. How do you know if you are on balance throughout the swing or not? What tells you that your balance isn't perfect? You may feel, for example, that at the end of your swing you are falling backwards slightly away from the target. Pay attention to whatever you feel most predominantly. Notice exactly when it happens, but keep swinging. Focus on what you feel, whether the balance increases by itself or not. Don't worry that it doesn't improve; if you keep swinging with attentiveness and trust, it will. Worry will rob some of your attention and interfere with the learning process.

One way to increase your sense of balance is to swing with your eyes closed. This will not only make visual feedback impossible but increase feedback from nonvisual factors. Another effective method is to decrease the pace of your swing until it is barely moving, checking the balance throughout. Begin by checking balance at the address position. Then gradually increase the tempo of your swing.

As your awareness of the intricacies of balance develops, you will notice that what tells you whether you are on or off balance is not changes in weight distribution but the relation of your center of gravity to the earth. The center of gravity in the human body varies with individual builds, but it is located in the general region of the abdomen. Instructors of the martial arts place enormous emphasis on awareness of our physical center, called *ki* in Japanese and *chi* in Chinese. Although I am not accomplished in the martial arts, knowing this simple principle has helped my own tennis game immensely, because it produces not only a heightened sense of balance but also increased power. It has provided similar benefits to my golf swing, and now my most reliable cues are those that have developed out of awareness of my center.

Without thinking about what your stomach should or shouldn't be doing, take some swings while placing most of your awareness on the abdominal region. Notice, as you do so, your sense of balance in relation to the ground. As you explore this sensation, you can feel the difference between being "up" and being settled low, or centered. It is well known to martial artists that when a person becomes anxious he usually "leaves his center" and goes "up." The slang expression "uptight" is an apt description of what happens when we lose mental or physical balance.

Finding Your Center of Balance

A simple balancing exercise frequently used in the martial arts will illustrate the value of focusing on the *chi* center.

Ask a friend to stand facing you about a foot away. Touch hands palm to palm and try to knock each other over by pushing hand against hand. It's a bit tricky; if you focus on resisting the push it's easier to be knocked off balance. Try to concentrate on your abdomen and flow with the situation. The secret to strength in this exercise lies in balance, not in force.

There are several situations in golf that tend to pull the body off balance—for example, downhill, uphill and sidehill lies. If you try to think how to compensate for these terrains, you will not find effective balance. Recognize, as you did in the pushing exercise, that there is a force tending to pull you off balance. Neither resist nor give in to it; merely find your balance in relation to the particular pull. Make balance your goal and allow Self 2 to learn how to find it. He will have no problem doing so.

Rhythm

Rhythm is easier to experience than to define. When your golf swing is rhythmic you know it, and when it's not you can tell immediately if you are at all aware. Because we can feel rhythm we can increase control over it.

Swing your club focusing on the rhythm that exists in your swing already, without trying to add any more. *Trying* to swing rhythmically can destroy it, just as trying hard to dance in time to music can throw off your dancing movements. The key to both is attentiveness.

A young woman who came to me for an Inner Golf lesson felt that although she tried hard to swing correctly, something was keeping her from getting good results. Watching her take a few swings, I found my attention drawn to the full stop she took at the back of her swing. Deliberately obeying all the "rules," she took the club back, stopped as if to shift gears, and then swung forcefully down toward the ball.

I asked Harriet if she liked to dance, and she nodded. "Then do a dance called the golf swing. Forget about results for a while, and all the rights and wrongs; just create a movement that has a pleasing rhythm to you." This was easy for her; inside of five minutes, her swing was completely different. She lost none of her effective elements of technique, but picked up so much rhythm and timing that her stroke really became a swing. Not only did power and consistency increase, but her obvious enjoyment in the movement itself was striking. "For the first time swinging this club isn't a chore that I'm worried about doing right, but something I like doing," Harriet said. "But I'm surprised that the results are there too. It's like hearing that you can do what you've always really wanted to, and it will work out okay." This seemed to me an apt definition of how the golf swing can be.

If you ask those who are most concerned about results—the pros—they will all stress the importance of rhythm. It requires body awareness; to feel the rhythm in your golf swing, you have to listen to your body. Some tennis players find that they play better with music in the background, and on ski slopes skiers wearing stereophonic headsets are not uncommon. Though golf is not generally suitable for musical accompaniment, it does have its own rhythm.

The golf stroke, like the tennis stroke, is basically a two-beat rhythm: back and forth. These two beats are fundamental to most movement—the rhythm of breathing, for example. We don't have to force it; it is there. Two common errors in swinging—failure to complete the backswing and forcing or rushing the downswing—are fundamentally errors of interference with that natural rhythm. Either we want the swing to descend before the backswing has been completed, or we doubt that the transition will happen without help and so we force it.

The club will come down and accelerate itself as the tension produced by the full backswing builds to its limit and begins to uncoil. The key is to let the swing's rhythm control itself.

Not only is paying attention to rhythm tension-reducing, but it is also a good way of freeing the body from the awkwardness and stiffness that result when trying to perform according to "do-instructions." Like balance, it can also distract Self 1, in playing conditions, from anxiety over results. Self 1 doesn't really have many ideas about how to achieve balance and rhythm, and consequently offers less interference in the guise of advice.

With trust, rhythm can be fine-tuned to an almost unlimited extent. Perfect rhythm would require full attentiveness, perfect oneness with the body, and no mental interference whatsoever. Practicing rhythm means tuning in to its subtleties until we can pick up its nuances. I can't really tell when the drummer in a jazz band is a little off the beat, but a musician can. He developed that skill by listening and focusing his awareness on rhythm. You can attune yourself to the rhythm of your golf swing in the same way.

Hearing Your Rhythm

An adaptation of the "da-da-da" exercise in Chapter 2 is useful for "hearing your rhythm." After a few swings, insert "da's" at the key places in your swing, such as the moment the club is all the way back, the moment of impact and the moment of swing completion. You can add as many "da's" as you like, but remember to keep your awareness on the club head so that you can say each one at the exact place in your swing that it represents. By listening to the "da's," you can sharpen your sense of rhythm. Do this exercise for about five minutes at a time as part of your range practice. Your own rhythm does not remain static from day to day, so it's not a bad idea to locate it again each time you play. Let the body find its own sense of rhythm for a particular day, or even for a particular shot. Your job is simply to let it happen and to stay attuned to it. If you do so, your swing will gradually find a basic rhythm that is suitable to your body size and type, temperament and skill level.

Tempo

Tempo means rate of motion. In the golf swing it is determined by the relative speed of the arms on the backswing and downswing. You can feel your tempo by sensing the rate of your backswing, downswing and follow-through.

Little is needed to improve tempo other than to become more aware of it, and to be alert to Self 1's slightest tendency to interfere. Self 1 can't really describe tempo; however, he can destroy it by trying to speed it up beyond the natural pace of your Self-2 swing, or by slowing it down too much through overdeliberateness. But simply being aware of the tempo of your swing can keep Self 1 from interfering.

As I experimented with my own tempo I found that if I took the club back too slowly, I increased my tendency to swing down harder with my right arm. Although in point of fact the speed of the backswing shouldn't affect the speed of the downswing, my Self 1 *thinks* it does, and makes up for a slow backswing by giving it the gun on the way down. I noticed that as I let the tempo of my backswing increase just a little, a slight momentum would build at the top of the swing that would heighten my sense of coil and increase my confidence that the club would descend at a reasonable speed. When my club came to rest at the top, I felt more inclined to force the club down to the ball. Bringing the club down willfully is nowhere near as effective as letting it descend as a response to the coiling of the backswing.

When practicing on the range, it is useful to explore different tempos, but when actually playing I would not recommend experimenting; merely be aware of your tempo as a focus for your attention. Consciously trying to influence tempo is likely to throw off your timing or some other aspect of your swing. If you think you would like a faster or slower tempo on a particular swing, translate that desire into a muscle thought by moving your arms in the desired tempo before the swing, and then trust Self 2 to do it.

Discovering Your Tempo

Experimenting with different tempos on the practice range will give Self 2 a chance to explore the feel of various speeds and choose what is best for you.

Take a few swings with your attention on tempo but without trying to change anything. Using a scale of 1 (slow) to 10 (fast) as a measure, rate your present backswing and downswing. How can you best differentiate between variations in speed? For me the left arm gives the best information about tempo. Without a club in your hand, feel the rate of your arm moving back, and then the rate coming down. Which is faster? By how much? Paying attention to the speed of the left arm gives a valuable clue, especially since—at least in my case—it is the overeager right arm that destroys the tempo.

After you have determined what your present swing's tempo is, experiment with several different ones (back 7, down 3; back 3, down 7; back 5, down 5; back 8, down 8; and so forth). By consciously swinging in these different ways, you are broadening the scope of your experience. Often this is a valuable method for going beyond our present limits, both physical and mental. Then let go of conscious control and let Self 2 swing, calling out the numbers corresponding to the speeds you feel. At first you will probably notice some variations.

Self 2 will be experimenting for a while to discover what feels and works best. Gradually he will stabilize at a consistent tempo as the learning process is completed. Then you should keep swinging for a while to groove your new tempo.

These three general aspects of the swing—balance, rhythm and tempo—are similar in that they relate to the whole swing, and are too complex for Self 1 to involve himself in. To focus awareness on them, you don't have to break down the swing or analyze its parts. Therefore they are excellent focal points for attention during play, when focus on a specific part of the body or aspect of the swing could throw your stroke off balance. Trying to conform to specific mechanical details during a swing under pressure is asking for trouble; yet too often this is what we try to do in moments of self-doubt.

It is also worth mentioning that experiencing balance, rhythm and tempo provide much of the enjoyment of golf.

The Setup Position

Much has been written in golf magazines and books about the setup position. This is one aspect of golf in which "do-instructions" are not so inhibiting because at least you have all the time you need to obey them. Still, aside from certain obvious fundamentals, there is very little agreement on the proper way to address the ball. Even if there were, going through a long checklist while setting up tends to make anyone feel a little stiff.

Having said that, I must admit that stance and alignment *are* important for the most consistent golf performance.

My main suggestion on this subject is that you allow yourself to experiment and don't become locked into an absolute doctrine. Use awareness exercises to experiment with alternatives in ball placement relative to your feet (both in and out and forward and back), with open, closed or square stance, shoulder or hip alignment, head position and amount of knee bend. The goal in each of these experiments is to find a position that (1) is comfortable for *your* body; (2) allows you to swing freely from a stable, centered platform; (3) gives Self 2 a vivid sense of the target line.

When setting up while on the course, it is especially important to let your body sense its position in relation to the target. Before hitting each ball, your body needs to know where the target is not only visually but through feedback from the position of your feet, hips and shoulders. Let it *feel* the target line, not just *see* it. One way to facilitate this is to move your feet in place several times before settling into your final position. This simple action, plus attending for a few seconds to the alignment of hips and shoulders, will tell your body where you want it to hit the ball, and thus help Self 2 determine what kind of swing will accomplish the result.

When a beginner first hears all the so-called rules of a correct stance, he can grow so concerned that he's doing something wrong on the setup that he's tense before he even hits the ball. After some experimenting I found that even if I didn't obey those rules, my Self 2 could hit the ball straight. This was a great relief to me. I even played around with radically open and closed stances, with the ball much too far in front or back. In the most extreme positions I couldn't hit the ball straight, but in all the moderate positions Self 2 seemed to be able to make the adjustments necessary to hit the ball toward the target. This built up my trust in Self 2 and made me feel a lot less intimidated by instructional dogmas. It also made it far easier to relax over the ball.

Still, there's no need to make it harder for Self 2 than necessary, especially if you are looking for consistency, so let him show you what's easiest for you. Use professional instruction or help if it helps, but make your Self 2 the final authority. After all, he's the one—not your teacher—who has to hit your shots.

Accuracy

Control over the direction of the ball is the major focus of most golf books. Although there are perhaps as many suggested solutions as there are books, there are only two factors that influence direction: the angle of the club face at impact and the path of the club head. From an Inner Game perspective, it stands to reason that the key to increasing your control over direction lies in increasing your feedback from these two aspects of the swing.

A golf ball can be hit out-of-bounds with a perfect grip, a perfect stance, a straight left arm and a still head—in short, with everything right, except that the club face is too open or closed in relation to the target. Conversely, a ball can be hit accurately with an awkward grip, terrible stance, bent arm and wobbling head—as long as the club face is square at impact. In fact, one of the few universally agreed-upon principles for accuracy in every golfing situation requires the club face to be square to the target at impact. For this reason, awareness of the angle of the club face is crucial in learning to increase accuracy. If the club face is either open or closed at impact, it will impart a sideways force to the ball, as well as sidespin, and produce either a slicing trajectory (open face) or a hooking trajectory (closed face).

Learning to sense the angle of your club face at impact on drives requires a greater degree of concentration than in putting because of the higher speed of the club face. Realizing that your club face was open after you see your ball slice into the woods won't help you to change it. The art of control comes from being able to acquire information from your body early enough during the swing so that the body can correct any misalignment *before* impact. This correction cannot be made consciously, but Self 2 can perform subtle last-minute adjustments below the threshold of conscious awareness if he is trusted to do so.

The path of the club head in relation to the target—not the angle of the club face—should determine the ball's initial direction. But sensing that direction is one of the most difficult kinds of awareness to achieve in golf.

Hit a few balls and guess their direction without looking. Ask a friend to check your accuracy. If you can't feel where the ball is going, it's hard to control it.

It took me a long time to truly sense my club-head direction by feel alone; I always had to look at my divot mark. Obviously, it was too late when I did so, but at least it told me that I was off line and that I should pay more attention in practice to this aspect of the swing.

One of the best ways to focus on your club-head direction is to practice making vastly out-of-line swings—far "outside-in" or "inside-out." Only by feeling the enormous difference between these two extremes did it become easier for me to sense the smaller differences.

There is much speculation about the cause of outside-in swings. To me, one reason seems predominant: it's more natural. Since the body is standing inside the target line, it is natural to swing across your body, or in the direction of the body. If you try hitting from an extreme inside position to the outside, your body is in the way. You can experience the same unnaturalness by trying to throw a ball outward to the right of your body (assuming you're a right-hander). It's much easier to throw a ball across your body, to the left.

An extreme outside-to-inside swing, which is therefore the more common error of the two, is destined to start the ball off the club head to the left. To compensate for this, the club face is usually open at contact, producing the beginner's banana ball that goes left off the club face before curving widely to the right. In an attempt to correct for the slice, the golfer often opens his stance toward the left; then the swing becomes even more outside-to-inside, and the slice correspondingly greater. Various compensations for this problem produce many of the swing patterns that test Self 2's ingenuity in hitting even a few decent shots.

Control of this flaw can best be gained by learning to sense the difference between outside-in and inside-out swings, and by learning to sense the difference between an open and closed face, both at setup and during the stroke itself.

Direction-Awareness Exercise

Exercises to develop control of accuracy and speed require subtle degrees of concentration, and should be used only on the practice range when the learning segment of the performance triangle is predominant.

Learning to discriminate the feel of the path of the club in relation to the target can be developed by aiming for different targets on the ball itself. Imagine the face of a clock on the top of the ball, with the point closest to the target representing the noon position. For an inside-to-outside, or draw, swing, aim at the 6:00 to 7:00 position on the ball and follow through in the 12:00 to 1:00 position. For an outside-to-inside, or fade, swing, aim at 5:00 to 6:00 and follow through at 11:00 to 12:00: It may help to imagine that you yourself are the ball. Which point of contact would give you the best trajectory to the target?

For true accuracy, awareness of the angle of the club face and of the path of the club head must be integrated. The effects of the spin imparted to the ball by an open or closed club face will cause it to veer to the right (open) or left (closed). Even with a square club face you will fade if the club comes through a little outside-in; if a little inside-out, you will draw. But these awarenesses have to be developed separately on the practice range. In play, it's best to surrender control and trust Self 2 to integrate what he has learned about both aspects.

Power

The first error most beginning golfers make is to try for power. By attempting to force power into the stroke Self 1 tightens too many muscles and, in so doing, restricts other muscles necessary to swing the club head through its arc. Overtightening freezes portions of the swing, and even if it doesn't lock the wrists completely, it definitely throws off timing and rhythm.

Compensation for this error causes the second major impediment to power, and the one most common among more experienced players. After many painful lessons learned from trying to hit the ball too hard, and with the encouragement of one of the most popular golf tips, the player tries to "swing easy." Fear of relinquishing control causes him to swing with too slow a tempo, or worse, decelerate as he approaches the ball. Learning to swing the club at different tempos is invaluable to the serious golfer, but slowing down the swing because of overcaution robs it of both power and accuracy.

Releasing optimum power on the swing comes from learning how to express your potential for it on the one hand, and discovering how not to interfere with it on the other. The actual bodily process of producing power is extremely complicated, involving the contracting and relaxing of pairs of opposing muscle groups with a rapidity and timing that stagger the imagination. Self 2 can regulate this process perfectly if he is not interfered with.

As a way to quiet Self 1 I find it useful to think of the generation of power as a flowing river. Strength lends additional power to the muscles if used properly, but it's more important to generate a river of energy that can flow through your body. Overtightening restricts this flow, and decreases power. I find that reminding myself before I swing to use energy, not strength, often results in a more powerful drive.

I learned a lot about the difference between muscle power and flow power through a demonstration of akido, a Japanese martial art. In the akido class, participants were paired off, and one of each pair was told to grasp his partner's arm above the elbow with one hand and his wrist with the other. Then he was instructed to try to bend the arm at the elbow while his partner tried to resist him by keeping it straight. Except where there was a gross mismatch in strength, the benders were easily able to fold their partner's arms. After I had succeeded in doing it to my partner, we reversed roles, and he proceeded to do the same while I strained with all my might to resist him.

Now the instructor asked the original benders to try again, but this time he instructed their partners not to try to resist. "Instead," he said, "use the bender's strength against him." When I tried to bend my partner's arm it seemed as strong as steel, and I couldn't budge it. He stood there looking completely relaxed, laughing at me as if he could keep his arm from bending forever. When it came my turn I thought to myself, I'll just relax and see what happens. What happened, of course, was that my arm bent immediately. I didn't really know what it meant to "use the bender's strength against him," but the next time I tried it anyway. It worked. I was amazed. Without straining, my arm was perfectly rigid, my fingers dangling loosely at the end of a relaxed wrist, but something was keeping my arm stiff as a board. I felt that I could keep it up much longer than my partner could keep exerting his pressure.

When I asked a physiologist what muscles keep the arm straight, he answered, "Not many—there are only a few extensors in the interior of the arm that keep the elbow from bending." So when I was trying to be strong, I not only overtightened and wasted a lot of energy but also sabotaged my efforts by tightening the biceps that serves the function of bending the elbow! Trying to "use my partner's strength against him" tricked Self 1 into trying to do something that wouldn't interfere with Self 2's understanding of how to keep himself strong. After I understood the trick, it was just as easy to achieve the same kind of strength with the instruction "Simply trust. Let your arm take care of not being bent."

Whereas strength is a function of the development and reflexive abilities of our muscles, power is generated by muscles contracting and releasing, and so it has more to do with coordination than with force. Therefore, though it is the speed of the club head that imparts power to the swing, this velocity is the result of a complex and well-timed sequence of muscle contractions that build up tempo from one muscle group to the next. It starts in the legs. The velocity of our leg movement is not great, but built on it is the forward momentum of hips, which in turn pull down the arms. The arms are also pulled down by their own muscles, and their velocity is the sum of the momentum building throughout the body and their own power. Then the wrists pick up that force, adding to it the momentum of their own uncocking.

Obviously, the intricacies of momentum are far beyond the abilities of Self 1 to master, especially in the two seconds it takes to swing a golf club. The entire sequence has to be coordinated by unconscious parts of the nervous system. All that can be grasped consciously is that the power swing is really a series of momentums, each building on another. No single one of them is very fast in itself, but the total velocity imparted to the ball is enormous when the timing is right. Imagine a man standing on the flatbed of an open railway car moving at sixty miles an hour who shoots a gun in the same direction at eight hundred miles per hour. The speed of the bullet when it impacts its target is eight hundred sixty miles an hour.

The timing of the muscle-releasing process is more important to power than the strength of any single muscle group. This is the reason why trying for power by flexing different muscles to the maximum can in fact impede the velocity of the club head.

Exercises for Increasing Power

To explore your own potential for power, swing your club with the intent of increasing the flow of energy through your body. Pay attention to anything that seems to be restricting this flow. Wherever you find the flow in your body restricted, pay attention to whatever is happening there. As you focus on it, it will free itself of its own accord. Don't tell yourself to relax; this will probably produce more tension. Do this exercise until you experience your body as a channel through which energy is flowing unrestrictedly. It doesn't help to push the flow; the best you can do is to let the water build up behind the dam, and then let it release. For me the exhilaration I experience with this release is one of the greatest enjoyments in the game.

Another way to experience the flow of power in your body is to tighten as hard as you can the muscles in the area of the stomach, and then let them release and stay relaxed throughout the swing. This will take conscious effort at first because in almost everyone there is a tendency to tighten at the center in moments of exertion. Relaxing the center introduces flow into the swing and generates a lot of power.

Increasing the stability of the swing will also enhance power. Beginners seem to believe that power comes mostly from the hands and arms. The experienced player knows, consciously or unconsciously, that the momentum that ends with the high speed at which the club head strikes the ball begins in the feet. Imagine what would happen to your power if you were suspended in a harness two inches above the ground. How much club-head speed could you generate? No matter how strong you are, the results would not be impressive.

To get a feel for the amount of stability you do have and how to increase it, here is an exercise you can do with the help of a friend. Take your normal setup position as if you were about to hit a drive off the tee. Ask your friend to test your stability by pushing you in the upper body, front, back and sides to see how easy it is to topple you off balance. Teachers of the martial arts are famous for using this technique to demonstrate to their students the value of a stable center.

Now make a conscious effort to ground yourself. Settle into your center as you did in the balancing exercise and let your belly hang as if it's resting on the ground, but without changing your physical posture. Relax any tension in your upper body. Ask your friend to try again to topple you, using the same amount of force. Unless your posture is already very stable, within a few minutes you'll experience a measurable increase in your stability. The greater the stability of the setup position, the more power and accuracy are introduced into the swing.

In golf the drive is one of the few opportunities we have to release our total power in action, and to me it's worth even a lost ball now and then to experience that sensation fifteen or so times a round. Driving is my favorite part of the game for this reason—not because I let myself swing fully, but because I allow myself to enjoy it fully. I've found that almost everything I let myself enjoy fully I soon am doing well, because enjoyment and learning go hand in hand. When they don't, usually it's because not much learning is taking place, and performance inevitably suffers.

There are many focal points on which to concentrate the attention that will aid in the production of more power, and any of them are helpful during practice on the range. Stick with one area for at least five minutes, but let Self 2 help you to find the focal point that he wants to stress.

Targeting

In *Golf My Way*, Jack Nicklaus writes of the importance he places on visualizing the target and the shot before hitting it:

> I never hit a shot, even in practice, without having a very sharp, in-focus picture of it in my head. It's like a color movie. First I "see" the ball where I want it to finish, nice and white and sitting up high on the bright green grass. Then the scene quckly changes and I "see" the ball going there: its path, trajectory, and shape, even its behavior on landing. Then there's a sort of fade-out, and the next scene shows me making the kind of swing that will run the previous images into reality. Only at the end of this short, private, Hollywood spectacular do I select a club and set up the ball.

Much has been written on the subject of visualization and mental rehearsal. These techniques can have a powerful effect on performance, but many people, including myself, don't "see" pictures distinctly when they visualize. The primary advantage to targeting in this way is that it can give Self 2 a clear goal in a language that it understands: imagery. Before putting, to tell yourself in words that you want the ball to go into the hole is much less effective than actually picturing the ball doing so. You will get the best results if you think of it as a way of communicating a request to Self 2. If you make it an order in the form of a picture from Self 1 to Self 2, you will induce doubt, and will *try* to accomplish what you visualized; probably you won't get the results you visualized, and will soon abandon the technique.

To me this is the most important issue in visualization: using it to make a demand on Self 2, or as a gimmick, undermines trust in Self 2 and your proper relationship to him. *Asking* Self 2 by offering an image of the results you want is very different from *demanding* them, and affects the success of the technique as well as your general state.

My son once approached me with this statement: "Dad, I want to ask you for something, but I don't know how. I don't want to just *demand*." I was a bit surprised and asked him what he felt the difference was between demanding and asking. He thought and then said, "Well, when you demand and don't get it, you get mad! But when you ask and don't get it, you may get sad, but you don't get mad." As it turned out, he got his raise in allowance, and I felt wonderful about it because I felt I'd truly been asked, rather than manipulated.

When visualizing the target, it is best to hold the image in your mind throughout the swing. If you were shooting an arrow, throwing a baseball or bowling, your eye would constantly be focused on the target. Since this is impossible with the golf swing, the best one can do is to "remember" the target constantly. "Remembering" does not mean trying to steer the swing; it simply means holding the position of the target as vividly as possible in your mind so that Self 2 can direct the swing.

Self-2 Targeting

I have so much respect for Self 2 that sometimes I think that picturing where I want my drive to go is presumptuous of me. I figure he knows better than Self 1 where to hit the ball. When I feel this way, I stand behind the ball and look down the fairway, letting Self 2 do the looking. I also let him decide whether to hit a fade or a draw to the left or right side of the fairway. It's exciting, and requires more trust than willpower. When I address the ball, I don't really have any idea where it's going, and I don't find out until it rolls to a stop. This is a good antidote to overcontrolling, especially to steering. How can I steer if I don't know where we're going? Letting Self 2 pick the goal is quite different from simply stepping up to the ball and hitting it anywhere; you make a conscious choice to let Self 2 make the decision, and then trust it, as well as its execution, to him. Self 2 understands whether or not I'm sincere in surrendering the target as well as the shot-making to him. When I have faith, he almost always surprises me pleasantly —often with a much better shot than I could imagine.

I remember one particular shot that seemed impossible to me on a day when I was playing Pebble Beach with Michael Murphy. I had admired Mike's book *Golf and the Kingdom* and had looked forward for a long time to playing with him. The fact that Pebble Beach put on its best weather for us was a much appreciated bonus. I had been playing pretty well up to the twelfth hole, a tricky, well-trapped par-three of 184 yards, where I hit a three-iron that faded into a trap ten yards in front and to the right of the green. The ball came to rest directly under the six-inch border of the trap. There was no way I could hit it toward the green without ricocheting off the border. "What on earth can I do in a situation like this?" I asked Mike, a much more experienced golfer. "Well, there's not much you can do but blast it out of the trap, and hope you can chip it close enough on your next shot to sink the putt and settle for a four." This made perfect sense, but somehow I just couldn't do the reasonable thing. Okay, I said to Self 2, I sure as hell don't know how to hit this shot. I don't even know where to aim. You hit it. When I addressed the ball, I found myself facing a good 70 degrees left of the pin. I swung down, without the slightest preconception, through a point about two inches behind the ball with three-quarters force. Almost immediately after contact with the sand my club banged into the trap border, but the ball itself bounced off the border in a direction 30 degrees to the *right* of the pin, and by virtue of spin and the break of the green, started a long curving roll toward the hole. I stood in awe as I saw it finally stop two inches from the cup. "I guess you should have hit it just a tad harder!" quipped Mike.

I leave it to the reader to do his own experimenting with Self-2 targeting. The key to success is a relaxed mind, faith and the effort to surrender to Self 2. Of course, not all your shots are going to turn out the way you would like, and when this happens, how you deal with the situation is important. If you blame your lack of coordination or intelligence, or berate yourself in any such way, you can expect repeat performances. If you don't sense the immediate cause of the error, don't dwell on it or try to analyze it; it is almost certainly due to some kind of self-interference. All you can do next time is to trust Self 2 more and put more effort into relaxed concentration. When you do, the past error doesn't affect the next shot.

Changing Habits

It is much easier to teach a beginning student than one who has adapted a lot of ineffective habits; it is one thing to learn a new skill, and quite another to change habits. How does one approach this problem in an Inner Game way?

Changing habits is not as difficult as *breaking bad habits*. Resistance is always hard. Therefore, especially with deeply ingrained bad habits, I recommend that you not try to break them. Simply leave them and start new ones.

A habit is like a rut in the nervous system. It might be difficult to repair a faulty groove in a record, but it's simple to move the needle a fraction. It is no more difficult to groove a new habit—unless you believe it is. All that's needed is an awareness of the boundaries of the old groove so that you don't get into it before you know it, along with the clear intention to create a new one.

Take the common example of the beginner's banana slice. There are many proposed remedies for this problem, but it still flourishes. Most solutions neglect the first step in changing a habit: to know the habit *as it is*. The banana swing is caused by an outside-to-inside swing with an open club face. But knowing this may not help you break the momentum of the habit. For a golfer to alter the pattern effectively, he needs to know *how* he slices—that is, he must be aware of slicing not just after the fact but at the moment that he slices. He must *feel* the outside-to-inside swing and the open club face. As soon as he can feel it while it is occurring, his body will be able to leave that groove and fall into another one.

The process with a student might go something like this. "John, I want you to hit some golf balls and make no effort to change your swing to keep from slicing. Just pay attention to your swing the way it is, and see if you can tell before you actually make contact whether it's going to slice or not."

John's reply might be, "Yes, I knew it was going to slice, because it always does." Then you can say, "All right, see if you can tell before you strike the ball whether the next shot you hit will slice more or less than the last one. Don't try to slice more or less; just see if you can anticipate, from feeling your swing, which it will be."

A big step has been taken here. John is probably convinced that you aren't trying to change him. There is no judgment, merely awareness and differentiation. As soon as he can feel the difference between a severe slice and a medium one, a learning situation has been created in which he can choose between two feels.

John will need also to become aware of the open face of the club. Perhaps he realizes that his club face is "slightly" open at contact but thinks that it is open to a degree of 1 on a scale of 1 to 5, whereas you can see that in fact it is more like a 4. Here you can safely give a "do-instruction" by asking him to hit some balls with a radically closed face. Then ask him to swing again without trying to control the club face and merely letting it find its own angle. Now that it is easier for John to feel the club angle, it will automatically be less open than before.

If Self 2 is given some alternatives, he will select from his own experience what feels good and what works. In this way the habit can be changed within a short time.

Body-Awareness Scan

To take full advantage of the curative faculties of awareness, a good practice is to tune up your body about once a month with a body-awareness scan exercise.

Begin with focusing your attention on your feet. Does anything draw your attention? Now focus on your calves, knees, thighs, lower body, upper body, right arm, left arm, wrists and head. This tune-up will give you information about which areas require specific attention and keep you from neglecting problems that may be affecting your swing.

Guideline for an Inner Game Practice Session

Ideally on the practice range the inner golfer should have a chance to stress each leg of the performance triangle; a session that should be enjoyable and conducive to learning, as well as to improvement of performance.

Of course, the following guideline is not meant to be a rigid schedule; experiment and discover what feels best for you. But it does give you an idea of what a productive practice session for an inner golfer might be.

5 minutes: enjoyment
Swing however you like. Loosen up, let go and set no goal other than experiencing the fun of swinging a club.

20 minutes: learning
Focus your attention on general body awareness for a few swings to see what part of the body or aspect of the swing emerges as a specific focus. Then concentrate on that area for at least five minutes. Begin each of the two or three awareness exercises you have time for by relinquishing attachment to results, and then gradually refine your awareness to achieve the necessary balance between letting go and awareness.

5 minutes: enjoyment
Take a break and hit balls for the pure fun of it. Reach for enjoyment by not assuming that hitting hard is the only fun; allow Self 2 to show you what he enjoys. You may be surprised.

Remaining time: performance
Use whatever time you have left to simulate playing conditions and to emphasize performance. Imagine actual golf holes; visualize the shot and select a club for each situation. Allow a longer period of time between shots, aligning yourself toward a different target for each one. Introduce psychological pressure by imagining more pressure than you would normally feel on the course. (This technique has the advantage of making real pressure less hard to handle.) Or set a goal for yourself and determine not to end the session until you achieve it.

The Role of the Teacher and Instructions

Some critics of the Inner Game approach have felt that I devalue the role of the teaching professionals, and that I believe that it is possible to learn the game without them.

It's true that many have learned golf without being taught; further, anyone can learn better on his own than with the kind of assistance that significantly interferes with the natural learning process.

But I value good coaching. In fact, I believe that it is better coaching that will increase the general quality of performance of most players. Though it is possible to play the Inner Game without assistance, it is more difficult to combat your own internal interferences all by yourself.

The main role of the Inner Game coach is to promote improved performance by facilitating the learning process. He does not need to do much teaching, but he does have to know how to help learning. Such teachers are valuable but are not often found. Speaking as a teacher, I have to admit that too many of us approach teaching thinking that we are the ones who know, and that the students are the ones who don't. If this psychological structure dominates the teacher-student relationship, relatively little learning from experience will take place. There is nothing wrong with experts and professionals, but learning is more than an exchange of information. Information is cheap. Insight is precious. There is value in being guided with insight through an experience from which you grasp your own insight.

If the teacher has the attitude that he knows and you don't, he will be quick to judge and to try to change you, quick to prove himself to you and to take credit for what you learn. You don't need this attitude developing outside of you—or even inside you from your own Self 1. You need someone who, from the depth of his own experience, trusts your Self 2—perhaps more than you do; someone who, from his greater experience, can intuit where you are in your own development and can help you find the best places on which to focus your attention. Finally, you need a teacher who helps you to discover your own learning goals, not his.

Good teaching is always nonjudgmental, trusts the human potential, is clear about objectives, and is unobtrusive. These are all basic Self-2 characteristics. When teaching is an ego trip, no matter how correct the information may be, the teacher will inject obstacles into the learning process that inevitably will be transferred to problems in performance. Therefore choose your teacher wisely.

A Lesson in Lesson-Taking

After a round at Los Robles Greens in Los Angeles, I went out to the range to hit some balls and was joined by Pete, one of the golfers in the foursome I'd just played in. Pete was a long-iron hitter with a 10-handicap who seemed to rear back and attack the ball. On the sixth hole he'd hit a nine-iron one hundred fifty yards downwind and sunk it for an eagle. He said he'd been having trouble with his drives; he was slicing all of them. I asked him if he wanted to try an Inner Game exercise that wouldn't tamper with his swing but would help his concentration. He agreed, and I explained the back-hit exercise to him. At first he couldn't do it at all, but when he started paying attention to the club head instead of trying to correct the slice, there was an immediate dramatic change in the trajectory of the ball. "Wow," he said, "it works! That's the first draw I've hit all day."

"Okay, but don't try to do it again. Just let the club head go where it wants."

Again Pete hit a draw. "This is incredible. I thought the stiff shafts of my new clubs were making me slice, and that I had to learn to really come through with them."

"The problem seems to be more that you *thought* there was a problem. Most of our problems come from trying to correct problems, and when we stop trying to correct them and just pay attention to the club head, the body makes its own corrections."

I could see that this was an entirely new idea to Pete, and that he wasn't buying it easily. Still, he went on practicing the back-hit, and I returned to practicing with my five-irons. Jack, another of our foursome, came over to offer Pete some help, and they began a very technical discussion. Pete started slicing again. Soon I heard him say to Jack, "Hey, watch this. I don't know why it works, but you ought to try this back-hit stuff."

After a while Pete came over and offered to give *me* a lesson. He wanted to teach me how to hit down into the ball on my irons, to take a divot from inside out and make the ball jump off the club.

He gave me about four "do-instructions" and I felt pretty awkward, but I was eager to learn. I knew that my irons weren't going as far as I could hit them. Actually, the lesson turned out well. He'd given a do-command like "Hit a goddamn divot this time!" and I'd translate this mentally into "Let's see how much earth my club takes this time, without trying to take any." Then there'd be a divot and Pete would say, "Good, do you see what that does? The ball jumped off the club, and look how far it went." Then he said, "Okay, this time stand farther away from the ball, and make the divot go in this direction." He placed a cigarette 30 degrees outside my target line. It didn't look possible to me; I'd never come close to swinging in that direction. All right, Self 2, I said to myself, somehow swing so that the divot goes toward the cigarette. I haven't the slightest idea how to do it.

After a few swings Self 2 got it. Pete was jumping up and down saying, "That's it! You're hitting it inside out!"

I knew that Pete's technical information was helpful, but I also realized that if I'd tried to follow his instructions literally, I'd probably have ruined my swing. I had to smuggle his tips safely past Self 1 somehow and hope that Self 2 got the picture. This wasn't easy, particularly because I didn't want Pete to think that I wasn't trying to do what he was asking, and I had no idea whether Self 2 would do it. But Pete must have thought I was trying hard to do exactly what he said because the results got better and the swing easier, and in the process I picked up a good ten yards per club on my irons. Pete left feeling that back-hit had cured his slice and that his technical advice had helped put distance on my irons.

I finished the practice realizing that what another person has learned from experience can help Self 2 to learn, and that it is possible to circumvent the doubt and overcontrol that usually attend "do-instructions."

9

OF SLUMPS AND STREAKS: THE SELF-IMAGE BARRIER

One of the most perplexing problems for any athlete is the slump. How do we get into them and, once in, how do we escape? Some of us don't slump, we just plateau, but it amounts to the same thing: the natural tendency to improve with time and practice reverses or simply stops for no discernible reason.

Almost all golfers will readily admit that the cause of slumps, especially if they are long-lasting, is mental. Working exclusively on the physical level to climb out of a slump usually makes it worse. Johnny Miller is a good example of a professional who at first didn't want to admit that the cause of his fall from top performance had anything to do with his mind. He asserted vehemently to the press that it was simply a mechanical problem with his swing, which he would identify and work out. But three years later he still hadn't solved it, in spite of the assistance of many technicians who thought they had spotted the problem. The technicians may have been right—but only about the symptoms. The cause is almost certainly mental. This is nothing for Johnny Miller or you or me to be embarrassed about. I don't know of a single golfer who has proved that his mind is no longer capable of getting in his way. In order to play the Inner Game, we have to admit that the enemy is always inside us and isn't always overcome easily. Only then do we have a chance to gain some of the lost control that Self 1 has wrested from us.

One day while I was watching an LPGA tournament at Rancho Park Golf Course in Los Angeles, Al, a member of the men's club who had read *The Inner Game of Tennis* and had been trying to relate it to his golf game, approached me with a question that had been plaguing him. Pointing out one of the women who had been playing well early in the tour and then seemed to fall apart, he asked, "How can you get out of slumps?" I wasn't feeling particularly analytical that afternoon, so my answer surprised me. "By not getting into them," I said abruptly.

Al paused. I knew what his next question would be, and I didn't know how to answer it.

"But what if you're already in one?" he asked on cue.

I'd thought a lot about the causes and cures of slumps, but had no pat answer.

"Slumps don't exist," I found myself saying. "We create them in our minds. Some people say they're in a slump after two bad shots in a row; others don't feel they're in a slump until they've played their worst for two months. Therefore you're in a slump when you think you are. The deeper you think it is—the more deeply you believe in it—the harder it will be to get out of it. A slump is a belief that poor past performance is going to continue, and the best thing to do is not to believe it. Stay in the present, and let each shot, good or bad, stay in the past. The past doesn't have power over the present unless you surrender that power to it. If you find that you *have* been believing that you're in a slump, stop believing this the instant you recognize it. You created the belief and you can un-create it."

I was a little surprised at the length of my answer, but it rang true. Al looked satisfied. "Just forget the bad shots and make each shot a new one," he concluded. "Yes, all the past is good for is that maybe it taught you something."

We each went our separate ways to watch the women professionals. But three hours later at the sixteenth hole, Al approached me again. "Tim, I have one other problem I'd like to ask you about. I'm a twelve-handicap; I play about twice a week. The other day I was playing in my usual foursome here, and I started off the day with par, birdie, par, par, birdie, par. By the time I reached the seventh hole, all I was thinking was, When is this going to end; it can't keep up much longer —and of course it ended on that hole. My question is, When you've got a streak going, how do you keep yourself from thinking it's going to end?"

I was struck by the parallel between Al's two questions, though he didn't seem to make any connection between them, and realized something I'd never seen so clearly before.

"That damned Self 1 gets us going both ways!" I exclaimed. "When you're playing badly, it tells you you're in a slump and will never get out, but when you're playing better than usual, it tells you that you're in a streak that can't last. It isn't even logical. On the one hand, it tries to get you to believe that negative experiences in the immediate past are bound to continue, but when the immediate past is positive, it tells you that your performance is bound to change for the worse!"

Although it's impossible to know to what extent the immediate past influences the present, this made it clear to me that what we *believe* about the past has great influence. Believing a streak is going to stop will interfere in some way with your capability to keep on playing your best. Further, believing that you're in a slump will increasingly interfere with the expression of your potential.

During a period of poor performance, when tennis professional Brian Gottfried was asked how he had fallen so far so fast out of tennis eminence, he replied, "Easy. I went from number 4 to number 5 to number 7 to number 14." He went on to say that the main problem was lack of confidence. "I played a few bad matches and started thinking I was in a slump. Then I started working on parts of my game that really didn't need it, and I got even worse. All the time it was just my head that needed the work." (Shortly after this interview Brian went on to reach the semifinals at Wimbledon as an unseeded player, losing to the undisputed champion, Bjorn Borg).

Some valuable advice given me by my own tennis instructor, John Gardiner, is useful in dealing with the problem of getting out of slumps and not interfering with streaks: "Never change a winning game, and always change a losing one." Of course, trying to keep a winning game going by analyzing what you're doing right will be sure to end any streak. If you want to see the effects of this, just ask someone who's in a streak what he's doing to play so well, and watch what happens to his game. Don't let your own Self 1 do the same thing to you.

Making radical changes in your swing on the practice range can help to pull you out of a slump. Once I saw Jack Nicklaus coaching Jerry Pate, who seemed to be having trouble with his game, to swing the club from his knees. Other approaches you can try include hitting left-handed if you're right-handed, or swinging slow if you normally swing fast. These experiments have the twin advantages of taking Self 1's attention off anxiety over results and giving Self 2 different feels with which he can refine your actual swing.

It is important to understand that Self 2 is *always* learning, and that he learns from both poor shots and good ones. Trusting in his potential rather than in Self 1's generalizations about your past performance will help you to see the past as it is, and to stay in the present on each new shot.

The Expectations Game

I once asked my dad why he played golf. "Because I enjoy it," he said enthusiastically.

"When do you enjoy it?"

"When I play well."

"How well do you have to play to enjoy yourself? Do you have to break eighty?"

"No, I have to play up to my expectations. If I play below them I enjoy it less, but when I play equal to or above them I enjoy it that much more."

This conversation started me thinking about expectations and how they influence a golfer's performance. It always seemed to me that my own score had a lot to do with my expectations of how I would play, although infrequently I would surprise myself by performing radically above or below what I'd estimated. I have also observed how the expectations of my tennis students influence their games. I knew that to make practical headway against the phenomena of slumps and plateaus of performance, I'd have to understand the dynamics of expectations—how and why we form them, and how they influence the expression of our potential.

In a recent round I played, I was determined to break 80. I decided that I would play nine holes, and if I broke 40 I would finish the remaining nine. I started well: par, par, par, birdie, par, bogey, par, for an even par going to the eighth hole. If I shot par in the next two holes, I would card my first 36. I hit a good drive—into a sand trap but with a good lie—took out my four-wood and proceeded to hit three consecutive balls out-of-bounds. I ended the nine holes with my accustomed six over par.

I saw the bind my expectations had put me in. The lower my expectations, the better chance I have to fulfill them; the better my performance, the higher my expectations will be. If I score well, I win some satisfaction but reduce the chances for satisfaction the next time. If I were to break 80, my expectations would skyrocket, and my chances for future satisfaction would be severely jeopardized by Self 1. This paradox provides the limiting factor of the expectations game. I tend only to achieve what I expect, and yet I don't dare expect too much for fear of getting it once or twice and then setting myself up for a lot of disappointment.

Essentially, an expectation is an arbitrary belief about the future—that I will miss or sink a putt, that my partner will hit out-of-bounds, that I will get the yips on my chip shot and so forth. Because we have hit out-of-bounds in similar circumstances in the past, we think we probably will hit out-of-bounds this time. But it is equally true that we have hit the fairway, so expectations are selective. Many people expect that at the crucial moment they will blow it, just because they did so a few times. But others believe that if they did something well once, it's probably what will happen again this time.

A good example of this response came up in a conversation I had with Tom Weiskopf about Jack Nicklaus, in which he praised Jack's positive attitude, saying that it was the most important attribute that made him a winner. Paired in a tournament with Tom, Jack needed to sink a ten-foot putt to keep the lead. He studied the roll for a long time, then stepped up to the ball, settled into deep concentration and putted. When the ball came to rest on the rim of the cup but failed drop, he turned to Tom and said, "I don't care if the ball didn't drop, I hit it in the hole."

The unknown in any situation makes us uncomfortable and anxious.

"When in doubt, tighten." By projecting our doubt about performance into the future with a negative expectation, we tighten our defenses against anxiety and disappointment. Some people fantasize negative concepts, others positive ones, but it is important to remember that both are not real.

Tennis players often use the warm-up as a way of measuring what their performance will be like on a given day, and golfers sometimes base their game expectations on their performance on the practice green. This tendency sabotages the intention of practice. I try to take advantage of this time to loosen up, get into the awareness mode and in touch with my sense of feel. When Self 1 uses practice to evaluate performance, the trying mode insinuates itself, and tightening and overtrying are inevitable.

The other day I played in a foursome, one of whose members commented as we walked down the first fairway, "Last week I ruined my stroke, and now my swing is totally out of synch. I'm really going to have to work it out during this round." How did he know this?

Similarly, if I start out with three poor shots, a voice inside may tell me, "You're way off your game today. Your swing is all screwed up." If I believe this, I do have a bad day all day—or at least a struggling one. All that really happened was that I hit three poor shots, and this doesn't say anything about my swing or about the future. But unconsciously I have set up negative expectations for myself, and as often as not I strengthen them by telling my partner, "I haven't played in two weeks, and last time I couldn't hit my hat, so don't expect much from me today." There's an obvious reason for this behavior: doubt. I don't trust that my game is going to work well, and confronted with the unknown future, I want to fill that doubt with a belief. If I pick too high an expectation, I'm liable to be disappointed, so I pick a low one. Thereby I accomplish two things: (1) I will have a sense that I know what's going to happen; (2) I will avoid disappointment. If I happen to do better than my expectations, I will make myself a hero by Self 1's standards.

As long as a player tries to combat doubt by manufacturing concepts about his probable performance and then trying to live up or down to those concepts, he will be caught in the expectations trap. Slumps will be the bottom line, plateauing the daily bread, and streaks short-lived and bittersweet.

What's the alternative? A wise friend of mine summed it up succinctly: "Blessed are those who have *no* expectations, for they shall not be disappointed." Playing without expectations doesn't mean playing without planning or without goals. It means having the courage to realize that you don't know what will happen. It means that instead of inventing an expectation to fill in the question marks in the future, you accept your ignorance: you set your goal, make your effort and see what happens. It's a much more exhilarating and satisfying experience than setting up expectations and then constantly measuring your performance against them.

The strongest tendency among golfers is to expect an "average" performance. If they play below that average, then they're in a "slump"; if they play above it, then they're in a "streak," which will probably end soon. The key to overcoming expectations lies in this simple maxim: Trust Self 2, not your past. Playing without expectations makes each shot a new opportunity for Self 2 to learn and to express himself. The goal is to release as much of that potential as possible, and then to let go and be surprised. The satisfaction and enjoyment I experience comes from the quality of the effort I make, from the learning I am absorbing, from my awareness of my swing and of the time between swings, and not just from the results.

Self 2 wants to express himself and to learn; Self 1 wants to be right. If you play with Self-1 expectations, you may not do any better than you expected to, but you give Self 1 the consolation that he was right about your performance. If you play without expectations, you may not be right about the future so often, but it will be happier.

The Self-Image Barrier

The limiting power of expectations becomes more serious when Self 1 incorporates them into the way you see yourself. Essentially our self-image consists of expectations we have about ourselves, and the basic self-image mistake is to overidentify with one's performance. The degree to which players identify with their golf games is brought home to me every time I play with strangers. The first question I'm always asked, after the usual social amenities are dispensed with, is "What's your handicap?"—a thinly disguised euphemism for "How good are you?" Most people's response to this question will be *"I'm* a four-handicap" or *"I'm* a fifteen-handicap."

During the time that I had a 12-handicap I played a round that brought this home to me sharply. The stranger with whom I was playing asked what my handicap was and we made a small bet. I was playing exceptionally well that day for a 12-handicapper, a fact that did not escape the attention of my companion. He made several sarcastic comments during our round, and I myself felt self-conscious about the discrepancy between my handicap and my performance.

At the end of the day the man owed me a dollar. When I thanked him, he asked caustically, "What're you thanking me for?" I told him I'd enjoyed the opportunity to play.

"Well," he replied in a disgusted tone, "I didn't. I never enjoy playing with sandbaggers." With that observation, he walked away.

Driving home after the game, I felt angry at the man's insinuation that I had lied about my handicap. Having told him truthfully that my handicap was 12, should I have played only as well as a 12-handicapper and fulfilled both our expectations?

Self 1's interest is in creating a self-image, and he loves to define himself. But his definitions are only limited imitations of your true Self-2 potential.

I often use the following demonstration in Inner Tennis clinics to illustrate the limiting power of self-definitions based on expectations. I ask for a volunteer from the audience who is a "three-ball player." No one knows what I mean, and finally someone asks, "What's a three-ball player?" I reply that a three-ball player is someone who says to himself after the ball has gone back over the net three times, Wow, this is a long rally! The audience generally laughs in recognition; nearly everyone has a limit, some of three balls, some of six or seven, after which that same thought pops into their heads. "And what happens shortly after the thought comes to mind?" I ask.

"You miss," the group choruses.

After getting my volunteer, I ask him to concentrate on the bounce-hit exercise. Because the concentration demanded to do the exercise accurately changes the game for Self 1 from one of expectations about performance to one of simple awareness, often the volunteer will hit the ball over the net twenty or thirty times without even noticing it. Interestingly, when the player does become aware of the length of time between missed shots, he often becomes a little confused, and his next attempt will probably once again reflect his comfortable image of himself as a three-ball player. Self 1 fears contradiction; he would rather be right and lousy than to surpass himself and be proven wrong.

Once a psychology student named Harry took a lesson with me and found his serve improved threefold using Inner Game principles. Afterward he was enthusiastic, but a few days later he called me and said in an agitated voice that he was about to play with a friend with whom he had a regular game. "What should I tell him about my serve?" he asked. "Should I tell him I had a lesson?"

"Sure, why not?"

"But if I tell him my serve is better . . . Oh, no, I couldn't do that!"

"Why not?" I asked again.

"What would happen if I told him about it and it wasn't there?"

He was terrified at the prospect of actually stating that his serve was better—as if uttering the words would banish his new serve forever.

Harry's dilemma brings to light a mental obstacle that might be called the self-image barrier. In a case like his, good performance is inconsistent with his self-image, and so in the interest of preserving this image, Self 1 interferes with the full expression of potential. To repeat: Self 1 would rather be "right" than effective.

An image is only a picture of something real. A self-image is only a picture of a real self. Just as a photograph is a two-dimensional representation of something three-dimensional and cannot capture every detail or perspective of the object itself, our self-image can never encompass our true potential. Whatever your image of yourself as a golfer may be, and however accurate it is as far as it goes, it can never be the *total* picture. Likewise, performance can never be a true picture of your potential, nor of anyone else's; your best performance is still only a small indication of the full possibilities of your Self 2.

Performance equals potential minus interferences. This equation is the essence of the Inner Game approach. Learn to distinguish between your lack of a certain talent and the presence of some obstacle preventing the release of your existing talent. Any golf shot is the result of an unknowable mixture of talent and your interference with its expression. This is the reason why it is wrong to identify with your performance. You are *not* your performance. Even if you hit ten slices in a row, it does not mean that you have a slice or that you are a slicer; it merely means that the ways you are getting in your own way result in slicing. Take away the interferences and the slice will disappear. If your swing is overly stiff, it's not because you are a stiff golfer, or that you are not fluid. It means that Self 1 is overtightening your body, which has the capacity to be fluid if Self 1 wasn't doubting you, or wasn't expecting you to be tight. When you find a way to evade the self-image barrier, suddenly the tightness is gone and the fluidity that is in your body right now is able to express itself. You don't have to *become* fluid or *become* more rhythmic; you only have to learn to get out of your own way so that your fluidity and rhythm can be expressed.

The Problem with Positive Thinking

A popular approach to dealing with a negative self-image is to "think positive," but this solution is not without pitfalls. The essential problem with positive thinking is that the other side of the coin is negative; it's impossible to have one without the other. In short, it is like a pendulum that swings to one extreme, only to reach its limit and swing back to the other.

I first learned this lesson while teaching tennis. I had decided that negative criticism was not helpful to the learning process, so for a while I gave only positive compliments when appropriate. Soon I saw that this didn't work, either. The student would hit three balls over the net and I'd say "Good shot" after each one. But if on the fourth shot I said nothing, the student would look up and ask, "What was wrong with that?" When you set yourself up as a judge and try only to give positive criticism, saying nothing automatically becomes negative. Seeing this, I simply stopped judging. I gave encouragement and expressed enthusiasm spontaneously, but didn't judge.

Self 1 can trap you in the same way by reminding you that you have hit some great shots. He tries to convince you that if you will listen to his analysis of how you hit them, it will be a simple matter to get the same results all the time. But my experience is that Self 1 will interfere with my ability to perform to the precise extent that I fall for his dreams of glory. Similarly, my fear of failure will be as deep as his ambitions are wide. Thus, much of what seems to be positive thinking is negative thinking in disguise.

Similarly, when we try to develop self-confidence by positive thinking—"I'm going to hit a great shot, I'm going to hit a great shot"—we are disguising a deeper self-doubt. Anyone who tries to talk himself into something does so because at heart he doesn't really believe it. A good putter doesn't go around constantly telling himself, "I'm a good putter." He simply putts, and putts well.

Once a man was playing a match against an arch-rival, and came to a difficult two-hundred-yard par-three hole that required a carry over water for most of the length of the hole. The man took out his two-iron and said, "This is going to be a great shot. I have all the confidence in the world."

"You're really sure you're going to carry the water?" his friend asked.

"Yes, I'm absolutely sure. I'm thinking positive. There's no way I can fail to hit that green. Just watch."

"Before you hit, can I ask you one question?" said the rival.

"Sure, ask away."

"Well, I was wondering—why did you put away the new ball you were using, and now the oldest ball in your bag is sitting on the tee?"

The way around programming doesn't lie in more programming. The images and opinions we hold of ourselves are already complex enough, and trying to counteract them often activates the very tendency we hoped to avoid. Imagine yourself as a short-tempered person; if you tried to change that image by repeating positive thoughts constantly it might go something like this: "I never lose my temper . . . I never lose my temper . . . I never lose my temper . . . GODDAMN IT, I NEVER LOSE MY TEMPER!" The inevitable blowup will be twice as big because you've fed it twice the energy; you've paid so much attention to repressing your temper that soon everything irritates you. Of course Self 1 will be swift to turn around and say smugly, "There! I told you you've got a rotten temper!"

What is wanted is a way to go beyond programming and reach the real self in order to be able to express what we are. Perhaps finding out what we really *are* is better than our most positive concepts of what we *should be*. In any case, we may as well admit that we are what we are and be it, regardless of what we think about it. What is needed is not to fight negative programming but to simply circumvent it. There is a surprisingly easy way to do this.

What If...

While teaching tennis, I learned that it was difficult to combat negative programming head on. If a person was convinced that he was a defensive volleyer, for example, it was hard to get him to attack the ball at net just by telling him to do so. Even attempts at reprogramming were difficult if the negative self-concept was a long-standing one. Although *I* might have the faith that the student's Self 2 was capable of hitting aggressive volleys, his mind would prevent its expression.

One day I found a way to circumvent this, and the student's potential immediately began to develop. Since the same technique has proven effective in golf, I will explain it by means of an Inner Game lesson I gave to a golfer who told me that he'd always had a jerky and unrhythmic swing.

Since many people exaggerate when they tell a teacher what's wrong, I expected that when I saw George's swing it wouldn't be as unathletic as he had described. I was wrong. Although he had played for over ten years and had an 18-handicap, it seemed miraculous that he could break 100. "I have to agree with you, George; those swings are not the epitome of smooth, coordinated movement. You weren't exaggerating." He looked a bit relieved that at least I could appreciate his concern. "But, of course, what I don't yet know is how you'd like to be able to hit the ball."

"Well, I'd like to be able to hit more smoothly and rhythmically—the way the pros do."

"Different pros swing in different ways. How would *you* like to be able to swing?"

"I'd like to be more—"

"No, don't *tell* me, *show* me. How would you swing?"

George started hitting shots. Immediately there was a marked increase in fluidity and rhythm, a different swing altogether. I gave no sign of surprise but, in a deadpan tone, remarked now and then, "Uh-huh, you'd like to swing a little more like that . . . Yeah, I see, more like that . . ."

By the time George had hit fifteen balls, his swing had transformed itself from that of a hacker to that of a swinger. I couldn't restrain my enthusiasm any longer. "Well, too bad you can't swing like that, George. Maybe someday!" George looked shocked as he realized what had happened. In his mind he hadn't been hitting smoothly; he was simply showing me how he would like to if *he could*.

George's next swing was a disaster, a replay of his earlier tight and awkward swing. "Right, that's how you do swing," I said. "Now show me again how you'd like to be able to."

Again the smooth swing appeared. George looked confused. The swings were completely different, yet he hadn't been taught anything new. "Which one is the real me?" he asked.

"It's your choice," I replied. "Both swings are there. The tight one is the one you thought was yours for over ten years, but the other one's been there all the time waiting to be let out."

That's how powerful negative programming can be. Self 1 is quite literal in his instructions. He will tell you a thousand times that you can't putt, and it will seem that you can't. Since everything you do to improve is based on the premise that you can't putt, nothing works for long; the identification with bad putting is too strong. Yet years of "I can't putt" can be circumvented by a single "But *if* I could . . ."

Likewise, a skier who hesitates going down a slope well within his capacity can be asked, "How would you ski if you weren't afraid of falling?" His style changes dramatically. A businessman who has been struggling with a decision to the point of desperation is asked, "If you knew the right decision, what would it be?" In both cases the "what if" often releases the potential that was being blocked by negative thinking.

Obviously this trick can't be used to develop something that is not already within you. All it does is avoid the expectation that something is not there which in fact *is*. It only works when there is some trust between instructor and student, for it is embarrassing for the student to see that what he had been striving for was available all the time.

There are a couple of ways to use this trick on the practice range. One is to hit the way you'd really like to, regardless of the outcome, as suggested in the putting chapter. A good way to make this exercise more enjoyable and more acceptable to Self 1 is to practice what I call the "movie-star drill." Pretend that you are starring in a movie about a golfer whose form you admire. You don't have to get the same results as that golfer; you merely have to pretend that your swing resembles his, and the director will splice in the shot later. Don't try to analyze how Jack Nicklaus swings and copy it; Self 1 will say, "I can't." Simply act the part of Jack Nicklaus.

We all tend to set expectations for ourselves that are commensurate with our past performance, even if they are optimistic ones. But when you play "what if" as Jack Nicklaus or Nancy Lopez, you'd be surprised what can sometimes be released when you really get into the role. You may not duplicate their swings, but parts of you that couldn't project beyond the self-image barrier of being only a weekend or average player emerge as soon as the barrier is circumvented in this way. Hidden parts of yourself are encouraged to simulate the attitudes and mannerisms of the pro.

Expressing Qualities

Self 1 tends to notice a quality that seems to be missing from our golf swings or our characters, and tries to replace it with some concept of the way we *should be*. All my life I've battled with my image of my own carelessness, and particularly in golf I've often wished I were more precise. Naturally, I've tried to improve in this regard, but until recently nothing seemed to work to make me more precise.

While working on this chapter it occurred to me that attempting to be precise puts me in the trying mode. Thereafter I stopped trying to put precision into my putting and chipping, which suffered most from this failing, and focused my attention on whatever precision was already there. My goal was to allow any precision I did possess its full expression. Through simple awareness my putting and chipping improved radically because I was giving all my attention to it.

On a piece of paper list five or more qualities that describe your golf swing—not its results, but the swing itself. Here are a few sample self-portraits: Tony—tight, overcontrolled, correct, careful, muscled; Margo—powerless, cautious, unsure, precise, smooth; Jim—loose, off-balance, wild, floppy, flowing.

Next, list some attributes you would like to see in your swing but which you feel it lacks. They don't have to be the opposites of your existing qualities, merely different. Tony's list might include "fluid, uninhibited, graceful, effortless and unthinking." Write down each of these desired qualities four times, encouraging Self 2 to express their essence as you write. The experience of expressing the word as you write it is much richer than simply writing the word. Like golf, writing is a physical action, and can therefore serve as a channel for the expression of Self-2 potential.

Another game that can be played with pencil and paper is one I call "paper golf." On a blank sheet of paper, mark points on the left-hand side to represent tees, and draw circles on the right side to represent holes. Placing the pencil on the tee, close your eyes and draw a line to the center of the circle. After you've done this a few times, pick one desired quality from your list and draw the line from "tee" to "hole" expressing that quality. Do this a few times for each attribute you feel you lack. How do these lines compare with the first set of lines? How do they compare with each other? Take a look at the shape of the lines, as well as their accuracy. Which qualities were the most fun to express? Next time you're on the driving range, take your list with you. Consider each quality separately and reflect on it. Search your memory for an image that expresses it. (For example, Tony might picture a river as he thinks of fluidity, or of a sapling bending in the wind as he thinks of gracefulness.) Then hold the image rather than the word in your mind as you swing. Don't *try* to express that quality; simply allow for the possibility that it already exists within you and let out whatever wants to express itself. Even if you think that little of the desired quality is coming through, notice whatever is there. Realize that you didn't force it to be there; it was already inside you. Continue with one quality until you have realized it to your satisfaction, then go on to another.

You will find that some of these desired qualities may improve your performance significantly, while others may make it worse. That's fine. You're not after performance right now; you're attempting to release certain generally desirable qualities. Then when you are actually playing, the qualities that you may need in a particular situation can emerge without conscious summoning.

Examples of qualities that you might want to consider include daring, trust, precision, finesse, mastery, gracefulness, coordination, rhythm, balance, power, straightness and cleanness. The beauty of this exercise is that you discover parts of yourself that you had assumed didn't exist. This widens the scope of your possibilities; you don't have to develop a set style but can adapt it to fit the circumstances.

One day, after working at expressing various qualities which I hadn't associated with myself, I conceived the idea of expressing "Tim Gallwey." It was quite a different experience; instead of *being* Tim Gallwey, I tried to express my picture of "him" as detachedly as I had the other qualities I'd chosen. This experiment may sound odd, but it gave me a feeling of freedom, a sense that I wasn't limited by any qualities, or even by the self-image conglomeration that is known as "Tim Gallwey." What I am is something more than my self-image and the qualities I can discern about myself. I can choose to present and express any of them.

"Utmost Sincerity"

When I began experimenting with expressing qualities, I naturally asked myself what was the most important quality to enhance golf. Many people would say self-confidence, and until recently I would have agreed if self-confidence is defined as reliance on Self 2. But there is an even more necessary quality on which the other attributes are based.

On the afternoon that I spoiled my chances for my best nine holes with four out-of-bounds on the eighth hole at Perfect Liberty Country Club in the Malibu Hills, one of the Japanese priests who tend the grounds approached me and asked me how my book was going. "You believe in using your brain more than your arm?" he asked.

"I believe in both arm and brain," I said, "but I want to play with less ego interference."

"That's the most important thing," he said diffidently. "We like to say, 'Always use *utmost sincerity*.' If I could do everything with utmost sincerity, it would be very beautiful."

The phrase struck a deep chord in me. Utmost sincerity is what's left when you stop trying to *be* anything, when there are no more expectations or pictures to live up to. For me it sums up something I've valued highly ever since I began my excursion into the Inner Game. For the first thirty years of my life I dedicated myself to making something of myself—to being something more than my current self-image. The day I really became a player of the Inner Game I turned 180 degrees from this pursuit to that of discovering more and more of what I already am. By and large this has been a process of "un-becoming" my images of myself. It's like peeling off layers to get closer and closer to a simple core.

And what's at that core? Sincerity—something I can't describe. No matter what pictures I paint of this core, they are inaccurate. It can't really be pictured because it's so profoundly basic, but the closer I get to it, the more I can sense that it is natural, strong and universal.

When that sincerity is the part of me that's predominant, I don't need to know if I'm going to play good or bad golf. I don't have to limit myself with expectations. I don't require any special results. Paradoxically, at times when I don't feel I need good results I can't seem to avoid them. The minute I grow greedy for them and try to hold on to them or make them happen, I tighten a little, try to force them, and find that they tend to slip away. But the more I experience "utmost sincerity," the more I realize that it is this quality—not the results—that feels good, and when I am in that aura I'm content to be what I am, and to enjoy it as it leads me beyond my Self-1 limitations.

10
"BREAKING 80" AND OTHER STORIES

During the nearly two years I spent on this book—roughly from the fall of 1978 to the summer of 1980—I kept a journal of anecdotes, reflections, letters I received from friends and strangers, my own experiences on the course—in short, anything that pertained to golf and the Inner Game. The entries are sporadic, partly because of my traveling schedule and other factors unrelated to golf, and partly because during this period I was ill twice, once for two months and once for three, during which I played not at all. What follows is some of the pertinent and more interesting entries.

4/16/79

Harry Graham approached me after an Inner Game learning demonstration, during which a forty-year-old man who had never held a tennis racket before learned to serve and keep the ball in play, using proper footwork and changing grips, in about twenty minutes.

"Seeing how easily you helped him learn tennis," Harry said eagerly, "I was thinking that you might be able to help me with my golf."

"What seems to be the problem?"

He proceeded to tell a story that I might not have believed if I hadn't been convinced of his sincerity.

"About five years ago," Harry said, "I took up golf for fun and relaxation. I used to get off work at three and be able to play a round before dark. I worked on the weekends when my friends played, so I always played alone. About a year went by before I had the chance to play with some other people. I was surprised that they all shot in the high eighties or low nineties, and they were astounded that I'd shot seventy-four. 'How do you do that, after playing for only a year?' they asked in astonishment. 'If you're that good already, you could probably easily learn to break par and earn your living on the tour. You should start taking lessons and go for it.'

"I didn't know how I'd done it; I didn't think it was any big deal to shoot par. I'd done it lots of times. In fact, that's what I thought 'par' meant—the score you were expected to make."

I looked at Harry incredulously.

"I thought par meant a kind of average score, and felt quite happy about being average after only one year. Of course, I was playing every day, mainly because I thought the game was so much fun and it really was a nice break from work."

"Well," I said, "that sounds wonderful. What's the problem?"

"Well, I got to thinking about what my friends had said and decided maybe they were right. It *would* be a nice way to make a living, doing what I enjoyed the most, so I began taking lessons and working on the mechanics of my swing. To make a long story short, my problem over the last four years is that I haven't broken eighty-five once and don't enjoy the game anymore. I've tried everything, and nothing has worked. I'm very frustrated."

"There's no way we can ever recover lost innocence, is there?" I said.

Harry nodded sadly. "I know. But is there anything I can do?"

Harry and I talked for some time about natural learning versus Self-1 learning and after a while he felt he could enjoy the game again. I left him realizing his story was a rare testimony both to the learning ability of a Self 2 without expectations and the power of Self 1 to interfere.

6/5/79

Went to the practice range with Tom Nordland and Linda Rhodes, both excellent golfers who are interested in learning to teach as well as to play Inner Golf.

We started doing the humming exercise to focus on tightness and locate any blocking of the fluidity of our swings. Watching my swing and listening to my hums, Linda observed, "The sound is mellow during your backswing, but then it has a sudden surge of tension on the way down toward the ball." She asked me if I could locate the tightness in the body that was responsible for the strain in my voice. I told her that I thought it was coming from my stomach. So she asked me to try to discover *when* the tightness occurred. I started giving her numbers for the amount of tightness I felt on each swing, but when she asked me to lower it, I couldn't. Finally she suggested that I deliberately tighten my stomach as much as I could. I found that after I released the contracted muscles, they seemed to relax more completely, and I could start swinging without any contraction in my stomach at all. From this we developed the maximum-tightness exercise described in Chapter 3.

Clowning around, we would approach the ball with every possible muscle tightened; then, before hitting, we would let go completely and feel the increased circulation coursing through our bodies. The swings that followed were as fluid as any I've ever hit.

It seems ironic to tighten in order to relax. But most golfers are so aware that they should be relaxed that they try to do so while addressing the ball, and then tighten involuntarily on the way down. It stands to reason that if you overtighten *first*, the same temptation to do so during the swing won't be there. Still, we couldn't imagine that we could ever force ourselves to go through this zombie-like over-tightening procedure when playing a serious match. But the more discreet way of doing it, as described in Chapter 3, will help you to relax during the swing.

6/18/79
St. Andrews Golf Club, Scotland

I flew to London on business but with the firm intention of heading up to Scotland to play the historic St. Andrews course. When my editor at Random House heard about my plans, he bet me ten dollars that I couldn't break 100 on the Old Course, whose generally adverse conditions of heather and weather make it one of the world's toughest.

The day I finally got a chance to play I flew to Edinburgh from the Inner Game Center in London, and rented a car at the airport to drive to St. Andrews. I barely made my 1:00 tee time. I played in a threesome with Peter and Daphne, an English couple who live on the first tee at the Canterbury Golf Course in Kent. I felt nervous as I stepped up to the first tee, where crowds of onlookers line up to watch. The souvenir scorecard described the hazards on each hole, complete with pictures. They were formidable. The first hole presents only one hazard, called Swilican Burn, a wide ditch full of water right along the edge of the green. I made an effort to concentrate, targeted, and landed left of center on the fairway. From there I hit a seven-iron twenty feet from the pin, but only ten feet from Swilican Burn. I wished I'd brought my own golf_clubs; the putter of the set I'd rented at the caddie house was much lighter than my own. I kicked the thought out of my mind, focused on the heel of the putter head and barely missed the putt. Par.

I'd come to St. Andrews on a day of rare good weather: 80 degrees, with a warm wind at our backs. Though I'd heard a lot about the beauty and majesty of this oldest course, I was nonetheless spellbound by its incredible meandering greens, like broad expanses of meadowland, and its treacherous and unusual traps. Some were eight to twelve feet deep; others had vertical sides that dropped six feet to fine white sand—more like small cliffs than lips. All bore provocative names: The Coffins, The Cat's Trap, The Principal's Nose. The sense of ancient tradition permeates the atmosphere; the town itself is built around the course, physically and culturally. I gave in to the magic of the place and the ambience of the day. I had anticipated pressure from my desire to make my one chance to play this course a good performance, not so much because of my bet with my editor as because I wanted to write about it in the book. (Self 1 was eager for renown.)

On the second hole I hit a hesitant chip shot for a bogey, parred the third and bogeyed the fourth. Then I noticed that I wasn't nervous anymore, and mistakenly I took this as a propitious sign. On the fifth hole I was a little discouraged to take three putts and a double-bogey; I was getting casual, at St. Andrews of all places! I went to the sixth tee without really shaking off my three-putt green.

Thus far I hadn't been reading the descriptions of the hazards on the scorecards, and my caddy, a Scot with wild reddish-brown hair tucked up under a plaid ski cap despite the heat, hadn't told me about them either. He would simply point his crooked finger to tell me where to aim. Trusting his experience and my own Self 2 to hit where he pointed, I had managed to stay out of real trouble for five holes. On the sixth, aptly named Heathery, Peter read me the description of the hidden bunkers. For the first time my caddie, Fred, offered some advice, telling me to keep right because I'd been hooking. I aimed right for a draw, forgetting to do the "da-da-da" with my swing, and the ball landed deep in the heather, nestling neither on the surface of the thick heather nor on the ground, but suspended midway between the two. I knew I would need a heavy club to budge it, so I asked Fred if he thought I'd be crazy to use a driver. He shrugged and said it might work. I swung hard, but succeeded only in driving the ball down to the ground no further ahead of where it had been. I switched to a sand wedge and this time managed to scoot it along ten feet, still in the heather. "Making progress," Peter commented dryly. Using the sand wedge again for the next shot, this time I moved it twenty-five yards, but at least I was out of the heather. My three-iron drove it one hundred and seventy yards to the left edge of the green—but this green was no ordinary one. I was still thirty-three yards from the hole, and would need to sink the putt for a double bogey. I hit fifteen feet past it, then missed the return putt, ending the fiasco with a quadruple bogey! Heathery had gotten to me!

It's this sort of experience that makes the hazards of St. Andrews so notorious. Daphne ran into similar trouble on the next hole, "High." The green is guarded by a bunker about eight feet deep, and Daphne hit into it. Peter told her to keep her head down and swing through. She strained, but stayed in. After three swings she said "Hopeless!" and picked up. She then had to ask Peter to haul *her* out of the bunker!

I ended the first nine with a 46, 10 over par. I was feeling generally settled, not nervous, and strangely unbothered by the pressures I'd anticipated. Peter was playing better than I and was ribbing me a little; I found his chiding helped me to increase my concentration. On the next six holes, I got two pars and four bogeys. On the sixteenth hole I pushed a drive OB and ended with a triple bogey.

Approaching the eighteenth hole after a bogey on seventeen, I was thinking that this would be my last opportunity to enjoy St. Andrews. I wanted to let out all the stops. Crowds were watching the golfers, mostly American tourists in plaid pants. I let go with my longest drive of the day, and then hit a six-iron twelve feet from the pin. I wanted to birdie the finishing hole but left it short.

Par on the first hole, par on the last. Almost poetic. I felt pretty good about both my inner and outer games. I'd scored a 90, and was able to find the often elusive balance between tensing too much and overrelaxing to the point of sloppiness.

Some barrier broke for me playing those eighteen holes. I knew St. Andrews was one of the toughest courses I could play, both for inner and outer games, and I had survived it. It was as if I no longer felt that I had to prove anything. Being in Europe had jarred me out of my usual routine and given me new perspectives, and although my desire to do well at St. Andrews could have been an opportunity for a lot of interference from Self 1, it hadn't turned out that way. The obstacles of the course created a natural pressure that I welcomed. I felt a healthy desire to pit myself against them and take golf beyond the limits of mere score. In the place where the game began I got a better sense of what golf could be. Some underlying self-doubt I hadn't been aware of disappeared, and I felt the effects of this even in my business dealings before returning to the States.

Coming home, I felt again a humility and appreciation for what the Inner Game could teach me, with golf as a medium for discovering both my own potential and my existing limitations.

8/4/79

Today Tom Nordland and I were in a threesome with Barry Elliot, a pro who hadn't played since he failed to qualify for the pro tour the year before. He was now thinking about going back to golf, possibly as a teaching pro.

Barry was raised on golfing technicalities and knows a hundred dos and don'ts for every swing in every possible situation. Predictably, his swing was mechanical, tight, and now, returning to the game, anything but consistent. He just couldn't seem to keep from hitting thin. He was obviously uptight, and becoming more tense as the day wore on and his former game refused to return. He was using the back-hit exercise, but admitted, "I really have no idea where the club is at the back of my swing. Nothing works for me, anyway."

"Then when do you say 'back?' " I asked.

"I say it when I think the club should be there, but I don't feel it."

I asked if he wanted to try another exercise.

"I'd try anything at this point," he said.

"All right, why don't you try hitting the next drive as if it really doesn't matter at all, how well you hit it or where it goes. Just hit it any way you want to."

Barry proceeded to drive fifty yards farther than anything he'd hit all day, but he didn't look self-satisfied as he watched the shot—only surprised.

"What are you going to do next time?" I asked.

"I'm going to try to do the same thing again, and hope for the same results."

"Maybe you'll get them, but the odds are you won't. You weren't going for results when you hit that shot, and if you start thinking to yourself, Hey, this method really works! it probably won't. You can't use 'not caring about results' to get specific results, can you?"

Barry looked puzzled. "Then what do you suggest?"

"Well, you could change games for a while. Up till now you've been playing the achievement game—hitting the ball 'right' to get the best results."

"Until recently that's the only game I'd ever played—especially on the golf course."

"There is another game, and it's not the only one to play, but it's a good one to try when you're frustrated. It's called 'fun-o,' and there are only two rules. One is that you hit each shot in whatever way is the most fun for you in that particular situation. The second rule is that you relinquish entirely any concern for results. You still play golf —that is, you go for the hole with the least number of swings—but your goal is the enjoyment you get out of each stroke, regardless of the outcome."

We all played "fun-o" for the rest of the round, and soon Barry was acting like a kid out of school. When I asked him what he was doing differently, he said, "I'm just doing the opposite of everything I've been told throughout my golfing career. It feels terrific. I'm using my right hand instead of my left, and slapping at the ball as if it were a hockey puck."

Barry enjoyed his rebellion for a couple of holes, whacking wildly at the ball. Then he grew tired of this and started hitting it the way he'd always wanted to. By the end of the round he was a different person.

After the game Barry told me, "I really dreaded playing again; I was sure it would take me a long time to reach my former standard.

Frankly, even as a kid I got into this game as a way to achieve success. I was always afraid of failure, so I practiced all the current techniques for hours every day. In twenty years of golf, I don't think I ever really played for fun before."

1/20/80
Chipping on the lawn:

I've learned a lot about golf just chipping on the lawn. Although I couldn't experience the feel of the full swing, I've become aware of what is essential about my swing, and this has made my time on the range and course much more efficient. What anyone needs to acquire in order to increase his learning rate in golf or anything else is how to get into the awareness mode and out of the trying mode. This can be practiced on any shot. Since it takes less energy and time to practice chipping than any other stroke (assuming you don't have easy access to a putting green), it is the easiest to practice to learn the secrets of golf.

I like to take a bunch of balls out to the lawn and chip them toward a target. All the elements of the game are there: my body, the club, the grass and the target. Most important, Self 1 and Self 2 are also there. The tendency to try to hit the target, to judge shots as good or bad, to get upset, to feel self-doubt or lapses in concentration, are all present. Perhaps you don't get the same pressure as out on the course, but there'll be enough to give you the essential practice in overcoming the limitations of Self 1.

To chip and chip again without thinking, without judgment, is pure, silent learning. The aim is uncalculated improvement. The target is only part of the stage set. If you can hit three balls in the awareness mode, without trying, without inner chatter—even Inner Game chatter—it is a significant advance. You can hit several hundred balls in an hour—which is several hundred opportunities to switch from Self-1 to Self-2 control and hundreds of chances to learn that you can trust Self 2. This will do more for your game and for your enjoyment than many rounds of hitting the ball around the course, thinking about what you're doing wrong after every shot. Forget about gimmicks; if you can't, at least seek gimmicks that are helpful—ones that help you achieve relaxed concentration, and stop tension and thinking. External gimmicks about technique will raise your hopes briefly and let you down; they keep your mind on unnecessary thoughts and put needless strain on your game. The tendency to seek such answers doesn't die easily, but the sooner it fades, the sooner you'll be free to begin to learn again.

To start, you need no technique other than back-hit or "da-da-da."

This gives a sense of rhythm conducive to relaxation and also helps you to concentrate on the club head. But chipping is also a good stroke on which to experiment with focuses that may suit you better.

After a session, notice how you feel, as well as your results. If you find yourself being self-critical, you have been in the trying mode. Judgment and frustration about not achieving results are part of trying for results. In the awareness mode you are playing a different game; your effort is focused only on experiencing each shot: the body, the club movement, the trajectory of the ball. Experience alike the shots that seem smooth or unsmooth; give the same attention to those that end up far from the target as to those that are accurate.

Remember, the more relaxed your mind is, the more aware you will be. Concentration cannot be achieved by tensing. Learn for yourself the difference between the natural effort to stay focused and the straining to do so. One will feel good and will increase your awareness; the other will produce tension. Proper effort feels good; it is not laziness, which will result only in boredom. Concentration produces a sense of aliveness, and from that sense will flow natural interest and enthusiasm.

2/21/80

Focus on the will is crucial: you have to know *why* you are playing. It can help to decide who or what you are playing for. Tom Watson won the L.A. Open playing for the wife of a friend who was in the hospital. Determination increases concentration and learning. When the will weakens, so does learning. Determination to win the Outer Game helps the dynamics of the Inner Game, but only if the determination isn't ego-centered.

In general, we need to find better reasons for playing.

2/25/80

Chipping on the lawn:

It's important to let go of each shot after you hit it. Trying to repeat a successful one or trying to correct a poor one gets you in trouble. Most errors in golf come from this. It is in compensating for past shots or trying to reproduce good ones that the momentum starts that eventually becomes our bad habits, for we hang on not only to the shots but to the tips that we think helped make them successful. That's a mistake; it takes away from the effort to concentrate and focus freshly on each shot. Tips don't work; concentration and trust do.

To increase the frequency of good shots, rely on awareness cues instead of technical ones. Awareness works like a light that shines on the ball and the body; it also has a specific focus and will often direct its beam spontaneously to a problem. Sometimes a pro can help you realize the best place to focus your attention, but don't let him tell you how it *should* feel, because then you will lose the more important sense of how it *does* feel.

Trust your awareness of your own body and develop your own awareness cues. Where does your attention want to focus itself, if you don't consciously direct it? Let it go there. The body has its reasons; each develops its own unique "feel" conducive to learning and to maximizing performance. This may differ from day to day or from shot to shot. Why not trust Self 2 to find its own most desirable focus of attention on any given shot or situation? Stay with this shot as long as learning takes place.

Your own cues developed from your own awareness are superior to those of the experts because they relate to *your* body at *your* present level of development. No golf book or pro can ever know your body as well as it knows itself.

Chipping on the lawn today, my attention went naturally to the back of my left hand. As long as I let it rest there, the feedback I received seemed to give me maximum feel about where my leading edge was, and to let me feel confident. This doesn't mean that it's my secret for chipping; it's merely what my body finds useful today. I have to be willing to let go of it, and may have to find another focus tomorrow.

4/4/80
Lunch with Michael Murphy
Ever since I met Mike at an Esalen Sports Symposium in 1973, I'd wanted to talk to him about golf. I admired and recommended his book *Golf in the Kingdom*. Mike is one of the acknowledged leaders in what has been called the human potential movement; he founded the Esalen Institute in Big Sur, and has a particular interest in sports and athletic achievement as a form of Western yoga. He shares my own interest in the role that sports can play in heightening consciousness. Still, we'd never managed to get together long enough to share our mutual interests until today. At the end of our meeting we both felt it had been too short, so we set a date to play Pebble Beach together on April twenty-ninth.

It would be impossible to reproduce our entire conversation, so excerpts must suffice.

On "Yips"
MIKE: The most excruciating moments in golf come while standing over short putts, the ones that are impossible to miss unless you do some-

thing grossly wrong. Something inside says, "You *will* miss; you'll do the impossible." And blink! You hit the ball sideways. It's the simplest movement fouled up, the most insidious opening to your demons. Those are the real character testers.

On Tips

MIKE: Almost any tip will work for a while, but none works reliably. Essentially they're like placebos, building confidence rather than being instrumentally effective. Yet most golfers and teachers make absolutes out of tips.

On Cheating

MIKE: Following the rules of golf impeccably is crucial to gaining the benefit from the game. Golf helps us by requiring us to conform to a discipline of mind that we benefit from—like yoga.

On the Difficulty of Golf

MIKE: Reflex sports are easier on the mind. You can overcome your inner demons with the adrenaline that is produced by rapid reflexive movements. You don't have as much time to become involved in your thinking. But in golf, as in no other sport, you have to face your demons. Professionals go through every torture of the mind; they have to deal with pressures without any way to dissipate them in violent action.

TIM: Yes, golf is like my children; it has its own ingenious ways of knowing my most hidden weaknesses and eliciting them.

On Self 1

MIKE: Just as Self 1 can grow anxious about not playing the Outer Game well, he can do the same thing by *trying* to have the right mental attitude. Like, "Uh-oh, I'm in Self 1 again. I've got to let go." Whatever we resist we strengthen. Bobby Jones used to escape Self 1 by humming a melody in his head while he played.

On Hogan and Nicklaus

MIKE: I think that Ben Hogan and Jack Nicklaus have a power of concentration that would have made them yogis. Having watched Hogan many times, I can tell you that he gave off a tangible aura felt by many in the gallery. I remember someone at the 1955 U.S. Open remarking that nearly everyone who was watching him seemed subtly hypnotized. There was an atmosphere around him you could cut with a knife. Without knowing it, he was a kind of meditation teacher for the five thousand people walking down those fairways with him.

On Precision

MIKE: The precision required in golf is murderous to those vulnerable to stress.

TIM: Yet the very nature of love is that it is precise. Sloppy love is something else.

MIKE: You ought to write about that in your book.

TIM: I don't dare.

4/29/80

At Pebble Beach with Michael Murphy

Mike and I kept our date to play at Pebble Beach. Both of us admitted to being a little nervous, knowing that it is always easier to share philosophy about Inner Golf than to succeed in demonstrating it on the golf course. The day before leaving Los Angeles for this course, I opened the paper to a cartoon that seemed expressly designed for the two of us. It pictured two yogis, scantily clad, sitting on their respective beds of nails. One is saying to the other with a contemplative expression on his face: "You know, there is only one true test of humility, and that is to play Pebble Beach from the back tees, with the wind blowing in your face . . ." When I showed it to Mike, we both laughed and felt more relaxed because we both knew that humility was the worst that could happen to us. Nonetheless, we decided not to play from the back tees!

Except for an occasional round, Mike hadn't played in several years, but I was amazed at the ease of his swing and at the degree of concentration he mustered when he was near the pin. He didn't hit so many greens in regulation, but he got a lot of pars, and ended the round with a birdie on the treacherous par-three No. 17 and a par on the long par-five eighteenth, giving him a respectable 82.

As for myself, I had decided that I didn't want Pebble Beach to intimidate me, nor did I want to fall into the trap of trying to impress Mike Murphy. Both of these had the potential to get to me if I let them. We had invited my father, who lives in Carmel and loves the Pebble Beach course dearly, to play with us. Just as we reached the club, I said to him, "I'm going to go for the enjoyment of the play today, no matter what games Self 1 wants to play. Pebble Beach is too beautiful and the companionship of Mike too rare to ruin the day worrying about how I'm playing."

By and large my resolve carried the day. It was threatened only at the times I began scoring better than I'd expected and started thinking about the possibility of breaking 80 at Pebble Beach. The thought "Wow, this would be great in the book" almost did me in a couple of times.

I had some jitters to overcome on the first hole, where I hit a long drive that was treacherously close to the woods on the right of the fairway. My only possible shot to the green was to stroke a four-iron low and to the left, hoping to fade it into the green, which was invisible from where I stood. The only problem was that I didn't know how to hit a four-iron low and fade it on purpose. It was my first chance to take a risk, and I did: "Self 2, I hope you know how to make this shot, because I don't, and I'm going for it." The shot ended up fourteen feet from the pin. Dad was on in three and sank a fifteen-foot putt for a par. Mike was on the fringe in two and two-putted. I was in the garden spot, with a chance for a birdie. Self 1 was a little intoxicated by my unlikely approach, and I failed to notice how fast the greens were, and so I hit my first putt past the hole by six feet. Coming back, I was thinking about making a par to at least tie the others, which proved to be an unnecessary and damaging thought, and had to settle for a bogey. This showed me how little detached I really was. I had a sinking feeling in my stomach as I missed that putt, and let my disappointment show. Mike responded to this: "That's good, Tim; it shows you care. One thing about this game; no one has too difficult a time really caring."

Mike and I both parred the second hole, but I hit an eight-iron approach on No. 3 over the green and across the road, a misjudgment that cost me two strokes. Self 1 said, "That's not fair. You hit a good shot. It never occurred to you it could go OB. That's going to ruin your chances." I thanked Self 1 for his comment, and remembered my initial intention to enjoy the day and do my best. The two-stroke penalty might teach me not to assume that you are ever out of the reach of trouble on the course, especially on one like Pebble Beach.

Mike finished the first nine with a double bogey on the ninth hole, which made his score a four-over-par 40. I was three over par after the third hole, and finished the round with par, bogey, par, par, bogey, bogey, for a 42. I was pleased with my score, but more pleased that I was truly enjoying myself quite independently of the number of strokes I'd taken.

On the second nine I started with three pars in a row, while Mike went three over par. On the twelfth hole, I made that impossible sand shot described in Chapter 8 that ricocheted off the lip of the trap to within two inches of the cup. When I hit my longest drive of the day on the 555-yard fourteenth hole, Self 1 whispered innocently, "You know, Tim, in spite of your forty-two on the first nine, if you keep going like this you could break eighty. You can get a par on this hole easily. Then you could afford a bogey on one of the next four holes and still come in with a forty-two—thirty-seven for a seventy-nine." I was attracted to this thought, and on my next shot I was overconfident. I hit a clean three-wood 220 yards, but it faded and dropped three feet outside the OB markers, on the front lawn of one of those beautiful fairway homes. My next shot came close to repeating the error, but landed three feet inside. Self 1 had managed to sabotage his dreams with a single shot.

Dad could see the disappointment on my face and consoled me with a story about Arnold Palmer, whom he had seen hit three shots on the same hole into an overhanging limb, each going OB near where I had. "The next day of the tournament that limb was missing from the tree," he said, "and it didn't look as if it had been sawed off!" I three-putted the green and carded an 8, but Dad's story made me feel better.

I was able to forget quickly and reengage my interest in enjoying each swing. I shot pars on the next two holes and bogeys on the last two, giving me a 42–42, 84. Mike shot a 42 on the second nine, which gave him an 82 for the day.

Throughout the day, I noticed that Mike took a lot of care with each shot. Even on two-foot putts he would study the lie carefully and prepare himself mentally as fastidiously as on more difficult shots. I realized that, for him, caring was a discipline that made the game of golf what it was. After a shot had gone astray, he would usually say something like "I lost consciousness in mid-swing," or "There was a big gap in my awareness on that shot; I wasn't very present."

Still, it seemed to me that caring too much can be as much a problem as not caring enough. Sometimes I care so much that I overtighten and mis-hit; other times I care too little and lose concentration and accuracy. For centuries Zen masters have wrestled with the problem of balance between these two extremes, and eventually generated the ideal of "effortless effort"—caring without caring. To the Western mind this paradox is enigmatic. It defies intellectual logic, but appeals to an intuitive sense that it is the true synthesis between the two extremes of caring too much and caring too little.

The answer here also seems to lie in the *nature* of the care—that is, what is doing the caring, and what does it care about? If what I am caring about is what Mike thinks of me as an inner golfer, or what my score will be, Self 1 is doing the caring, and he is more interested in my image than in my experience. But if my caring takes the form of a natural desire to do my best for the fulfillment inherent in the action, then Self 2 is caring about expressing himself to the fullest, which is appropriate to the situation at hand. Effortless effort: the absence of Self-1 trying, and the natural expression of Self-2 effort. It's a state of mind that can only be achieved by constantly choosing Self 2 over Self 1 whenever the choice is clear. Golf is an arena in which both selves vie constantly, and, more than in almost any other game, the feel of the action and its results gives a strong indication of whether it was Self 1 or Self 2 who was in control.

5/2/80

Letter from Gary Peterson, PGA professional and Inner Golf teacher, Normandale Golf Club, Edina, Minnesota:

My friend Don was in recently for a golf lesson. He was once a 4-handicap player, but in recent years has put most of his energy into building a successful business. Now that he has more time for golf again, he finds that his handicap has soared and wants badly to bring it down. Don made it clear to me at the outset that he'd been seeking the advice of top professionals around the world, and attending week-long golf camps; in his opinion, no local pro would be likely to have the experience and expertise to compare with the people he'd been spending time with. With that, we walked to the practice tee.

Don hit several times, and his problem emerged in each shot: it went to the left every time. "Look, Gary," he said, "even my divots go left."

How much does he really know about his shot? I asked myself. "Don, how do you know your shots are going to the left?"

"I can see the ball go thirty to fifty feet left of where I was aiming every time," he answered defensively.

"How about your divot? When do you first know that it's gone left?"

"I can *see* it, Gary."

"When?"

"After I've looked at where the ball went."

It was obvious that Don was doing what so many of us in golf do: he was only seeing results. He couldn't wait to see that ball go left, then inspect the divot his club carved to the left of his intended target and say, "I told you so!" I knew from my Inner Game teaching experience that if Don could increase his awareness of what was happening *while* it was happening, he would be able to change it without a conscious effort. I asked him to pay attention to the exact moment his club carved the divot. At the moment that the instruction to Don became "Feel it happening," he stopped trying to change his bad shot and began focusing on what needed his attention all along, his swing. Soon he was able to swing feeling the divots being carved, even in directions other than to the left. The balls would fly in the corresponding direction, and in a short time he could go straight, left or right at will.

In our next lesson I asked Don to focus his attention on the leading edge of the club head. As his awareness of what he felt the leading edge was doing throughout the swing increased, he was able to have it do what he wanted it to do without trying. He described his results as incredible, something he had not seen in several years, and concluded that his swing wasn't so bad after all. He even made the concession that local professionals were okay, and was delighted with this process known as the Inner Game.

6/18/80

Reflections on doubt and the will:

The reason that doubt is such an enemy is that it attacks the will itself. Anxiety and fear are emotional and psychological disturbances that make functioning more difficult, but doubt weakens the will, which is at the center of our being. Doubt can cripple a person's desire to act, think or even to live.

To perpetrate doubt in the educational system or in parent-child or manager-employee relationships is one of the most debilitating— though unconscious—crimes against human potential. The cost of not recognizing it is high, not only for the individual but for the group or organization. When doubt becomes institutionalized and its forms become the norm, the will of an entire country or even a culture can be weakened. When a culture loses its will to greatness and dignity, negative forces hold sway, and the individuals in that culture cannot find either protection or meaning for their lives. The seeds of decadence generally emerge out of the ground of doubt.

6/30/80

Letter from Barry Green, lead bassist for the Cincinnati Symphony Orchestra:

My great success with bass violin students has been instructing them in Inner Game techniques of concentration, increasing their awareness as a means of listening to themselves, working with increments to break habits and build new ones, and combating nervousness and fear. I have helped myself with all of these ideas, as well as revitalizing my interest and concentration. I've found new ways to combat boredom playing in a symphony orchestra. I am truly a changed person.

My tennis game has undergone a revival. Inner Game techniques of improving concentration have been extremely successful. The master tips are equally helpful. In general I'm not a "winner" in any sport, and have only achieved consistent success in music. It has always baffled me that I could do one thing well and would always choke in athletic competition, although I do not have any physical handicaps. However, my tennis improved so much that I beat the friend I play with ten times in a row. The first time I lost was when Self 1 finally got to me. I told my opponent, "The reason you haven't beaten me is that you haven't read Gallwey's books lately, and aren't applying the techniques of the Inner Game." I thought I'd learned it all—after which he promptly crushed me and my ego, 6–1, 6–1. I really had to work hard to get it all back. The next day I was finally able to quiet Self 1 and regain concentration. Since then I have continued a long string of victories into the present.

My golf game was another new experience with inner techniques. In Puerto Rico I played Dorado Del Mar, a difficult course. I'm a poor golfer, mainly because I've played only about once a year for the last fifteen years. I rarely score par, but can maintain a consistent game with bogeys and some double bogeys. This was inconsistent with how well I knew I could hit the ball, but I just couldn't drop putts or put a string of good shots together.

Well, at Del Mar my game got better with each hole. I'd decided not to keep track, but since I wasn't blowing any holes I wrote the scores down. At first they were all bogeys and double bogeys. Then, as I got the feel of the club head, the swing and the path of the ball, I began to enjoy swinging, always concentrating on relaxing my mind and body. When I stopped trying hard, things started to change rapidly. The most amazing change was in putting. I was getting pretty close on long putts and dropping all the shorter ones, an accuracy in perceiving distance that I'd never experienced before. I parred the last five holes. My colleagues told me that they could feel a "wall of concentration" around me to the point that I appeared to be in another world. They said that if a bomb had dropped on the next tee, I probably wouldn't have heard it.

7/16/80

Testimonial from Tony Coleman, a PGA Club professional and Inner Golf teacher from Eau Claire, Wisconsin:

Before I began play in the Wisconsin Medal Play Championships in Manitowoc, Wisconsin, for my PGA section, I faced a crisis. The previous week had been the most disastrous week for putting I'd ever encountered. In a 27-hole weekend tournament I had three-putted eleven times and four-putted once! I had gotten myself into such a negative state during this tournament that I began to think I would miss every putt, and sure enough, I even missed a twelve-inch putt.

The night before that little tournament the idea had begun to ferment that I could miss a short putt. All year I had been putting well, but suddenly doubt in my ability surfaced. I *did* miss a few short putts that night, and during play the next day those misses stayed in my mind and I actually started expecting to miss. The doubt grew and grew, and my putting became worse and worse. During the round I thought of quitting, but a golf pro can't do that. I finished the tournament dejected and embarrassed.

At the PGA event the following week, part of me felt that I should try to figure out what was wrong with my putting and try to change it. Instead, I decided to let go, stop trying, and trust Self 2. Before every shot, and especially before every putt, I reminded myself to trust and let go. I would set up, pull the trigger and see where it went—and it went very well indeed.

In previous PGA Medal Championships, I had never finished better than fiftieth place. I would always tell myself, Hey, you're in the PGA Championships, and these guys are playing all the time and of course they're better than you. This time that thought never occurred. When it was over, I had shot 71–76–73 for a 220 total and eleventh place! The "71" and the total were my best performances ever under such pressure conditions. My putting had never been better. I had three three-putts, but they were all from at least sixty feet away. I made all of my short putts and never missed when I had to make one.

7/22/80

Today I went out to play Perfect Liberty. I didn't really have time to play eighteen holes, but I promised myself that if I broke 40 on the first nine, I'd play the second. I was becoming increasingly aware that my last chance to break 80 before submitting the manuscript to my publishers was approaching. I had maybe another four weeks, and knowing this didn't exactly reduce the pressure.

I was playing with Tom Nordland and two other golfers, all of whom were going to complete the round. To walk away after nine holes would be embarrassing, but before we started I told them the conditions I'd imposed on my game.

I started with a bogey on the difficult uphill first hole, hitting a four-iron to the fringe of the green but failing to get down in two. Still, I felt relaxed going to the second hole and absorbed in the technique I had chosen, a combination of three exercises (described in detail in the next chapter), which at this point I had practiced relatively little.

I parred the next five holes and could feel the tension mounting as I approached the eighth tee. I was aware of the score and that breaking

40 was within reach, although the last two holes at this course had often been my downfall. A three-wood well hit on the dogleg eighth hole would put the ball into a dry water hazard in the middle of the fairway. Although I'm not particularly fond of my two-iron, Self 2 selected it as the best club for the situation. "The ball is already there, ten yards short of the water hazard . . . I can see it there . . . now, how would you like to swing this two-iron?" I asked myself.

I heard the answer in my own head: "As if I knew how." And that's exactly how I swung. I hit it as if it were my favorite club. I felt wonderful as I swung; the swing was effortless, the crack off the club was clear and I felt almost no vibration from the impact in my hands. The shot was clean, and the ball landed uncannily near the exact spot of grass where I had pictured it. I could do nothing but marvel at seeing what Self 2 can do without self-interference. That shot gave me added confidence in the technique, and I parred the hole after missing a twenty-foot putt by half an inch.

To say I was truly confident on the ninth tee would not be accurate. The thought did pass through my mind: Wow, you could hit the drive OB and *still* break forty.

"That's right," I answered, overlooking the fact that this thought could only have come from Self 1, "I've got it made." Of course my drive faded just enough to hit on the top of the hill a few feet on the wrong side of the OB marker. I waited to see if by luck it would roll down, but it stayed put as if defying me.

Two shots later I was on the fringe of the green needing to chip close enough to one-putt to break 40. I remembered how only a few months earlier this situation would have scared me to death; at the very least I would have been thinking of some technique to keep me from yipping. But I hit the shot without a thought. Confidence in myself and in this latest technique was growing and I felt very little pressure. The chip almost went in; I had only a two-inch tap for my 39 and a chance to play another nine.

From time to time during the second nine I thought, I should be feeling more pressure than I am . . . I wonder when it's going to hit. But it never did. I didn't play spectacularly, but I made only a few mistakes. I missed a few birdie putts, failed to get out of a sand trap once, and hit another drive OB, putting me three over par, with a 78 for the round.

However, my enthusiasm for breaking the "80 barrier" was dampened by the fact that I did so playing the same nine holes twice. The second nine would not be completed until October, and for this reason I didn't feel I'd legitimately broken 80. But it felt good just the same.

8/7/80

Played with the Thursday Thieves today. When I went to the practice range to hit a few warm-up shots, Don Shields, a television script writer to whom I had given an Inner Game golf lesson and a copy of *The Inner Game of Tennis* the previous month, waved at me enthusiastically. "Where were you last week?" he asked. "It was the triumph of my golf career."

"What happened?" I asked.

"I shot a sixty-eight!" he said. "The first time I've ever broken par, and I've been playing this game for over thirty-two years, ever since I was nine years old! I don't exactly know what worked, but I've become a believer in Self 2. He's really there, if you just let him hit the ball. All this time I've been thinking that I had to use my intellect, but obviously I don't. I thought less and played better than I ever had. I finally figured out that my body has hit hundreds of thousands of balls since 1948, and that I can trust it. I also realized that I never enjoyed the game more than when I didn't have to put up with the continual chatter of Self 1. Since then I've been shooting in the seventies conconsistently, which isn't bad for an old ten-handicapper like me. It's a dream come true."

9/1/80

A few weeks ago I sent my father a rough draft of the first part of this book, and last night I called him for his comments.

Obviously eager to give me his reactions, he said, "It really made sense to me. I decided, To hell with trying to use this stuff as a gimmick . . . I'm really going to give it a try. I went out to play last week and started with two bogeys. I was hitting good drives but making mistakes. Then I told myself, Mistakes don't really matter. I just want to feel calm and happy. I'm just going to enjoy myself, *feel* as much as I can, and not even think about the score.

"I proceeded to shoot a par and another bogey, then six pars in a row, and ended with a seventy-nine! It was the first time in six years I've broken eighty! I never got tense, and I was having fun. I didn't even add up my score until the end. But I had no double bogeys, and no three-putt greens. And more fun than I can ever remember having!"

Although Dad had always been open-minded about the Inner Game —mainly because I was his son—he'd been skeptical about its practical value. In effect, his attitude had been "I'll accept it if it gets results instantly and every time, but I'm not sure I trust it enough to really work at it." Reading the book pushed him over the edge and he was excited by his whole new approach to the game, which meant more to him than just one good score.

Dad went on, "Of course I went out to play three days later knowing that I was going to expect to do really well. I started out with a double bogey, par, double bogey, and thought that I'd lost the magic. Then I reminded myself that I didn't really care about the score; I wanted to have the fun and the same kind of feelings I'd had last time. I began doing the back-hit exercise again—I'd thought I was beyond that after my seventy-nine—and ended up with an eighty-two, parring the last four holes, and had even more fun than when I'd shot seventy-nine. And my back, which usually bothers me, didn't seem to hurt at all, even on the last holes. I've been playing golf for a long time, but I've never enjoyed it so much. It's a whole new game."

Dad's enthusiasm moved me even more than his Outer Game success. I could tell that he had passed the point of treating the Inner Game as a gimmick and realized that it was a fact of the game of golf. He was playing it consciously, and it was adding a dimension that had been missing for him. My congratulations were sincere, but I couldn't help adding, "The only thing I don't understand is why people who are only reading about Inner Golf are breaking eighty while its author hasn't yet been able to break the barrier."

"Maybe you're trying too hard," Dad said, delighted to be able to turn the Inner Game back on me. "Maybe you're letting the pressure of the book get to you. Forget about the book and enjoy yourself."

I had only three more chances at most to play before the completed manuscript was due. The first time I played I scored an 82, but after a quadruple bogey on the second hole my hopes had been serious diminished. The last two rounds were at Camarillo Springs, a par-71 course, and I scored an 81 and an 80! Tantalizingly close, but not what I needed. I was playing well, but always seemed to make enough mistakes to ruin my chances. I knew that I was being too score-conscious, but breaking 80 had been my Outer Game goal from the outset, and it was hard to forget. Intellectually I knew that it wasn't *really* important, but I couldn't make it seem unimportant to my emotions.

9/7/80

Business took me to England, and it was three weeks before I had a chance to play again. "Where's the 'Breaking Eighty' section?" my editor at Random House called to ask after I returned. "You did break eighty, didn't you? We can still put the section in if you can get it to us by the end of the week." I told him I had broken 80, because I had, but I didn't tell him that in my own eyes I hadn't done it legitimately on an eighteen-hole, relatively unfamiliar course. I had one last chance on Sunday to play, write it up, and send it in. I knew that the situation was bound to put pressure on my performance, and I hadn't played in three weeks, so my chances didn't look good. I didn't feel confident, but I had no choice but to go for it.

I called Tom Nordland, and he invited Jon Wright, a 2-handicap player from Santa Barbara, and Alan Forbes, who'd had a low handicap but hadn't played much in the past five years. We played Camarillo Springs because it was near Santa Barbara. Everyone knew that this was a "do or die" day for me, but considerately acted as if it were just another round.

I had a chance to practice for fifteen minutes before our party was called out to the tee. My shots on the range lacked consistency, but I didn't mind; I spent the time loosening up and getting my mind tuned in to the feel of my body. I was going to trust the Inner Game and accept the results, whatever they were.

I decided that I was going to stick to the exercises that had worked at my home course, and which are described in more detail in the next chapter. We were directed to play the second nine first. I parred the tenth hole with a good drive, a six-iron to the green and two putts. I was surprised and hopeful. On the eleventh, a sharp dogleg to the right, I was asked about the best line. Although I suggested that the smartest line was not to try to cut off any of the dogleg but to go down the middle, when I addressed the ball a treacherous whisper suggested I try to save distance by hitting over the trees. The drive felt good and went right on line, but began to fade toward the end of its trajectory. I thought it had landed safe, but hit a provisional ball just in case. I walked confidently down the fairway but grew alarmed when I didn't see my first ball. Then I saw one under the trees, identified it as mine and realized that I'd lost two precious strokes. I must admit that this event got to me. Although I hit my approach to the green, my first putt stopped five feet short, and I missed the second for a triple bogey 7. Three over par after only two holes.

At this point Self 1 came up with a strong and clear suggestion: "Why don't you just ignore the OB? Give yourself a five—that's what you really deserve. At least it would give you a chance to break eighty!" It was a novel idea, since I'd never been tempted to cheat on a score before. Perhaps Self 1 had never felt he had so much at stake. On the twelfth hole, a 163-yard, par-three, into the wind, I hit a five-iron to within 10 feet of the pin and sank the putt for a birdie. Then Tom Nordland, who was keeping score, asked me, "So what did you get on the eleventh hole?"

I took a deep breath. "I want to say five, but in fact I got a seven."

"So now you're only two over par," was all Tom said.

On the next hole, I had a fifteen-foot putt for a birdie. I stayed with my exercises. Knowing that the ball was in the hole, I putted with authority. It felt pure and dropped in the center of the cup. I parred the rest of the holes, playing without mistakes until the last hole of the nine, a 180-yard par-three. I remember remarking to my companions that this was a deceptively difficult hole into the wind. I used a three-wood, but skied it to the left, failing for the first time to get to the green in regulation. I had to hit over a sand trap to the pin, a simple 50-yard pitching wedge—simple, except that I didn't take the wind into account sufficiently. I hit the shot high and it seemed to come backward, hitting the corner of the trap and rolling back into its center. I took three more shots to get down, giving me a three-over-par 38, with still a chance to reach my outer goal. With the exception of a couple of slips I was also close to attaining my Inner Game goal—playing under considerable pressure with little self-doubt. In fact, my only slips seemed due more to overconfidence and sloppiness than to underconfidence and anxiety.

We ate a hurried sandwich before being called out to the tee for the second nine. Of course, everyone reminded me that I was still in the running, and so I was surprised not to feel pressure. Instead I was keyed up to concentrate and continue my Inner Game exercises. My play seemed to become more confident. Before each shot I made a conscious decision to trust my body with the shot. "Show me how you can hit the ball," I said each time. And more than ever before, Self 1 really stayed out of it. I could feel my swing vividly, but I wasn't trying to control it. I had pars for the first three holes, a bogey on the the 490-yard par-five, then two more pars. But on the par-three seventh hole I ran into trouble. I hit a six-iron smoothly, and it felt great, but I saw it drop one foot over the edge of a water hazard near the green —unplayable. My heart sank. John said, "It looks like you don't really want to break eighty." I couldn't help wondering if I was going to let Self 1 sabotage me this late in the round.

I knew the chip shot to the pin was crucial, but I stuck with the exercise, putting as much trust in Self 2 as I could. The pitch was crisp and clean, ending up six feet from the pin. However, I missed the downhill putt and reluctantly carded a double bogey.

Two holes to go. I decided to play each shot with as much trust in Self 2 as possible, and to concentrate on improving my skill with the technique I was employing. On each hole I was on the green in regulation, with birdie putts within twenty feet. I missed them both, but got the pars and ended up the nine with a three-over-par 39, and a total score of 77!

Of course I was happy and relieved to be able to send my publishers the promised "Breaking 80" section in the nick of time, but the real thrill of the last few holes came from the concentration and trust I was able to maintain in the face of potential pressure. I hadn't choked; somehow I knew that I was going to do it this time. When the demands of performance might have made me tense and self-centered, I was able to stay calm and take an interest in the games of the others in the foursome. My energy was concentrated on striving for excellence—not in order to card a particular score, but for the exhilaration of surrendering to Self 2.

At the end of the round I didn't feel particularly excited or proud; in fact, the absence of mental pressure and ego-satisfaction seemed the bigger victory for me. After the round I gave Alan an Inner Game lesson to help him with a slicing problem. His swing corrected itself within ten minutes, and I felt just as good about seeing the Inner Game work for him as I did about my own score.

As I reflected on this breakthrough in score, I realized that if it represented an achievement at all, it was not in the 77 itself. Many players have shown that it is possible to break 80 after only two years of play. Two years ago when I had set out to explore the Inner Game of golf, my goal was not to achieve the lowest score possible; if it had been, I would have played at least three or four times a week. What I had really wanted to establish was that steady improvement was possible for the golfer who only has time to play once a week or less. I had no doubt that more play produces better scores, but I also trusted that with more effort put into following simple Inner Game principles Self 2 could learn more in less time and have more fun doing it. I was more interested in reestablishing faith in the human learning process than in achieving a given score. Thus far my golf experiences have taught me increased admiration for the wondrous capabilities of Self 2 and, I have to admit, a healthy respect for the persistence and ingenuity with which my Self 1 interferes with those capabilities.

9/7/80
An entry from Tom Nordland, Inner Golf instructor, living in Los Angeles:

Tim breaks 80!
It has been two years since Tim and I started playing golf together. When I moved to Los Angeles from Minnesota, I thought I had done so in order to become involved with Inner Tennis, so it was a pleasant surprise when I learned that Tim was going to write a golf book. It is

my better game, and at the high point of my amateur days I held a 2-handicap at the tough Wayzata Country Club in Minneapolis. I also once won an IBM office tournament and the privilege of playing in the 1967 Minnesota Pro-Am. My partner turned out to be Al Geiberger.

When we started playing together, Tim had a long way to go. His swing was upright and uptight, and he had a unique way of lifting his arm and cocking his wrists as he swung the club. Although his typical shot was a slice, sometimes he would overpower the ball with his stronger right arm and pull the ball far to the left. He could hit the ball a long way when he connected just right, but his swing allowed for little consistency. His short game was equally erratic and showed that he hadn't played the game much. He would take "Mulligans" and "Gimme's," and fix his lie if it wasn't to his liking. I gradually let him know that serious golfers don't touch their ball between tee and green, and that they count every stroke.

At the start, Tim's scores were in the mid- to high 90's consistently. Gradually, as he played more and practiced Inner Game exercises, his scores started dropping, breaking 90 and then moving toward 85. His improvement came from the fact that though he was playing only once a week, he was able to effectively use concentration techniques he had transferred from tennis to golf. But I had wondered if he would lower his score much more unless he played more and took some lessons. Although he had originally planned to take a lesson once a month, his first experiences with professional instruction weren't satisfactory. "My head gets clogged up with instructions, and I just don't have the time to devote to taking my swing apart and putting it back together," he said. So much for lessons.

Then Tim's business commitments began interfering with the regularity of his golf. When I reminded him of the need to play the game frequently if he hoped to improve, he replied, "There are a lot of golfers who can't play regularly. I'd rather prove that the average golfer can continue to improve with Inner Game techniques as well as the guy who can play all the time. Anyone knows that with enough practice he can improve. Besides, I can practice concentration anytime I remember to."

Tim started playing less and scoring better. I think it was after he came back from playing St. Andrews in June, 1979, that I first noticed a change in his swing. Suddenly he *looked* like a golfer, rather than a tennis player trying to play golf. He was hitting the ball straighter and more solidly than he ever had, and with less effort. He had developed some consistency. I don't know how it happened; there was simply a breakthrough. Tim said that he'd known it had to happen.

For a few months Tim was playing in the low 80's consistently, and I thought that it wouldn't be long before he broke 80, having played a scant forty rounds from the time he was shooting in the high 90's. Then in the fall of 1979 he was laid up with an illness that drained his energy and kept him off the course for three months. When he resumed, his scores shot up to the high 80's and he had to gradually regain the consistency he'd attained earlier. He took the setback as an Inner Game challenge, and seemed more interested than discouraged. By the following summer he was again shooting fairly consistently in the low 80's.

On September 7, 1980, we played Camarillo Springs Golf Course, northwest of Los Angeles, with Jon Wright and Al Forbes. The course is a relatively short par-71 but fairly challenging, especially with the strong wind that was blowing that day. We all knew that this was a "must" situation for Tim; time had run out on his book deadline. It was a real pressure situation, but Tim looked calm and composed as we teed off.

On the first hole, Tim reached the green nicely with a drive and a midiron and two-putted easily. He had hit both shots with authority, and I sensed he was up for the challenge. On the next hole, No. 11, he was explaining his "doctrine of the easy" drill to Jon, tried to cut across a dogleg, and hit his drive out-of-bounds by a few feet. He reached the par-four hole in two with his second ball, but three-putted for a triple bogey! I hoped he wouldn't be too discouraged, and his five-iron tee shot on the next hole, a par-three, showed that he wasn't. He hit it about eight to nine feet away and sank it for a beautiful birdie. He also birdied the next hole and almost birdied the fourteenth, leaving him one over par after five holes. He was playing beautifully.

After hitting the next three holes in regulation and getting easy pars, he came, still one over, to the par-three eighteenth, which was about 180 yards into a strong and sometimes gusting wind. Tim hit a three-wood and skied it about halfway, his first really bad shot of the day. His 50-yard pitch shot was held up by the wind and landed short in a trap; he blasted out fourteen feet from the pin, and missed the putt for a double bogey and a 38, three over par.

On the first six holes of the front side Tim made only one bogey, the rest being pars. Some of them were tough because of the strong wind, but Tim was playing without error. His concentration was relaxed and steady. If he didn't reach a green in regulation, he was usually close enough to chip and putt for par. I was amazed by his accurate chipping all day long. During this interlude I wanted to ask him how he was feeling, but didn't want to increase the pressure on him. Usually in such situations we made it a point to tease each other, but today was different. I sensed that Jon and Al felt the same way. We talked about Inner Game drills and concentration, and avoided talk of his score.

The third-to-last hole, the seventh, was the crucial one. It was a medium-long par-three (155 yards), but again the wind made it difficult. Tim hit a six-iron, didn't catch it fully, and landed in a water hazard. After taking a drop on the line-of-flight into the hazard he was still forty to fifty yards from the green and lying two! I had been in similar situations before and knew that if he got nervous here and missed his recovery shot, he could easily get a double or triple bogey and blow the round. I watched with interest.

Tim didn't take much time, and hit a beautiful, fluid approach shot, pin-high about six to seven feet from the hole, as nice an approach shot as I've seen under those circumstances. At that moment I knew that he was going to break 80. Though the putt lipped and he got a double bogey, it didn't matter; he had proved he could handle the pressure. He was now only six over with two holes to play. Neither tensing nor playing safe, he made pars on the last two holes, hitting the greens in regulation and two-putting. After he hit his second shot 150 yards to the green on the last hole and thus assured himself of his goal, we watched in amusement as he spent several minutes quacking at a flock of ducks in an adjacent pond. I wished I'd had a camera. The picture of the serene golf course at dusk, the lovely pond with its mallards, the mountains in the background and the happy golfer with his bag on his shoulder seemed to symbolize something about the game, the recreation it offers and the reasons we play it.

10/17/80

A late entry, submitted when this book was in galleys:

Perfect Liberty opens its second nine and celebrates with an invitational tournament. My first club tournament.

I played with three strangers and felt some pressure, but welcomed it. I mis-hit my approach shot on the first hole but sank my chip for an auspicious beginning. On tee #5, the #1 handicap hole, I asked Self 2 for power, let out all the stops, and hit an exhilarating drive that ended up winning the long-drive contest. I got into trouble late in the round trying to take a shortcut on a blind hole, and ended with a triple bogey. Tom Nordland finished early and came out to heckle me on the last two holes, but his chiding helped my concentration. I barely missed a birdie putt on seventeen and sank a twenty-footer for a birdie on the last hole. My gross score of 80 tied the best score of the day on this difficult, very beautiful and unplayed course, and I won the handicap competition.

At the awards ceremony there I was, smiling broadly for the camera, just as I had after winning tennis tournaments at fifteen. But now, twenty-seven years later, there was a different kind of glow burning within, and a far different sense of victory.

11
BREAKING
THE GOLF ILLUSION

Looking for a Game Worth Playing

After a lecture on the Inner Game of golf as part of a UCLA Extension Continuing Education program, a middle-aged businessman approached me and asked urgently, "Can you give me a particularly strong concentration exercise that can keep me from becoming nervous on the last two holes?"

"Are you sure it's a concentration focus that you need?" I asked, guessing that he might be looking more for a gimmick than a real solution to his problem.

"Yes," he said. "There's really nothing wrong with my game until I get to the end of the round. I've been playing all my life, and I love the game. I have a four-handicap, and I believe in everything you say about the Inner Game, but I never par the seventeenth or eighteenth holes. Sometimes I'll even double or triple bogey them."

Over a cup of coffee, Joe began to speak about his game in general. "You know," he said, "I don't really have problems dealing with pressures in my business or home life; I seem to be able to handle anything that comes my way pretty easily. In a funny way, golf is the only part of my life that *really* matters to me. Every time I play it's like a microcosm of my life. When I tee off on the first hole, I'm born. On the first few holes I'm growing up; on the middle holes I'm in my prime. And then . . ."

"Then at the last holes you approach death. No wonder you have trouble concentrating!"

Joe laughed. "I suppose you're right," he said. "Seriously, though, can you give me something to help maintain an old man's concentration through the eighteenth hole?"

"Well," I ventured, "don't you think that maybe if you reconsidered the meaning you attribute to the game—"

"No!" Joe cut me off abruptly. "Don't take away my game! That's what gives meaning to golf for me. Even if letting go of it were the only way I could score better, I wouldn't do it. I want to win the game *I'm* playing," he said with intensity.

Joe's candor struck me. His story may seem odd, but I could see a parallel to what was happening in my own golf game. I realized that virtually everyone is playing his own private game within the game. Golf has its own individual meaning for each person who plays it. In some ways it is like a Rorschach inkblot: each person projects his subjective interpretation on it. Joe was aware of his game and chose to protect it. But I wonder how many of us are as aware of the games we play within the framework of eighteen holes.

In truth, golf is not a mental game; rather, it is a physical game requiring concentration. Although I believe that most golf errors have mental rather than physical causes, this cannot be blamed so much on the game itself as on the games we play *within ourselves* while playing golf. It is not golf that tells us we have to be nervous while standing over a three-foot putt. The tension that players experience stems not from golf itself but from the supposition that the game has some importance worth feeling pressure about. If we so chose to, we could feel uptight about how well we walked or drove a car. The ego seems to become threatened whenever it feels it is being measured. When no ego games are played, there is no ego pressure.

The different games that golfers project while playing golf each have their own individual twists. Some of them are:

(1) Competition: Played primarily to beat others; the score is only important relative to how others do. A sense of "reality" is often added to this game by betting money on the outcome.
(2) Perfection: Played to attain a personal ideal. Feelings rise and fall relative to how one's score or form approaches perfection.
(3) Image: Played purely for the image we create for others. It's not so important to score well as to leave the impression that we can and sometimes do.
(4) Friendship: Score and form are unimportant in comparison to companionship.
(5) Fun: The game played purely for the fun of it.
(6) Expectations: A very common game, played simply to do as well or slightly better than one's expectations. It has a built-in interference because it's an easier game to win with low expectations, which are attained only by poor performance.

Underlying many of these games is Self 1's fundamental game called "Let's show people how good I am," a variation of an even more fundamental game called "I doubt I'm good enough." When these games are fueled by Self 1's questioning of Self 2's competence, they give rise to doubt and the kinds of tension described in this book. The doubt springs from the Self-1 game we are playing within the game of golf.

When we get nervous or frustrated or feel the tension of doubt, we should ask ourselves what game we are playing, and whether it is worth winning. If you can see that it isn't, in time your tension will be reduced. If it is clearly a game worth playing, then you will find yourself able to employ more of your potential. To return to the same fundamental point: clarity of purpose is all-important. Know what game you really want to play, and how it fits in with your broadest life goals. From this motivation follows, confusion declines, concentration increases—and with increased concentration and motivation, anything is possible.

My Game Within the Game

When I started to play golf again, I wondered about my own motivations. On the surface it was obvious that I was playing as a necessary part of my exploration of the Inner Game dimensions of golf so that I could write about the experience. But I also realized that no matter how many "professional" reasons I came up with, I felt stirrings of that same compulsive drive that as a child made me turn down a chance to play with the gang in favor of hitting golf balls by myself. Doing well at the game obviously had an importance to me that I didn't fully understand.

As I began to integrate Inner Game practices into my game, my compulsion to achieve decreased a little. I played with less frustration and mental interference and began to enjoy golf more. As I shook off the negative emotions that used to get in my way, my mistakes stopped compounding themselves and my performance grew more consistent. I seldom had a string of bad shots or a really disastrous round.

At the same time, I knew that I hadn't gotten to the bottom of what motivated me to try to do well at golf. I could tell that something was wrong because I often found myself becoming overly excited when an Inner Game technique worked especially well. I wasn't thrilled because this would enable me to write a better book and help thousands of golfers play better; rather, I was excited by the possibility that perhaps *I* could be a really good golfer. Then I would fall into the trap of trying to make Inner Game techniques work to achieve results instead of letting results occur naturally as a side effect of playing the Inner Game. Sometimes I noticed, for instance, that I was one-putting many more greens when using Inner Game exercises. Then that insidious voice in my head would pipe up, "Wow, if you can do this with such little practice, with a little more work you'll be breaking par, and then . . ." and off I'd drift into dreams of glory.

Why? If the previous chapter were called "Breaking 70" instead of "Breaking 80," what difference would it really make? I realized that in my own game there was a narrow line between playing golf as a game and using it as a vehicle to prove something. When I simply played the game, I did well, but whenever I played to win or to show how good I was, I almost always experienced self-interference and the ball didn't fly so straight.

The crucial issue seemed to be how I related to results. When the external results seemed important, I tended not to attain them as readily as when I felt they didn't really matter. I realized that in many ways this paradox carried through into my life as a whole: I did best when results didn't matter; when they seemed important, I often did poorly.

In the course of writing this book I realized on a conscious level that winning the Outer Game isn't as important to me as winning the Inner Game. Clearly, the true importance of any game lies in what happens to the *player* more than in what happens to his score. Having realized that, I knew that I didn't want the frustration and self-contempt that golf is notorious for evoking, and I escaped these emotions by telling myself that playing good golf wasn't truly important to me. If I played well, fine; if I didn't, so what? But "pretending" that results weren't important in order to get better results wasn't the final solution, for it didn't really work. Although imposing this attitude on myself decreased tension, I often felt I wasn't making my best effort in golf. Other golfers seemed to experience more mental disturbance than I did, but in spite of this they often made more effort and even concentrated better. When I adopted this "I don't care" attitude, I noticed my game would tend to become too casual. Yet when I began scoring well, I found myself again growing tense and over-controlled. I didn't feel that a median position between too casual and too tense was needed as much as a breakthrough in understanding.

Almost Perfect Liberty

One of the most exhilarating moments in all my golfing experiences occurred one evening on the ninth tee at Perfect Liberty Golf Course. Starting at 4 P.M. after a day of writing, I had been unusually concentrated in my practice of "da-da-da" and wasn't aware of my score at all. As I approached the ninth tee, I checked my card and found that I had taken only thirty-two strokes—even par. I had a good chance to score my best nine holes ever. Of course I started thinking how good such a success story would look in the book. Looking down the narrow fairway, a longish downhill hole with OB on either side, I remembered that I had ruined many a good score on this hole before.

Then something clicked inside me; I realized it *really* didn't matter one iota whether I hit the ball OB or not. This may not sound like an event of epic importance, but it was to me. For a moment my heart knew what I grasped so well intellectually: the results in golf were not real. There was something else that was much more real, and how I scored on the course wasn't it. I can't say what made this perception so clear, but I remember an incredible sense of freedom as I stepped up to the ball and, concentrated but without concern, took a full swing. The ball left the club with a crack that seemed louder than any I'd heard before, and soared off to the right, heading right toward the OB markers on the side of the hill. I remember thinking that it looked as if it would go OB, and at the same time knowing more certainly than my eyes could see that it wouldn't. Part of this was knowing that it really didn't matter if the ball *did* go OB, and part of it was the feel when I'd hit it. But before the ball even began to draw, hit the side of the hill and roll down onto the fairway, I let out a loud whoop. I felt a sense of victory that didn't come only from seeing a shot land well. Externally, I've hit better shots; internally, it was my best ever. In that moment there was a triumph that went far beyond managing to swing a stick correctly to make a ball go where I wanted it to. I had broken through an illusion. I felt as if I'd been freed from a tyrant. I could see that I had been trying to please the tyrant demanding external results because he rewarded me with praise and pride when I did what he wanted, and punished me with feelings of self-contempt and helplessness when I didn't. But with that drive I had told him I didn't want to play his game anymore. He had taken the fun out of games and the art out of work, and was an obstacle to getting the very results he demanded. His rewards weren't real and offered nothing but the illusion of happiness. I saw all this clearly as I walked to my ball. I felt no stronger, not even more confident, merely a lot less vulnerable.

The sun was setting behind the hills as I sank a four-foot putt for a par. I had scored my first par-36 for nine holes, and I felt no excitement. Yet I felt wonderful. I'm not ashamed to say that my eyes teared in gratitude.

For me, and obviously for many others, the illusion of the game had become so powerful that it had seemed real. Many people don't even like to speak of golf as a game. "You're going to have a hard time convincing the average golfer that his score isn't the most important thing," cautioned my father. "It's the score that makes them feel good." But it's believing that the results are so important that also creates most of the misery I see on the golf course. There *is* more to golf than the score. I've felt it, and I know there must be others who recognize that games are far more than results.

The Nature of Games

All games have certain qualities in common. They are limited in time —that is, they have designated beginnings and ends. They are also limited in space; they are played within specific physical boundaries. They have goals, and obstacles that must be overcome to reach them. They are always limited by a set of rules.

But the fundamental attribute of games is that they are simulations. Games are *pretend* realities, played within the context of something more real. For example, Monopoly simulates the real estate business. A child may leave his "real" world of school and come home to play with friends. For three hours they enjoy a fantasy of buying and selling real estate; some become millionaires while others lose everything. But when the game is over, all the money and properties go back into a box and the children reenter the "real" world to get ready for dinner. The next day the game may be hide-and-seek instead of Monopoly, but the function of the game as a simulated reality is essentially the same.

Games and play are a natural part of human life in every culture, from the most primitive to the most advanced. Children's games are an intrinsic part of their learning and growth processes, as well as a rich source of enjoyment. Potentially, adult games offer the same benefits. Precisely because they are simulated realities, they are conducive to learning and enjoyment. If you *really* had to worry about losing two thousand dollars for landing on Boardwalk, it wouldn't be much fun—and you also wouldn't be apt to learn so quickly.

Learning occurs most naturally in a setting where mistakes can be made without dire consequences. Yet learning and growth also require the acceptance of challenge, and the motivation to reach a goal is not always easily attained. Hence the value of a game lies in its ability to create an illusion—that is, to provide a separate reality in which you can experiment and take risks without great penalties for failure. Simulated challenges, simulated obstacles, simulated pressures—all of these are for the purpose of enjoyment and of learning better how to meet *real* challenges and overcome *real* obstacles in the presence of *real* pressure. Games prepare the player for the moments in his life in which he can afford no mistakes, when results are all that count. (For example, it is better to learn tightrope walking a few feet over a net than over the Grand Canyon.) In addition, the game can be an expression of skill for the sake of excellence. It can be art.

The power of illusion makes the unreal seem real and the real seem unreal. Pretending is part of the richness of life: common examples include movies, poems, Halloween masks. As long as you don't mistake illusion for reality, there's no problem. But some people have a hard time believing that John Wayne wasn't really a cowboy or that Vincent Price is not a real villain. In a small town in India the members of the audience became so involved in a film that they rose out of their chairs and attacked the bad guy to protect the heroine, leaving the screen ripped to shreds. Yet you have to pretend that the movie or mask or game is real in order to benefit from it; as Coleridge said in another context, there must be a willing suspension of disbelief.

Two golfers who are good friends decide to go head to head against each other in match play. In effect, they agree to pretend that they are enemies. The contract is: you pit all your effort and skill against me, and I'll do my best to beat you. What's the purpose? By pretending to be adversaries, they can experience the excitement and challenge that comes from combat. Great effort is made, concentration is called for, and each player can discover the limits of his potential without exposing himself to potential harm. Thus the competition is a form of cooperation, an agreement to maintain the golf illusion during the match. Although there is only one winner of the *game*, both can enjoy the real benefit of playing it. Thus, in *reality* both can win.

Competition against other players and the course itself calls forth one's best effort, and making this effort is not only enjoyable but conducive to growth and learning. The golf illusion suggests that getting the little white ball into a slightly larger black hole with a minimum number of strokes has real importance. Clearly, golf holes don't really need golf balls hit into them, and the world won't be a better place if everyone begins shooting par. Skill with a club is confined in its usefulness to the boundaries of the game, but on the course the same power of illusion that gives the game its value can seduce the player into believing that the illusion is real and that what happens is of great importance. But if golf stops being a game, it loses its benefits. Thus the player who starts a round thinking that it really matters if he has the ability to hit the ball into a hole with a stick ends by experiencing real frustration and real anxiety during the round, and can walk off the course feeling discouraged. But in Monopoly, though I may experience anxiety as I approach Boardwalk, it is largely feigned, since I have not lost track of the fact that my trouble exists only within the game-reality. I may even lose $2,000 and pay my opponent with feigned displeasure, but I don't worry that my account at Wells Fargo has truly been reduced. In this way I enjoy the pretend-frustration and pretend-excitement as the wheel of fortune changes. But if for a moment my situation in Monopoly became real for me, my frustration, anxiety and discouragement at losing would be very different. If you mistake the game for reality, you are subject to all the real pressures that you are playing the game to avoid.

An Aid to Breaking the Golf Illusion

The illusion that golf is important is so strongly ingrained in most players that it would be fatuous to think that it might be broken simply by an argument presented in a book. If you feel that you are experiencing more anxiety and frustration than the game warrants, and would like to take a practical step toward breaking the golf illusion, I have a challenge for you that can be helpful as well as enjoyable. This experiment may sound like strong medicine, but then so is the disease. The next time you're playing with friends, make a promise to yourself that you will not score better than ten strokes higher than your average score. The second rule is that you can't tell your friends what you're doing; you must give them no indication that your intentions are different from what they are on any other round. Having decided that your external results are going to be disastrous, you are now free to hit the ball any way you please. My suggestion is that on each shot you aim to get as much enjoyment as possible from it. Forget about all the rights and wrongs, shoulds and shouldn'ts and swing the way you want to on every shot. Play with golf instead of letting the game play with you. For example, you might find it fun to aim the ball out-of-bounds and see if you can draw it into the fairway, or to select any club in the bag you feel like using instead of the one dictated by your lie or position. When putting, enjoy yourself, take risks and don't be overserious. In short, do whatever you wish in the certain knowledge that you are going to take a lot of strokes. You might even adopt the philosophy that since swinging can be so much fun, the more strokes the merrier. Be inventive about how you enjoy this round, and also about how you keep the secret from the other players.

This exercise may seem childish, but so is the illusion that makes most of us frustrated on the golf course. Its aim is to provide a tangible example that nothing drastic occurs when you don't achieve results in golf. Lightning doesn't strike even when you flagrantly disregard the game's purpose, and it's a wonderful relief to know that pressure exists only to the extent that you invent it on the course. Another benefit of this exercise is to allow you to experience the fact that *in itself* the golf swing can be fun. My father believes that many golfers feel that the only fun is in achieving desired results, but this exercise allows a player to see the extent to which he can have fun *without* results, as well as with them. Thirdly, the experiment gives you an opportunity to observe the reactions of your friends to your disaster. At the end of the round, will you feel that you *have* to tell them in order to save face? Will it even matter to them? What if you never let them know? To what extent have they bought the golf illusion? Can you play one game and let them play theirs without feeling tension?

Obviously, this medicine need not be employed every round you play. I would use it only when I felt the illusion was becoming too strong—that is, when the game was getting to me. (It's much better than vowing to quit.)

Obviously, golf would lose its purpose if you continued to play as if results had no importance, or if you consistently aimed for results that were worse than your capabilities. Having broken the illusion, it is now time to create it again, but this time consciously.

Re-creating the Golf Illusion

After a golfer has shattered his illusion that results have real importance in golf, to the extent that he neither becomes overly excited when he achieves them nor upset when he doesn't, he must take another step to gain maximum benefit from the game. *Knowing* that results have no importance, he must now *pretend* they do. Pretending that winning has importance is essential to making one's best effort and to receiving the most pleasure from the game. You may ask, "Why destroy an illusion just to rebuild it?" The answer is that only a thin line separates pretending to believe in an illusion and *actually* believing in it. On one side of the line the illusion works for you; on the other it works against you. To create the golf illusion consciously can be a lot of fun and involves avoiding *real* pressure, as well as finding a much higher degree of motivation.

For instance, the same golfer who vowed to shoot ten strokes higher might this time set his goal at scoring three strokes better than his handicap. To add a sense of importance to achieving this goal he might pretend that succeeding would win him $100,000, a desired vacation, a place in the next PGA tour or anything else he might fancy. He could even imagine that attaining his goal would mean that he was a more important or valuable person. Or he could dedicate it to someone who means a great deal to him, just as knights of old honored a lady whose affection they wanted to win. Pick an illusion that you think will cause you to make the maximum effort, no matter how absurd it is. But never lose sight of the fact that you created this game, that it is illusionary, and that you can dispel it anytime you wish.

By this device a golfer can have the best of two worlds. He can reap the benefits that come only from making maximum effort and avoiding the disappointments, anxieties and frustrations that result from believing that the outcome of the game has any real consequence. Tension is overcome by playing games consciously as games; sloppiness and lack of effort are overcome by pretending the game is real.

It is necessary for each player to experiment to find a balance between the two extremes. If he finds that he is playing with too much tension, he can consciously choose a game that decreases the importance of results; if he finds himself too casual, he can play one that heightens the round's sense of importance. By picking your own game within a game, you have a tool that gives you control over your state of mind.

My Favorite Game Technique

Since the breakthrough on those nine holes I parred at Perfect Liberty, I knew that there was more satisfaction to be gained from golf than the pleasure of good results. Thereafter I began playing the game more for the experience it could give me and for what I could learn while playing. I enjoyed playing without doubt or fear of failure, and whenever I achieved this state of mind I knew that it was the only game for me.

But Self 1 is subtle and years of programming lend it a definite momentum; the Inner Game is not won in a single battle. The next week when I played again, the same course looked much the same way as it always had, and I could feel a familiar inner pressure to perform. I even caught myself thinking, I wonder if I'll play even better now that I've really seen through the importance of results!

At this point in the practice of my own Inner Game, I began using a technique that combined many elements of the Inner Game into a single practice. I have no name for the technique; it is a composite of "the doctrine of the easy," targeting, and expressing qualities. Before I address the ball, I look at the situation and let Self 2 pick the target. I see the ball already there and convince Self 1 that the results are already accomplished. You might say that I pretend that the desired results have already occurred. This leaves Self 1 with nothing to be tense about or to doubt. It is the ultimate in the doctrine of the easy— what could be easier than to do something that has already taken place?

Now all that is left is to enjoy hitting the ball. In effect, I say to myself, Now that the ball has already landed where you want it, how would you like to have hit it there? Then I express the quality I want to experience by hitting the ball the way I really want to, allowing Self 2 to express himself to his full limits.

If I begin to notice that in the absence of tension I become too casual, I focus more effort and concentration on expressing the epitome of the qualities I want to experience. For example, I may pretend that it is of the greatest importance that I express my utmost in precision on a particular putt. You will find that although this imaginary demand to *express* precision does not create the tension involved in trying to *achieve* precise results, it requires concentration and trust—and, *as a by-product*, leads to precise results. If I feel too tight, I might choose to express fluidity in my swing, setting my goal as being fully aware of the flow in the swing—all the time "knowing" that the results are already achieved.

This exercise encourages me to stay in the awareness mode and has given me such pleasure that I almost haven't cared that it also has improved my scores. It takes me into a state where I can enjoy golf, play it well and learn—all at the same time. When I'm really focused on the technique, I experience something akin to pure action. The satisfaction comes from the action more than from the results, even though the results give direction to the action.

The point cannot be overemphasized that golf is a goal-oriented game. The value of the target in golf is to give direction to your effort and energy. The target itself offers no real satisfaction, which comes only from expressing your energy concentratedly in a single direction. In this sense, the goal is all-important. When the results achieved are far below the limits of your capabilities, then you have an indication that something is out of balance. In this sense, I can begin to appreciate poor results. They are symptoms of the presence of one or another form of Self-1 interference, a signal that I have something to learn, an obstacle to overcome. Without them the motivation to keep on learning would diminish. Just as I can be grateful to feel pain when I stick my hand into fire, I can feel glad that poor results give me a warning that I may be falling back into a Self-1 illusion. Then I can take steps to dispel it before becoming trapped again.

So in the final analysis, I hold to one effort—to express my best in the direction of the game goal, not for the sake of that goal but for the experience of excellence expressing itself. As long as I hold to that aim and let my satisfaction come from it, I am free of the limitations and frustrations of the golf illusion and can fully benefit from the game by always wanting to make my best effort. My punishment for not doing my best is immediate and simple: I don't feel the excellence. By not making the effort to concentrate and relinquish control, I don't get the pleasure that comes when I do. Thus, both my "reward" and my "punishment" are immediate and indivisible, and they don't emerge from frustration, thoughts or expectations. Both are natural and serve to heighten performance, learning and enjoyment.

The Future of the Game

Though the rules of golf are relatively static, the use and meaning of the game varies with each individual and is affected by changes in the culture. I believe that in the next ten years there will be significant changes in the way golf is taught and played.

Already golf instructors I have spoken with admit that there is relatively little more to be learned about the mechanics of the golf swing; what teaching professionals need most is to learn how to help their students put into practice what is already understood about the swing. The focus is shifting slowly to the art of learning, as opposed to debating the content of what should be taught. There is a growing admission on the part of even the master technicians of golf that breaking down the elements of the golf swing and putting them back together again is a difficult and generally ineffectual way to master the game. There is also a growing recognition of the role of tension and other mental obstacles in golf. In short, we are seeing a shift of attention from the physics of the game to its psychology.

This shift from the outer to the inner in golf reflects a general rebalancing occurring in the culture at large. There is a growing realization that physical control over our external environment is limited. Without an ability to solve problems on the mental level, technology cannot get to the root of the causes of wars, crime, famine or our general dissatisfactions. It seems clear that the breakthroughs of the next age must come in the form of advances in our individual and collective abilities to tap existing human capabilities, and to overcome the negative internal forces that interfere with their expression.

It has been interesting for me to see an awakening in the business world to the topic of human as well as professional development of employees. There is much interest in the way that the Japanese culture has been able to establish levels of productivity and cooperation among its workers that make competing with them difficult. Just as there is more to learn from golf than golf, there is more to the workday than simply getting the job done. Besides attending to results, two questions must be asked: (1) What is the worker learning while performing? (2) What is he experiencing? These questions will provoke steps that can solve the serious motivational problems that stifle efforts to raise productivity levels.

As our culture undergoes a necessary rebalancing of its outer and inner games, sports in general can find a new raison d'être. Potentially, sports have a greater value to a culture than as a mere outlet for releasing tensions or providing heroes. They can become the laboratory in which research and experimentation about human motivation, performance and self-interference take place. Ancient cultures used sports to benefit and strengthen themselves. The Inner Game is hardly a new one, but we are pretty rusty at playing it. Sports can be a safe arena in which we relearn its importance, and increase our skill in it. Sports can be both the showcase and the laboratory in which the culture can learn increasing self-control.

Golf has a particular role to play in this scenario. Admittedly, its players are not known for their openness to change; indeed, it is said that it is a conservative game played by conservatives. But it is in fact a game popular with a broad cross section of the population, and one that demands self-control. A businessman who learns how to cope with stress on the golf course can save his management a lot of suffering and his business a lot of money. Likewise, a student can grasp the elements of learning and self-confidence on the golf course in such a way that it has a permanent effect on his life. Everyone should learn to respect that thin line existing between what is real and what is a game. As a culture, we would then come to understand the true value of competition. In short, the Inner Game aspects of the game of golf described in this book are exactly those issues that the culture at large needs to grapple with. If golf allows itself to become a medium for such experimentation, it would more than justify its existence.

This shift of attention will have a great significance for golf instructors. It will no longer be sufficient for a teacher of the game to be a good player and to know the mechanics of the swing. Forward-looking teachers will attempt to develop an understanding of the learning process. If they do, they will be more valued than in their old roles as swing mechanics, for they will be teaching such valuable inner skills as concentration, self-trust, will and awareness. The best of them will be held in the same esteem as the Zen masters of Japan who taught judo, akido, archery and even flower arranging—not just as skills useful in themselves, but as vehicles for learning self-control. Such teachers will be recognized as making valuable contributions to the quality of a student's entire life.

There is always resistance to change. Some golf professionals may respond to this book as some tennis and ski instructors responded to other Inner Game books; they may say that a knowledge of mechanics and a lot of practice is all that becoming skilled in a sport is about. But resistance to new methods is to be expected and, in some ways, serves to strengthen the forces of change. Frankly, I don't think the game of golf can maintain its present popularity and acceptability if it doesn't change. It can't even claim to be a good form of physical exercise, especially since the advent of carts. There are obviously cheaper and less time-consuming ways to enjoy recreation with friends or to spend a day in a natural setting.

But how many better ways are there to engage in the universal and ageless contest against oneself? If the game is played as Bobby Jones claimed to play it—as a conquest of oneself—it becomes truly recreational. It is a break from the routine and patterns of daily life that can truly enrich our existence. What players learn about themselves on the course can be transferred to every aspect of their lives, and can thus benefit the culture of which golf is only a small part.

Such a perspective would give the game a significance that would make it worth all the time and effort we enjoy putting into it. Although I don't expect this new way of looking at the game to take place overnight, it could happen quickly in an era of mass media. But whether it comes gradually or as a revolution, it will take place, and golf will become more fun, more natural and more in tune with the way games are meant to be played—in dynamic balance between the inner and the outer.

Goal Clarification in Everyday Life

I have found that understanding the performance triad (performance, experience, learning) can help in clarifying my goals in *any* activity in my life, or even in its fundamental direction. It helps when I ask myself, What do you *really* want? and then make conscious choices. The question always guides me to what I want to *do*, to *learn* and to *experience*. When I notice that one of these is missing or is significantly low, I start thinking about how to redress the imbalance. I don't have to analyze much, for I let my Self 2 lead the way. It all becomes very simple and natural, and very different from the kind of life where Self 1's interest in maintaining his self-image or promoting his sense of importance is running the show.

One person can never really tell another what goal or objectives to pursue because it's an individual matter. So is the particular method we each have for understanding what we want. All I want to say on the subject is that I know that much more can be attained from the game of golf than is ordinarily gained by most players, and that the same is true of life: much more can be discovered than is generally even being sought. I myself feel that I've only dipped my little toe into the ocean of what human life can be; yet even that slight experience has been much richer than what I was led to believe was possible. When I was a child I felt life was going to be wonderful; as I grew up I learned to associate maturity with a stoic acceptance of less from life than I wanted. Now, as neither a child nor a stoic, I'm finding that there's no true longing that cannot be fulfilled. Where there's a will there *is* a way, and we don't have to be afraid to go for it. The worst that can happen is that we may learn that we really didn't want what we thought we did, or that it can't be found where we were looking for it—in which case we keep seeking until we find it. The self-doubt that cripples the will now seems to be weaker than the faith that knows that life's fulfillment is far beyond my Self-1 dreams, and that is attainable if I make a sincere commitment to pursue it.

About the Author

Ever since TIM GALLWEY missed a heartbreakingly easy volley on match point in the National Junior Tennis Championships at the age of fifteen, he has been fascinated with the problem of how human beings interfere with their own ability to achieve and learn. His search for practical ways to overcome the mental obstacles that prevent maximum performance led to the basic discoveries first described in his best-selling classic, *The Inner Game of Tennis*. The principles and methods of the Inner Game were next applied to skiing, and *Inner Skiing* revolutionized the approach to the teaching of that sport. With the completion of *The Inner Game of Golf*, which Mr. Gallwey calls "my most difficult Inner Game challenge," he is spending most of his time, in the Los Angeles offices of the Inner Game Corporation, developing an Inner Game approach to such diverse fields as selling, management, stress, diet, music and the quality of work.